D0992245

Liberal Party Politics

JN
1129
.L45
L49
1983

LIBERAL PARTY POLITICS

Edited by

VERNON BOGDANOR

Fellow of Brasenose College, Oxford

Clarendon Press · Oxford
1983

Tennessee Tech. Library
Cookeville, Tenn.

359561

Oxford University Press, Walton Street, Oxford OX2 6DP

London Glasgow New York Toronto
Delhi Bombay Calcutta Madras Karachi
Kuala Lumpur Singapore Hong Kong Tokyo
Nairobi Dar es Salaam Cape Town
Melbourne Auckland

and associated companies in
Beirut Berlin Ibadan Mexico City Nicosia

Oxford is a trade mark of Oxford University Press

Published in the United States
by Oxford University Press, New York

© Vernon Bogdanor 1983

All rights reserved. No part of this publication may be reproduced,
stored in a retrieval system, or transmitted, in any form or by any means,
electronic, mechanical, photocopying, recording, or otherwise, without
the prior permission of Oxford University Press

This book is sold subject to the condition that it shall not, by way
of trade or otherwise, be lent, re-sold, hired out or otherwise circulated
without the publisher's prior consent in any form of binding or cover
other than that in which it is published and without a similar condition
including this condition being imposed on the subsequent purchaser

British Library Cataloguing in Publication Data

Liberal Party politics.
1. Liberal Party
I. Bogdanor, Vernon
324.24106   J1129.L4
ISBN 0-19-827465-3

Typeset by Hope Services, Abingdon, Oxon
Printed in Great Britain by
Billing & Sons, Worcester

A Whig is a perfectly sensible Conservative.
A Radical is a perfectly sensible Labourite.
A Liberal is anyone who is perfectly sensible.

J. M. Keynes 1926

Preface

The purpose of this book is to analyse the traditions, structure, and policies of the Liberal Party. The electoral prospects of the Liberal Party have, of course, been transformed by the Party's Alliance with the Social Democrats, but *Liberal Party Politics* does not seek to predict the future. Nevertheless, the possibility that the Liberal Party will come to play a more important role in British politics constitutes an excellent reason for analysing the Party as it is today.

Most of the essays in *Liberal Party Politics* were first presented at a conference sponsored by the Social Science Research Council and held at Nuffield College, Oxford in March 1982 and *Liberal Party Politics* is in a sense complementary to *Conservative Party Politics*, ed. Zig Layton-Henry (Macmillan, 1980), and *The Politics of the Labour Party*, ed. Dennis Kavanagh (Allen and Unwin, 1982), which also resulted from conferences sponsored by the SSRC. I would like to thank the SSRC for its generosity, while stressing that it is, of course, in no way implicated in the conclusions which the contributors have reached.

The contributors do not share any particular political standpoint. Some are themselves Liberal activists or supporters of the Alliance, while others would regard themselves as opponents of the Liberal Party. Yet all of the contributors have subordinated their political preconceptions to the interests of academic inquiry; and I am most grateful to them.

I am grateful also to David Butler for encouraging this project from its formative state to its completion; and to Michael Steed and Anthony Teasdale for many stimulating discussions on the Liberal Party.

August 1982   Vernon Bogdanor

Contents

The Liberal Party 1931–1982

A Chronology

1931, October: General Election. Liberals divided into three groups: (i) Liberal Party, led by Sir Herbert Samuel, winning 33 seats: (ii) Liberal National Party, led by Sir John Simon, becoming indistinguishable from the Conservatives, winning 35 seats: (iii) Independent Liberals, Lloyd George's family group, reunited with Liberals in 1935, winning 4 seats. 3 Liberals and 2 Liberal Nationals in Cabinet of National Government formed after the election.

1932, January: Liberal ministers accept the 'agreement to differ' whereby, while remaining in the government, they are enabled to speak and vote against its tariff proposals.

1932, September: Liberal ministers resign from government (although remaining on government benches) in protest against Ottawa agreements on Imperial Preference.

1933, November: Liberal MPs cross the floor of the House, joining the Opposition.

1935, November: General Election. 20 Liberals returned. Sir Herbert Samuel defeated at Darwen, Sir Archibald Sinclair elected leader.

1936.   Reorganization of party structure. Liberal Party Organization established in place of National Liberal Federation. New Party Constitution adopted.

1940, May: Liberals join Churchill Coalition. Sir Archibald Sinclair appointed Secretary of State for Air.

1945, May: Liberals leave Coaltion. June General Election. 12 Liberals returned. Sir Archibald Sinclair defeated at Caithness and Sutherland. Clement Davies elected Liberal leader.

1950, February: General Election. 9 Liberals returned. 319 out of 475 Liberal candidates forfeit their deposit.

1951, October: General Election. 6 Liberals returned, only one having faced a Conservative opponent. Clement Davies declines offer of a place in Churchill's government.

1955, May: General Election. 6 Liberals returned.

1956, September: Clement Davies resigns leadership. November, Jo Grimond elected leader.

1958, March: By-election victory at Torrington, the first for twenty-nine years.

1959, October: General Election. 6 Liberals returned.

1962, March: By-election victory at Orpington.

1964, October: General Election. 9 Liberals returned.

1965, March: David Steel wins by-election at Roxburgh, Selkirk, and Peebles.

1966, March: General Election. 12 Liberals returned.

1967, January: Jo Grimond resigns leadership. Jeremy Thorpe elected leader.

1969, June: By-election victory at Birmingham, Ladywood.

1970, June: General Election. 6 Liberals returned.

1972, October: By-election victory at Rochdale.

1972, December: By-election victory at Sutton and Cheam.

1973, July: By-election victories at Isle of Ely and Ripon.

1973, November:	By-election victory at Berwick on Tweed.
1974, February:	General Election. 14 Liberals returned on 19.3% of the vote.
1974, March:	Liberals reject offer of Coalition with Conservatives.
1974, July:	Christopher Mayhew crosses the floor, leaving Labour and joining the Liberals.
1974, October:	General Election. 13 Liberals returned on 18.3% of the vote.
1976, May:	Jeremy Thorpe resigns leadership. July, David Steel elected leader by an electoral college representing all Liberal constituency associations.
1977, March:	Lib–Lab Pact lasting until July 1978.
1977, December:	Proportional representation for European elections rejected by Commons.
1978, January:	Special Liberal Assembly conditionally endorses Pact.
1979, March:	Liberals win Liverpool, Edge Hill by-election.
1979, May:	General Election. 11 Liberals returned on 13.8% of the vote.
1979, November:	Roy Jenkins's Dimbleby Lecture calling for realignment.
1981, March:	Social Democratic Party formed.
1981, June:	Joint Liberal/SDP policy statement. *A Fresh Start for Britain.*
1981, September:	Liberal Assembly endorses Alliance with Social Democrats.
1981, October:	William Pitt wins by-election at Croydon North-West, the first Alliance victor.

The Electoral Fortunes of the Liberal Party: 1931–1979

Election	Total Vote	Candidates	MPs Elected	Lost Deposits	% share of Total Vote	% Vote per Opposed Candidate
1931	1,403,102	112	33.	6	6.5	28.8
1935	1,422,116	161	20	40	6.4	23.9
1945	2,248,226	306	12	76	9.0	18.6
1950	2,621,548	475	9	319	9.1	11.8
1951	730,556	109	6	66	2.5	14.7
1955	722,405	110	6	60	2.7	15.1
1959	1,638,571	216	6	55	5.9	16.9
1964	3,092,878	365	9	52	11.2	18.5
1966	2,327,535	311	12	104	8.5	16.1
1970	2,117,033	332	6	184	7.5	13.5
1974 Feb.	6,063,470	517	14	23	19.3	23.6
1974 Oct.	5,346,754	619	13	125	18.3	18.9
1979	4,313,811	577	11	284	13.8	14.9

Source: David Butler and Anne Sloman: *British Political Facts 1900–1979* (London, 1980).

Leaders of the Liberal Party, 1931–1982

1931-1935	Sir Herbert Samuel
1935-1945	Sir Archibald Sinclar
1945-1956	Clement Davies
1956-1967	Jo Grimond
1967-1976	Jeremy Thorpe
1976-	David Steel

Introduction

Vernon Bogdanor

I

'Go back to your constituencies and prepare for government',
urged David Steel at the end of his speech to the 1981 Liberal
Assembly at Llandudno, the first Liberal leader for over half
a century able to adopt such a battle-cry with any degree of
credibility. The last purely Liberal government in Britain
ended in May 1915 when Asquith 'at a hastily arranged
meeting after only fifteen minutes' discussion' in an operation
'as secret and as obscure as any deal that could be conceived'[1]
established a Coalition government with the Conservative and
Labour Parties. The last Liberal Prime Minister, Lloyd
George, was toppled by the Conservatives after the famous
meeting at the Carlton Club in 1922. Since then, Liberal
participation in government has been confined to periods of
national emergency — 1931-2 when the Liberals joined the
National Government, and, against the wishes of Lloyd
George who declared that if he was to die, he preferred to die
on the Left,[2] remained in it after the general election only to
be discarded when they had served their purpose; and 1940-5
when they formed part of Churchill's wartime coalition.
On three other occasions since 1922 — in 1924, in 1929-31,
and 1977-8 — the Liberals have sustained minority Labour
governments from the Opposition benches, yet this did not
prove to be the springboard for a Liberal revival.

It is, therefore, sixty years since the Liberals have been a
party of government; and as early as 1928 Keynes could say
with justice that 'If one regards the existence of the Liberal
party as a route to power, I agree that one is probably

---

[1] Cameron Hazlehurst: 'The Conspiracy Myth' in Martin Gilbert (Ed.): *Lloyd
George* (Englewood Cliffs, 1968), p. 149.
[2] Quoted in John Campbell: *Lloyd George: The Goat in the Wilderness, 1922-
1931* (1977), p. 301.

wasting one's time.'[3] Yet this is not to say that the Liberal Party or Liberal ideas have been wholly without influence. For, even if it was no longer *in* government, Liberal opinion has frequently made itself felt *upon* government, especially perhaps in foreign affairs. The outcry against the Hoare–Laval pact in December 1935, when, three weeks after an election fought on the principle of collective security, the government proposed to reward Mussolini with a large chunk of Abyssinian territory; the long-delayed resentment at the policies of Baldwin and Neville Chamberlain which turned middle opinion from the Conservatives in 1945 when the electors, according to Harold Macmillan, voted not against Churchill, but against the ghost of Neville Chamberlain;[4] and the moral revulsion against the Suez operation of 1956 — all are evidence of the continuing influence of Gladstonian ideas in politics.

But Liberal influence has by no means been confined to foreign affairs. In domestic policy, the two most influential figures in twentieth-century Britain have been Keynes and Beveridge and both were Liberals. Liberal opinion has had a weight totally disproportionate to its numbers. Keynes indeed believed that although only about 10 per cent of the electorate could be classed as 'natural radicals' distinct from Labour in mentality, feelings, and class sympathies, yet, 'No important reforms will ever be carried in this country without their intellectual, moral and numerical support.'[5]

The Liberal Party, therefore, has not been a minority without influence. Perhaps, however, one central consequence of its decline has been to have made the Labour and Conservative Parties more liberal. For it is a paradox that the Liberal Party began its long decline in a democracy which was beginning to realize liberal ideals. The Party 'buried itself with a kind of triumph: because Britain as a whole is liberal, the Liberal Party dies'.[6] The Liberal Party was

[3] John Maynard Keynes: *Collected Writings*, Vol. xix (Cambridge, 1981). Letter to J. L. Garvin, 9 February 1928. p. 733.

[4] Harold Macmillan: *Tides of Fortune 1945–1955* (1969), p. 32.

[5] Keynes: *Collected Writings*. Vol. xix. Article in *The Nation and Athenaeum*, 8 November 1924. p. 327.

[6] Jean-Jacques Chevallier: Preface to Albert Mabileau: *Le Parti liberal dans le système constitutionnel britannique* (Paris, 1953). My translation.

unable to crystallize the tendencies of public opinion into a
new party programme, precisely because, in Britain, institutions, parties, and even political leaders themselves were
seen as fundamentally liberal.

Liberalism, as Michael Brock shows, has always been an
optimistic creed. Yet the revival of the Liberal Party did not
occur until the waning of optimism about Britain's future.
It is pessimism concerning the country's prospects combined
with disillusionment with the performance of the two major
parties which, as John Curtice makes plain, has led to the
Liberal Party again being seen as a viable party of government.
For, as the pressures of economic failure persuaded the major
parties to abandon the post-war consensus, itself the intellectual product of Beveridge and Keynes, it was no longer
quite so plausible to believe that the Liberal tradition was
safely embodied in the Labour and Conservative Parties.

It is the Alliance with the SDP which has made the Liberals
seem a party of government again. Of course, it is far too
soon to predict whether the high hopes of the Liberals are
likely to be realized or once again disappointed. Yet the
future of the Alliance will depend in no small degree upon
the attitudes and preconceptions which Liberals bring to it.
So far, the role of the SDP, the Liberal Party's rather more
glamorous partner in the Alliance, has been emphasized.
But the Liberal Party with its long history and roots which
lie deep in Britain's political culture is of equal importance to
the success of the Alliance. An analysis of the Party's past
traditions, present structure, and future prospects should,
therefore, cast considerable light on new trends in British
politics. That, at least, is the standpoint from which the
contributions to *Liberal Party Politics* have been written.

II

The essays in this book fall into four well-defined yet interrelated groups. The first, comprising the chapters by Michael
Brock, Peter Clarke, and William Wallace, discuss the ideology
and traditions of the Party. They seek to discover whether
there is a continuous Liberal identity such that an elector
who was a Liberal during the era of Gladstone or Asquith

would also feel at home in the party of Jo Grimond or David Steel. There then follow two chapters — by Michael Steed and John Curtice — dealing with the electoral strategy of the Party, and the basis of its electoral support. A successful strategy depends, of course, upon an accurate understanding of 'the sources of the Party's electoral appeal; but the type of appeal it is able to make is itself shaped by the Party's traditions and history.

The next two chapters by Dennis Kavanagh and Philip Norton discuss the contemporary organization of the Liberal Party, a subject conspicuously neglected in the literature on British politics, and relegated by Robert McKenzie in his classic work on *British Political Parties* to the indignity of a three-page appendix. In their analysis of the structure and organization of the Party, its finances and power relations, and the behaviour of its MPs in the Commons, Kavanagh and Norton are therefore charting new ground.

The final section of the book discusses the main Liberal policies. In his Llandudno speech in September 1981, David Steel referred to 'the four corner-stones of the great reforming government I expect us to form with our Social Democratic allies'. They were (i) industrial reconstruction; (ii) social reconciliation; (iii) a new constitutional settlement; and (iv) Britain's international role. Andrew Gamble's chapter discusses Liberal economic policy and how it relates to Liberal social attitudes; my own chapter analyses Liberal thinking on constitutional matters; while the chapter by Brian Keith-Lucas and Stuart Mole shows how Liberal policy on decentralization has been translated into practice. Alan Butt Philip's chapter analyses Liberal policy towards the European Community, the main external theatre within which Liberals might hope to exert practical influence. The conclusion attempts to answer some of the questions raised by the various essays, and to chart possibilities for the future.

III

Liberalism, like other modern political ideologies, is a creed with a long history. Its elements can already be discerned in the writings of Locke, Montesquieu, and Spinoza. Yet it was not applied to the organized adherents of a political creed until the second decade of the nineteenth century. In its earliest uses, the term 'liberal' meant simply 'generous' as in Isaiah 32:5, where we are told that 'the vile person shall no more be called liberal, nor the churl bountiful'. A commentary on Isaiah tells us that 'The Hebrew word for liberal originally meant exactly that — open-handed, generous, magnanimous. In the East, it is the character which above all they call princely.'[7] There is, therefore, considerable historical justification for Michael Brock's view of the nineteenth-century Liberal Party as the Party of freedom and hope.

According to Halévy we find 'liberal' used 'for the first time as the designation of an English party by the *Courier* in August 1819';[8] and its early use was strongly tinged with derogatory intent. 'We have too high a respect for the noble qualities of British jurisprudence to imitate our Liberals.' The term 'liberal' was first officially adopted by a political party in the General Election of 1847. But the formation of the Liberal Party is usually held to date from June 1859, when in a meeting at Willis's rooms, Whigs, Peelites, and Radicals joined to form the new Party.

As a political creed, Liberalism was a response to the slow undermining of traditional sources of authority, both religious and secular, by the twin forces of industrialism and the democratic spirit — what Tocqueville characterized as 'equality of conditions'. Liberals welcomed these forces as both liberating to the individual spirit and as conducive to social progress. 'The beneficial effects', wrote Mill at the age of seventeen, 'produced upon the human mind and upon the structure of society by the revival of science and by the cessation of feudal darkness have been so obvious that there is scarcely room for the smallest discussion.' 'The spirit of commerce and industry' was, he declared, 'one of the greatest instruments not only of civilization in the narrowest, but of improvement and culture in the widest sense: to it, or to its

[7] Revd. George Adam Smith: *The Book of Isaiah*: Vol. i (13th Edition, 1901), p. 258.
[8] Elie Halévy: *History of the English People in the Nineteenth Century*: Vol. 2. The Liberal Awakening, 1815–1830. p. 81 fn.

consequences, we owe nearly all that advantageously distinguishes the present period from the middle ages.'[9] For, by undermining traditional sources of authority, 'the spirit of commerce and industry' offered the individual the possibility of choosing his own way of life unencumbered by traditional restrictions. But, although potentially liberating, this beneficial result would not occur automatically. For 'human affairs are not entirely governed by mechanical laws, nor men's characters wholly and irrevocably formed by their situation in life. Economical and social changes, though among the greatest, are not the only forces which shape the course of our species.'[10] Michael Brock's essay discusses the Liberal tradition in the period of its ascendancy, the years when, in Newman's words, Liberalism was 'scarcely a Party. It is the whole lay world.'

Historians still disagree as to the nature and significance of the 'New Liberalism' of social reform which took hold of the Party after the death of Gladstone, and formed the intellectual basis for many of the reforms of the 1906 Liberal government. In Peter Clarke's view, the New Liberalism 'represented a discovery of the old liberal values in a collectivist context'. As such it also had a powerful appeal in the first two decades of the twentieth century for many who would today be called social democrats. Indeed, the formation of the Alliance between the Liberals and the Social Democrats may well tempt us to look at the history of these years in a different light.

The conventional view of the relationship between socialism and liberalism in Britain was that the one superseded the other after the First World War. During the years from Attlee to Harold Wilson, it was plausible to believe that social democracy had become the main ideology of social reform in Britain. Peter Clarke shows that an alternative view is possible, that social democracy and liberalism, far from being inherently conflicting political traditions, were closely

---

[9] J. S. Mill: Speech on the Utility of Knowledge, 1923, reprinted in *Autobiography of John Stuart Mill* (World's Classics Edition, 1969), p. 267; *Tocqueville on Democracy in America, Vol. 2* in Gertrude Himmelfarb (Ed.): *Essays on Politics and Culture by John Stuart Mill*: (New York, 1962), p. 263.

[10] J. S. Mill: *The Spirit of the Age* in Himmelfarb, op. cit., p. 264.

interrelated. Thus, the secret electoral pact agreed in 1903 between Herbert Gladstone, the Liberal Chief Whip, and Ramsay MacDonald, Secretary of the Labour Representation Committee, could have formed the basis for a permanent Progressive Alliance which would have absorbed all that was best in the liberal and socialist traditions. It was the First World War, which rendered such an Alliance impossible; and, in particular, the Liberal Party's failure to secure electoral reform which would have allowed the Liberals and Labour to work together rather than destroying each other at the polls. The result of the dissolution of the Progressive Alliance was to be Conservative electoral dominance throughout the inter-war period.

It was during these years that many Liberals, Keynes amongst them, came to believe that the party divisions of the day were artificial, and did not reflect the real division of opinion on concrete issues. In the 1920s, Labour saw the politics of the Left not as a Progressive Alliance against the Conservatives but as a division between 'socialists' and 'capitalists', the dividing-line being the issue of public versus private ownership. This, for many Liberals, was entirely unreal. The crucial divide ought not to be based upon attitudes to the ownership of industry but upon how to manage an industrialized society, whether by the traditional methods of reliance on impersonal forces such as the balanced budget and the Gold Standard, or by policies of economic planning and intervention which, however, would fall well short of socialism. The division between these two streams of opinion – between economic conservatives and economic radicals – did not coincide with the division of parties. All of the parties – including the Liberals – contained politicians of both persuasions. Yet the economic conservatives, under Baldwin and MacDonald, remained in power – while the Liberals, under the leadership of Lloyd George, put forward many of the proposals – notably in the famous 'Yellow Book', *Britain's Industrial Future* (1928), – which pointed the way to the management of a modern industrial society. All this, however, proved to have little practical influence during the inter-war years. For it was the tactical priorities of the party struggle which stood in the way of a natural division of opinion in the country, and prevented the adoption of economic policies which might have provided a cure for unemployment.

Many of the Liberal ideas worked out in the 1920s were taken up by groups such as PEP (Political and Economic Planning) and the Next Five Years Group, representative bodies of 'middle opinion'[11] in the 1930s. They also formed the basis for the social and economic consensus adopted by governments after 1940. Yet this did not help the Liberal Party which, between 1932 and 1956, seemed to have no role in British politics. The immediate post-war period was one of powerful social cohesion when ideological conflict was at a discount; in Butskellite Britain there seemed no place for the Liberal Party. In the era of centrist politics, there was no room for a centre party. Yet, it survived. The Party's independence was tenaciously preserved by its least fashionable leader — Clement Davies — who declined Winston Churchill's offer of a place in his 1951 government.

The choice of Jo Grimond as leader of the Party in 1956 proved, as William Wallace shows, a turning-point in Liberal fortunes; and, just over a year later, at Torrington, came the first of the by-election successes which were to mark successive Liberal revivals, each one reaching a higher peak and receding to a higher plateau than the last. Grimond's accession to the leadership coincided with the first serious questionings of Britain's post-war economic performance, and the Suez crisis which served to undermine the consensus on foreign policy. Further, it seemed as if class lines were at last beginning to unfreeze, slowly but gradually, and this could only work to the advantage of the Liberal Party. Grimond, indeed, based his hopes of a Liberal revival upon the supposed growth of a 'new class' — the professional salariat and the affluent worker, apparently disenchanted with the Conservatives, yet unable to identify with the Labour Party's traditional class appeal.

Grimond gave the Liberals a strategy; the strategy of realignment. In his view, the party system dispersed the forces of radicalism into three parties while giving power to the conservatives in the two major parties. A more natural

[11] Arthur Marwick: 'Middle Opinion in the Thirties' in *English Historical Review*, 1964.

division of opinion would be between a radical and a conservative party with perhaps a small socialist party on the extreme Left. This was an attempt at recreating the pre-1914 Progressive Alliance in very different conditions. In Grimond's view the Liberal Party would, with the aid of the Labour Right, replace Labour, riven with internal contradictions, as the main Left-wing alternative to the Conservatives. Yet, as John Curtice shows, this strategy presupposed that the Liberals could attract, as the Labour and Conservative Parties had done, a solid block of Liberal identifiers; something which was to prove more difficult than Grimond had imagined. For the decline of class feeling, and the weakening of the tie between class and party, seemed to be leading not to the realignment which Grimond hoped for, but to de-alignment, a weakening of trust and confidence in parties and political institutions generally, from which the Liberal Party was unable to gain any permanent advantage. Moreover, as Michael Steed demonstrates, the supporters of the Grimond view never explained how the Liberals could become a new radical force when so much of their electoral effort was concentrated in Conservative areas. The same problem, of course, faces the Alliance today.

Dennis Kavanagh's essay on Liberal Party organization is concerned not only to elucidate the structure of the Party, but also to uncover the differences between the formal organization and the real distribution of power within the Party. He shows that there is no clear focus of decision-making within the Party and that the unwieldy and complex structure is often ignored when important decisions, such as the allocation of seats between the Liberals and the SDP, need to be taken. The Party claims allegiance to principles of power-sharing and decentralization; but, to what extent does the working of the Party conform to these principles embedded in the Liberal ethos; or are there the same tensions between parliamentary leaders and extra-parliamentary activists which have proved so difficult for the Labour Party to resolve?

Philip Norton shows the difficulties which Liberals face in a Parliament geared to two-party 'adversary' politics, where the Liberals find it difficult to develop their own distinctive standpoint; nor can they easily use Parliament as a forum to inform the electorate of Liberal policies. Moreover, because of the electoral system, Liberal MPs tend to come from the far-flung rural periphery, and not from the areas where most Liberal voters and activists live. Their priorities have been fundamentally local, and therefore they have been singularly unsuccessful as compared, for example, to such independent-minded MPs as George Cunningham. Nevertheless, Norton brings out that the central concern of Liberals in the Commons has been less with socio-economic issues than with questions of civil liberties, minority rights, and constitutional reform. They have, therefore, played a valuable role in ensuring that such issues are not submerged by the debate on how to manage the economy.

It is in their concern with these essentially political and constitutional issues that a continuing Liberal identity, linking the concerns of the twentieth century with those of the nineteenth, is displayed. My own essay attempts to show how a concern with the political and the constitutional was a defining characteristic of Liberalism in the nineteenth century, and has maintained this importance today. For Liberals, precisely because they have shared J.S. Mill's view that the value of democracy lies as much in its educative effect on the voter as upon the economic and social benefits which it might bring, have always been as much concerned with political structure as with policy. It is the way in which things are done as much as what is done which the Liberal seeks to alter. What is needed in the Liberal view, are policies designed to allow all groups to identify with the community as a whole. Only in this way can a sense of common interest, the mainspring of progress, be created.

Since 1974 at least, proportional representation has been the corner-stone of Liberal policy, and it has been part of the programme of the Liberal Party since 1922 when it ceased to be a party of government. For, although defended by Liberals on idealistic grounds as increasing the opportunities available to the voter and ensuring the just representation of minorities, proportional representation also suits Liberal self-interest since it is an obvious pre-condition of the Liberal Party exerting influence on government again. In recent years the case for proportional representation has become stronger as single-party governments elected on smaller minorities of the popular vote find the regeneration of the British economy a task beyond their powers. Yet Liberals have unintentionally weakened their case by linking it to the notion of an overall 'constitutional settlement' which, as I try to show, is a dangerously misguided as well as illiberal notion.

Decentralization, as Bryan Keith-Lucas demonstrates, has, for a long time, been a central theme in Liberal constitutional thinking. Liberals believe in devolving powers to local government; they have supported parliaments for Scotland and Wales since 1949, and regional devolution in England since the mid 1960s. While, therefore, in a book about the Conservative or Labour Parties, it would be perfectly possible to omit discussion of local government, a book on the Liberal Party would be incomplete without it. Indeed, not only do ideas of decentralization and devolution lie at the core of Liberalism, but, because Liberal electoral fortunes have been so much more dependent on success at local level than is the case with the two major parties, local elections have been of greater importance for the Liberal Party. This is well brought out by Stuart Mole in his account of community politics. He shows how it led to a new strategy after the electoral débâcle of 1970, and how this strategy has come to conflict with the Alliance strategy being pursued by David Steel and Roy Jenkins. Indeed Jenkins has in the past been a critic of community politics, believing that politicians ought to draw together and synthesize popular aspirations rather than merely exploit grievances.

Community politics, the strategy of many Liberal activists, means clarifying the identify of the Party, and rejecting the politics of 'moderation' and 'the centre ground'. 'It is no accident,' wrote one Liberal activist, 'no accident at all, that the Liberals who are the most active campaigners, the practising community politicians and activists, are by and large the most suspicious of the Social Democrats;' they regard those favouring a merger with the Social Democrats as 'enemies of Liberalism'.[12] Such views may gain credence if the Alliance's electoral appeal fades; for many Liberals will

---

[12] Tony Greaves: 'The Alliance: Threat and Opportunity' in *New Outlook*, September 1981, p. 20, p. 22.

be tempted to say that they could have done better on their own without the need to make the compromises entailed by the formation of the Alliance.

Too often, as Andrew Gamble shows, the central issues of economic and social policy have been edged out by abstract discussions of political and constitutional reform. Yet Liberals have by no means entirely ignored economic and social problems. Liberalism has always rejected what in the nineteeth century it called 'the old false principle of class representation,'[13] and it has seen itself as a philosophy of social harmony. Yet this harmony is not something likely to occur naturally, but requires intelligent government intervention. For this reason, Liberals also reject the philosophy of the free market which they see as the opposite heresy to that of class conflict. The Liberal philosophy is that of the middle way. What remains in question, perhaps, is whether Liberal values can be reconciled with the economic policies which the Party has put forward — an incomes policy together with *dirigiste* policies of economic intervention and modernization. There is a conflict here which the Party has not yet been able to resolve.

In foreign policy, the Liberal Party has been distinctive since the 1950s through its support for British entry into the European Community, and its commitment to a federal Europe. Because the European Community involved the abolition of national frontiers, support for it could be reconciled with the traditional Liberal doctrine of free trade. Alan Butt Philip traces what is on the whole a smooth progression of Liberal thought on the subject of Europe. Yet, at the end of his essay, we can see that nagging doubts about the European Community affect even Liberals. For, only a very optimistic, or perhaps blinkered observer could genuinely believe that the European Community is actually moving in a Liberal direction today. Many of its activities, indeed, as well as its governmental structure seem profoundly antithetical to the spirit of Liberalism. Nor does the Community seem wholly compatible with a political approach which stresses the values of localism and community politics.

[13] Quoted in Peter Clarke: *Lancashire and the New Liberalism* (Cambridge, 1971), p. 164.

This dilemma — of how to preserve Liberal values in what seems a deeply illiberal world — is present, to some extent, in all of the essays in this book. Themes such as decentralization and participation lie at the heart of Liberalism. They presuppose an electorate which is at least potentially liberal — tolerant, fair, and able to be convinced by rational argument. Is such a philosophy appropriate to the Britain of the 1980s, racked as it is by mass unemployment, falling production, and inner-city strife? Has not the Liberal Party, indeed, gained in strength precisely because liberal values are no longer so deeply diffused throughout British society? And if so, can there be a real future for the Party? That is the question which the essays in *Liberal Party Politics* have tried to answer.

1. The Liberal Tradition

Michael Brock

The attempt to delineate the traditions of a political party is enough to daunt any historian. In the first place, while the portrayal should be sympathetic, no thinking person can be a partisan and no more. E. C. Bentley recorded an argument between two of his friends in which one pronounced: 'To put it shortly, you have a cross-bench mind.' 'You may put it even more shortly,' the other replied: 'I have a mind.'[1] Secondly, in the perspective of history who looks either effectively conservative or effectively radical? Nothing has accelerated change more than the attempt to conserve too much. Nothing has retarded reform in one era more than the great reform of the last: it is the institutions erected through a sweeping and successful reform which are most liable to obstruct later changes. Thirdly, a century of franchise extension has transformed all British political parties. The electoral system in which the Liberal party began was still oligarchic by today's standards; the electorate produced by the 1832 Reform Act numbered a mere 800,000 in a population of more than twenty-four million. Finally, can any leader be picked out as the supreme representative of the Liberal party's traditions? Gladstone began as 'the rising hope of those stern and unbending Tories':[2] Lloyd George held the premiership by leave of the Conservatives.

It is a truism nowadays that the members of any government have only the most limited opportunities to put party programmes into effect. There is nothing new in this. Only one popular leader is recorded as having managed, when given office, to perform exactly what he had promised without any omission. That was Cleon, an Athenian leader of the later fifth century BC. He promised to take Pylos from the Spartans within a stated period. He did so; but

---

[1] E. C. Bentley, *Those Days* (1940), p. 198.
[2] Macaulay's phrase: *Edinburgh Review*, lxix.231 (Apr.1839).

this seems to have been something of a fluke.³ Historians sometimes imply that executive effectiveness is four-fifths of statesmanship, so that Sir Robert Peel becomes the exemplar against whom other Victorian public men are judged. As for political parties, they are seen as 'coalitions of convenience'⁴ differing from each other, not so much in ideology, as in social composition, and consequently in perceptions of self-interest and in the accompanying rhetoric. If Victorian Liberalism is approached in this way, nonconformity, provincialism, and the Celtic fringe are given the emphasis. All these perceptions have their value. Yet parties differ profoundly from each other in long-held attitudes and inclinations; and, in the long run, these differences matter.⁵

The term Liberal was used in politics for a whole generation before it became a party label; and a glance at the formative period for the liberal tradition in the 1820s is of use. The liberals of that time were characterized by three attitudes which may perhaps be held to enshrine the enduring essence of Liberalism. They were hopeful rather than fearful; they valued freedom supremely and hated coercion; and they believed moderation and reason to be the prime requirements in the ordering of human affairs.

These principles may look like those of the preacher who was 'agin sin' (that being the only feature in the sermon which Calvin Coolidge saw fit to disclose). This view would be mistaken. Those three attitudes or inclinations were not by any means universal in the 1820s; and they are not unchallenged in politics today.

To understand the first attitude involves glancing at the people who were hopeful in the 1820s. From the Terror of 1793 onwards, the French revolution and the Napoleonic wars generated fears in Britain on an enormous scale. The governing class had looked across the Channel and seen what happened when a popular assembly was given an inch and took a mile. They resolved to keep all such dangerous ideas

³ Thucydides, *Peloponnesian War*, iv. 27–40.
⁴ J. Vincent, *Formation of the Liberal Party, 1857–1868* (1966), p. 258: the phrase could be applied to other parties at other times.
⁵ The Liberal and Conservative parties did not differ greatly from each other in social composition until Home Rule split the Liberals in 1886; but each party had developed its own characteristic attitudes many years before that date.

of popular government out of Britain: the lesson, they concluded, was not to give an inch. In the 1820s a younger generation of Whigs and Liberal Tories took a cooler look. They were inclined to come to the opposite conclusion. Revolutions, they thought, sprang from a refusal of change until no reform could be kept under control, until every reform became a desperately dangerous concession. 'They who resist indiscriminately all improvements as innovations', said George Canning, 'may find themselves compelled at last to submit to innovations although they are not improvements.'[6]

That was the authentic voice of Liberalism. The periods of Conservative ascendancy during the nineteenth century were those in which the electorate was gripped by powerful fears. The first such period has just been mentioned. There were two others, the earlier dominated by Sir Robert Peel, the later by Lord Salisbury. Both followed extensions of the franchise promoted by the Conservatives' opponents. Britain's progress towards democracy was frightening to upper- and middle-class Victorians. They lived in a country where those who were reckoned, and who reckoned themselves, working class constituted the large majority; and they did not appreciate what a wide variety of political attitudes the term 'working class' might cover. So they feared that the establishment of anything like manhood suffrage would mean a permanent working-class ascendancy in almost every constituency; that only the most strenuous and united resistance to radicalism could keep their country off the road to ruin. 'We shall see the result of the elections . . . From all that I see and hear, I am afraid that . . . such a dose of Democracy has been introduced generally into the Constitution that there is no room for anything that is not radical or at all for Monarchy', said Wellington.[7] In the three elections which followed that of 1832 Peel steadily increased Conservative strength until, a mere nine years after the Act which was

---

[6] K. G. Feiling, *Sketches in Nineteenth-Century Biography* (1930), p. 49.

[7] Wellington to Camden, 8 Dec. 1832 (K. G. Feiling, *Second Tory Party* (1938), p. 403). See also Peel to Goulburn, 3 Jan. 1833 (C. S. Parker, *Peel*, ii (1899), 212–14) and note 9 below. W. E. H. Lecky's *Democracy and Liberty* (1896) gives an idea of the fears aroused by the third Reform Act and by Gladstone's championship of Home Rule. Lecky was a Liberal Unionist and thus one of those impelled towards the Conservatives by alarm at Gladstone's policies.

thought to have shattered his party, he won a great majority: (he was indeed in 1841 the first British Prime Minister to gain office as the direct result of an electoral victory). Lord Salisbury's Conservative party was in office for seventeen out of the twenty years after 1885: their ascendancy just outlasted him. During those twenty years the Liberals never had an effective majority in the Commons.

Thus all three of the great Tory or Conservative periods — the ascendancies of Lord Liverpool, Sir Robert Peel, and Lord Salisbury — began in fear; and they ended when these fears grew faint. When that happened those Conservative coalitions fell apart. The uniting factor was alarm: once it was removed there were devastating quarrels. By contrast the Liberals flourished predominantly in the more hopeful and sanguine periods — during the years of mid-Victorian prosperity and in the decade immediately before the 1914 war. The event which, more than any other, gave the Victorians that confidence was in the strict sense a non-event. It was the fact that Britain was almost the only European country not to be involved in revolutionary outbreaks during the Year of Revolutions, 1848. The Great Exhibition of 1851 was a celebration by people who judged that they had tamed the industrial monster: they reckoned that they had gained the benefits of industrial production without suffering from the political turbulence which rapid social change was engendering elsewhere.[8]

A look at the great Victorian statesmen makes the contrast unmistakable. Prophecies of doom were a recurrent staple for Peel, for Derby, and for Salisbury. A month after the passing of the 1832 Reform Act Peel predicted 'that apprehensions would prevail for the security of property — apprehensions which were likely to affect considerably . . . the productive powers of the country — and that the political excitement would continue as rife, and the political unions as flourishing and noisy, as ever'. In March 1851 Lord Stanley (as he then was) told Croker that if his party did not win the impending election 'we must go through the ordeal of Cobden and Co., if we escape a republic'. The year before the 1884 Reform

---

[8] See G. M. Young, *Victorian England: Portrait of an Age* (1936), pp. 77–87.

Act, Lord Salisbury published an article, 'Disintegration', in
the *Quarterly Review*.[9] Disraeli built his career on the defence
of the corn laws, on the proposition that to allow free imports
of corn represented too much of a risk. His account of the
opening Corn Law debate in January 1846 depicts the
protectionists as 'tortured' by 'visions of deserted villages and
reduced rentals'.[10] Even Joseph Chamberlain, that other
great Conservative maverick, ended with dire warnings about
the destructive effects of continued adherence to free trade.
The issue of women's suffrage is often said not to have been
a party question. This statement, though correct, is somewhat
misleading. Both of the great parties were divided on it;
but the lines of division are worth noting. The Conservatives
supplied most of those who opposed any large addition of
women to the electorate.[11] Some of these Conservatives
objected on what might be called old-fashioned masculine
grounds. Nearly all of them feared the results of universal
adult suffrage *per se*.[12] And when leaders defected to the
Conservatives they did so because their fears had increased.
Graham realized in the 1830s that the Reform Act had not
turned out as he hoped. Lansdowne and Hartington joined
the Conservatives during the 1880s when seized with the
fears characteristic of Irish landlords during the agrarian
troubles.[13]

The leaders opposite provide a striking contrast. What
everyone noted about Lord John Russell was his confidence.

[9] M. Brock, *Great Reform Act* (1973), p. 206. Jennings, *Croker* (1884), iii.
231. Salisbury's *Quarterly Review* article 'Disintegration', Oct. 1883, has been
republished in *Lord Salisbury on Politics*, ed. P. Smith (Cambridge, 1972), pp.
335-76.

[10] See the account in Disraeli, *Lord George Bentinck* (1852), p. 70.

[11] Only 29 of the 219 votes for W. H. Dickinson's Bill, 6 May 1913, came from
Unionists. Though supporters of women's suffrage, Bonar Law and Balfour
abstained in deference to the balance of views in their party. Dickinson wanted
all householders and their wives over the age of twenty-five to have the vote.

[12] See Violet Markham, *Return Passage* (1953), ch. xii. 'To double the ignorance
and inexperience of the men by further blocks of still more ignorant and inex-
perienced women seemed to me folly. . . . As a Liberal . . . I had now and again
an uncomfortable feeling that I had stumbled into a hotbed of reactionaries.'

[13] Lansdowne resigned from Gladstone's government in 1880 in protest against
the Compensation for Disturbance Bill. Hartington left the Liberals with many
others in 1886 when he opposed Home Rule.

He would have been willing, as Sydney Smith remarked, to have built St. Peter's, commanded the Channel Fleet, or to have operated on a patient for the stone (and would not have been deterred by the collapse of the sacred edifice, the sinking of the fleet, or the patient's death).[14] In Palmerston this confidence was of the most obvious and ebullient kind. In a more subtle way, Gladstone showed the same characteristic. He was shedding fears throughout his career. And when Lichnowsky did his character sketch of the British Prime Minister with whom he had dealt, this was the element in H. H. Asquith's style which emerged most sharply: you could not rattle H.H.A. Lichnowsky noted that this steadiness was fortified by a weekly round of golf.[15]

This is not intended as an attack on the Conservative tradition. None the less to suggest that this tradition has been based to a great extent on alarms and fears does not present the Conservative party in a wholly sympathetic way. There is something chilling about a group whose feet, when they are marching to success, are, in Curzon's phrase, 'positively glacial'; (he was, incidentally, referring to Bonar Law).[16] It should be stressed, therefore, that every political attitude or inclination has its dangers. In the high Victorian times confidence easily degenerated into complacency. Dickens's Mr Podsnap was surely a Liberal. In 1914 many Liberal MPs were confident that stories of German war plans were circulation-boosting scares by the Northcliffe press, or part of a Tory plot to enslave the working class by introducing conscription. During the very last days of July 1914 'a very active Liberal Member' accosted the Foreign Secretary in the Lobby to say that Britain must not 'in any conceivable circumstances' go to war. 'Suppose Germany violates the neutrality of Belgium?', Grey replied. 'For a moment,' Grey recorded, 'he paused, like one who, running at speed, finds himself suddenly confronted with an obstacle, unexpected and unforeseen. Then he said with emphasis, "She won't do it." "I don't say she will; but suppose she does." "She

---

[14] Spencer Walpole, *Russell* (1889), i.287n.
[15] Lichnowsky. *Heading for the Abyss* (1928), p. 69. The passage originally appeared in *My Mission to London* (English edn., 1918).
[16] H. Nicolson, *Curzon: the last Phase* (1934), p. 324.

won't do it," he repeated confidently.'[17] Such incidents may easily be overstressed. By the last week of July 1914 the cabinet had a fair idea of the dangers ahead; but in a fast-developing crisis its members had little time to deal with the long-held illusions of back-bench Members. Moreover, an inclination to look forward with hope rather than foreboding is far from being the only source of illusion. As will appear a little later, the Conservatives were, by and large, as blind as any Liberal MP to the dangers to which Britain stood exposed when the Archduke and his wife were killed at Sarajevo.

Secondly, a love of freedom and a hatred of coercion have been central to the Liberal tradition. Once again, let us look at the other picture. The English, said the Duke of Wellington, are a very quiet people; and if they are not, there is a way to make them quiet.[18] What Ireland needed, said Lord Salisbury in the 1880s, was to be governed. She needed a 'government that does not flinch, that does not vary'.[19] Those were pre-eminently Conservative sentiments. The opposite attitude, the more libertarian stance of the Liberals, was closely allied to the one of confidence just delineated. The Liberals of the 1820s were confident because they recognized, and rejoiced at, what they called 'the march of mind' or 'the spirit of the age'. They had just witnessed a revolution in the techniques of newspaper printing. Instead of fearing its effects, as the Tories were inclined to do, they welcomed the prospect of a wider diffusion of news and comment. Above all, they saw in improved education an enlargement of the area of freedom, an unshackling of the human spirit.

Once again, there is a danger of reversing Dr Johnson and of writing so that the Tory dogs do not get the best of it. Let me record therefore that at least two Conservative leaders, Sir Robert Peel and Arthur Balfour, were notable proponents of educational reform, A. J. Balfour being one of the most effective political leaders for that purpose in the whole history of this country. But the general picture on the

[17] Grey, *Twenty-Five Years* (1925), i.338.
[18] *Morning Chronicle*, 17 May 1832 (Potter's speech).
[19] Lady G. Cecil, *Salisbury*, iii (1931), 303: from St. James's Hall speech, 15 May 1886.

Conservative side was rather different. In December 1831 Lord Lowther wrote that mechanics' institutes and news-rooms produced 'the greatest mass of floating discontent that pervades this country and France'.[20] His views were not merely those of the backwoodsmen. When Sir Robert Peel spoke optimistically at the opening of the Tamworth Reading Room, John Henry Newman wrote to controvert Peel's thesis that the extension of knowledge was always a desideratum.[21] Moreover, it is worth noting what the stakes were perceived as being in the denominational struggle which bedevilled English education for so long. The Conservatives wanted educational advance if, but only if, the schools stayed in safe hands; and for them the Church of England was safe. The parson could be trusted to inculcate a proper deference in the young, whereas the nonconformist minister was suspect, in that he might represent the thrusting, insurgent element in society.[22]

These two attitudes — the inclination, on the one hand, towards confidence and liberation, and, on the other, towards precaution and strong government — are discernible through-out the whole period between Waterloo and the outbreak of the Great War. They are naturally most obvious early in the period, that is, in the days before each of the parties began to ape the other in wooing those later to be called 'the marginal voters'. The essential difference between reformers and anti-reformers in 1831 was one of stance and inclination. Facts of a sort were bandied about. There was some evidence on the Reform side that standards of education and political knowledge had improved among middle-class people to the point at which they ought to be entrusted with votes.[23] Against such arguments the anti-reformers could cite many signs which suggested that this extension of the franchise

[20] A. Aspinall, *Politics and the Press* (1949), p. 12.

[21] See Newman's seven letters to *The Times*, 5–27 Feb. 1841 (all but the first signed 'Catholicus'), and *Apologia Pro Vita Sua*, Note A. proposition 18.

[22] One of the Conservative Members for Liverpool (Visc. Sandon) referred to the Church of England in his election address, Dec. 1834, as 'an institution which diffuses respect for the laws of God and man'.

[23] It was clear, for instance, that, despite the stamp and paper duties, news-papers had become more informative during the last few decades and had reached farther. In 1813 *The Times* was printed at 250 sheets per hour, in 1827 at 4,000 per hour: A. Aspinall, op. cit., p. 7.

would straightaway be exploited as the springboard for the next.[24] None of this was crucial. Even now almost all major political decisions have to be made on inadequate data. A hundred and fifty years ago they were made on the basis of the few facts which could be scratched together and presented to Parliament.

What counted in those days was 'the weather in the soul'. Jack Althorp, later 3rd Earl Spencer, the Leader of the Commons who, more than anyone else, put the Reform Act on the statute book, had quite a good head. He had a Cambridge 'First in Maths' to his credit,[25] though his only other qualification for the Chancellorship of the Exchequer was some well-kept kennel accounts. But it was not his intellectual qualities which riveted Whigs, liberals, and radicals firmly to him. They followed because they saw that his heart was in the right place. The Tories had done little or nothing to educate the people; and they were now using that lack of education as a reason for denying people the vote. Althorp's reaction to that was, in the Churchillian phrase: 'Up with this I will not put.' In times of crisis political decisions may well turn on the kind of risk which the people in office are inclined to take. Althorp and his friends were hostile to repression and unafraid of political change. They and their Liberal successors may well have overestimated what could be done by education to give an enlarged electorate wisdom. When all the disadvantages of an evolutionary, as opposed to a revolutionary, political tradition have been weighed, however, it was fortunate for Britain that in 1832 Althorp and his colleagues had Liberal inclinations and that these brought them down on the side of change.

The third strand in Liberalism listed above was that of moderation and reason as supreme political requirements. Ever since classical times people have seen a connection between the Greek motto 'nothing in excess' and a disposition towards

---

[24] 'Others will outbid you,' Peel told the ministers in the Commons, 3 March 1831, '... at no remote period. They ... will quote your precedent for the concession, and will carry your principles to their legitimate and natural consequences.'

[25] This refers, strictly, to the Trinity College exam, Althorp being exempt, as a nobleman, from the University public exam: D. Le Marchant, *Althorp* (1876), pp. 74–82.

rational discourse and rational solutions. If we look back to the beginnings of Liberalism it is not hard to see why the creed was connected with an attempt to enthrone reason in political affairs. The die-hard Tories of that time had an unfailing resource when their fortunes flagged — no popery. This amalgam of religious bigotry, xenophobia, and fear of the competition of cheap Irish labour was a considerable force in nineteenth-century England. And the Tories of Lord Eldon's time were not averse to calling in the mob, so long as the mob showed no capacity to take independent, or insurgent, initiatives. There was no rational basis for the no-popery cry against which the Liberals contended. The Catholic Emancipation measure of 1829 was a perfectly safe one. It did not increase the Pope's power in Britain. It merely rectified an obvious injustice by allowing a Roman Catholic to take his seat as an MP.

In the Liberal trilogy of 'Peace, Retrenchment, and Reform' the first item had long been regarded as paramount. During late Victorian and Edwardian times the Liberals contended against the more bellicose and irrational aspects of imperialism — 'the fiend of jingoism', as Gladstone termed it.[26] The imperialism of the Kipling era was a complex phenomenon and to attempt any assessment of it would lie far outside the scope of this article. Many of the Liberal accusations hurled at it were just. In its more extreme manifestations it was profoundly unrealistic and at least one of them — the Jameson Raid — did great harm. The music-hall imperialists wanted to feel that they belonged to a powerful and beneficent Empire; but they were not willing to pay the heavy price which those postures exact. They tried to paint the map red on the cheap. Instead of having plenty of British troops on hand, under tight control, to make sure that the Uitlanders in the Transvaal were not ill-treated, Joseph Chamberlain allowed the Uitlanders to conspire with a force over which he had practically no control at all, namely the private army of Rhodes's Chartered Company commanded by Dr Jameson. The result, both in the Jameson Raid and the Boer War, suggested that the most starry-eyed Liberals

[26] Morley, *Gladstone* (1903), iii.173.

were more realistic about Imperial wars than were their Kiplingite opponents.

'Tory democracy', Gladstone wrote in 1885, 'is demagogism ... living upon the fomentation of angry passions, and still in secret as obstinately attached as ever to the evil principle of class interests.'[27] Liberals objected, with justice, to the attempt to divert the electors from their own real interests — from their needs in education and social welfare — by jingoism or appeals to race pride. There was too much sleight of hand about imperalism whether in its military or its economic phase. No major policy proposal has ever been dissected for the electorate's benefit more devastatingly than Joe Chamberlain's tarriff-reform scheme. The series of speeches in which H. H. Asquith demolished it represent the high-water mark of rational analysis in British platform speaking.[28] Asquith's case was sound. Was the tariff meant to keep out the foreign food and goods? Or were they meant to come in over the tariff barrier, and so to produce a large revenue which would pay for social reforms without an increase in direct taxation? There was no satisfactory answer to the question. When Lloyd George began to raise the money for the social reforms by the taxation proposals in his 1909 budget, there was much outcry about the demagogy of his Limehouse speech. The charge was not unjust; but Lloyd George's welfare scheme itself was farther removed from demagogy than the one which it replaced.

The most dangerous field for imperialist demagogy lay in Ireland. When Gladstone sought to reverse the Union with Ireland by introducing Home Rule and restoring a parliament to Dublin, the Conservative response was cynical and unhesitating. 'The Orange card' is 'the one to play', wrote Lord Randolph Churchill in February 1886; 'please God it may turn out the ace of trumps and not the two'.[29] Lord Randolph's prayer was answered. Belfast was then fast becoming a proud and prosperous city. Bringing its Protestants under the authority of a Dublin parliament would have been

[27] Ibid.
[28] See (J. L. Garvin and) J. Amery, *Joseph Chamberlain*, vi (1969), 474–79, for an appraisal of Asquith's speech at Cinderford, 8 Oct. 1903.
[29] Winston Churchill, *Lord Randolph Churchill* (1906), ii.59.

immensely difficult even if the Conservatives had confined themselves to constitutional methods in opposing the change. They exercised no such restraint. There can be no defence for the moves which Bonar Law and Carson made and encouraged between 1912 and 1914. The only plea in mitigation which can be made for the way in which they enlisted their private army in Ulster, and armed it in the Larne gun-running, is that, unlike later generations, they did not have examples before them to show all the dangers of the game which they were playing. All this was going on in the summer of 1914. Early in that year the Conservatives came close to using their Lords majority to obstruct the Army Annual Act; that is, they came close to removing the statutory basis for the discipline of the armed forces. The remark made earlier that in 1914 they were as blind as the most optimistic Liberal MP to the dangers which Britain was about to meet is not an exaggeration.[30]

The statement that Liberalism has stood for the application of reason in politics entails a definition of rationality which is not too high-flown or philosophical. (The only considerable philosopher in recent British politics, A. J. Balfour, was a Conservative.) The antithesis is between the politics of reason, on the one side, and those of unreason and passion, those of demagogy, and those of extremism, on the other. Reason is used here to connote reasonableness, as well as rationality in the stricter sense. The politics of reason, in that wide sense of the phrase, are the most essential ingredient in any political system.

[30] For statements that the Ulster Protestants would rather be ruled by Berlin than by Dublin, see *Morning Post*, 19 Dec. 1910, 9 Jan. 1911 (Andrews, Craig); *Parl. Deb.* xlvi.464, 471 (Bonar Law, 1 Ja. 1913). For eulogies of the Kaiser in the Conservative press, see *Evening News* (a Northcliffe paper), 17 Oct. 1913; *National Review*, lxii.298.

2. Liberals and Social Democrats in Historical Perspective

Peter Clarke

The central argument of this essay is that the British political tradition of radicalism and reform does not simply fall into a distinction between liberalism and socialism. That this is *part* of the story we may readily accept. But the development of the British Left (or radicalism) has, it will be argued, been profoundly influenced by persons who were both liberals and social democrats.[1]

The origins of the term social democracy constitute our first puzzle. It was used virtually interchangeably with socialism in the late nineteenth century (and socialism often interchangeably with collectivism for that matter). In *Fabian Essays*, published at the end of 1889, we find Graham Wallas writing of 'a tentative and limited social democracy' as his political goal.[2] This usage was characteristic. Likewise in 1907 Bernard Shaw stepped in to clarify the 'proper sense' of the term, that is, to refer to a socialist who was also a democrat; and thus it covered 'all socialists who postulate democracy as the political basis of socialism'.[3] In practice, this meant the pursuit of state collectivism by parliamentary methods. In *Man and Superman* Shaw supplies a trenchant exchange sufficiently exemplifying this point. When Straker says of Duval, 'Oh, you're a Social Democrat, are you?', the Anarchist sarcastically comments: 'He means that he has sold out to the parliamentary humbugs and the bourgeiosie. Compromise! that is his faith.'[4]

Shaw, however, also acknowledged that there existed 'a transient misunderstanding', namely that Social Democracy

---

[1] Some of what follows, especially the historical treatment of L. T. Hobhouse and J. A. Hobson, is more fully substantiated in my book, *Liberals and Social Democrats* (Cambridge, 1978).

[2] G. B. Shaw (Ed.), *Fabian Essays in Socialism* (1889), p. 147.

[3] Bernard Shaw, 'The impossibilities of anarchism', in *Socialism and Individualism* (1908), p. 28.

[4] Bernard Shaw, *Man and Superman* (Penguin edition, 1976), p. 115.

should be equated with doctrinaire Marxism and the stance of the Social Democratic Federation[5] (founded in 1884 and briefly identified as the Social Democratic Party between 1908 and 1911). There was the German example, too, since the SPD was indisputably Marxist during this period. In fact, until the First World War, references to social democracy generally had a Marxist connotation, leading some historians to assert that modern social democrats have no right even to their name! Its usage only became current in its modern sense after 1917, when the Russian Revolution produced a clear rift in the socialist movement. By the 1930s the label had become commonplace in European ideological debate, and accepted as such even by the backward British. Thus Evan Durbin speaks ironically of 'a miserable social democrat like me',[6] though it is interesting to see that by preference he termed himself a democratic socialist — a problem of terminology to which we shall return.

But even before 1914 there was a significant effort to establish the concept in a non-Marxist sense, especially in the writings of Hobhouse. Thus when he urged the Liberals to take up social reform in order to confront the House of Lords in 1907, he claimed: 'the road to political democracy in England lies through what, in a broader sense than is usually given to the term, we may call social democracy'. A passage on the same tack in 1911 shows why he put it this way: 'Political changes, then, which have given us constitutional democracy, have paved the way for what, if the term were not limited to a rather narrow theory, we might call a social democracy . . .'.[7] This really brings us to consider the relationship with liberalism. For the essence of Hobhouse's argument was that the historic task of the old Liberalism was the achievement of political democracy, whereas the province of the new Liberalism should be social democracy. Thus it was an explicit recognition of the salience of the economic problem in politics.

---

[5] *Socialism and Individualism*, p. 28.

[6] Evan Durbin, *The Politics of Democratic Socialism* (1940; 5th imp. 1957), p. 208.

[7] 'The moral of failure', *Nation*, 25 May 1907, p. 478; *Social Evolution and Political Theory* (New York, 1911), p. 183.

The economic policy of the old Liberalism of the nineteenth century can broadly but not unfairly be described as that of *laissez-faire*. It saw the creation of the free market as an end in itself; how it worked was no matter of political concern. The proper role of the state ended with the establishment of the formal conditions of economic liberty, of which anyone might take what advantage he chose. This economic analysis was reinforced by moral attitudes — the exemplary paradigm of self-help and individualism, with a commendation of responsibility, foresight, and thrift. In the late nineteenth century this was often backed up by Social Darwinism, or at least a selective invocation of Herbert Spencer's maxim about the survival of the fittest. At any rate, it was no job of the state to help the failures. This was either because they were bound to fail for biological reasons, and served thereby a eugenic function; or because they deserved to fail for moral reasons, and had only themselves to blame since the remedy for their plight lay in their own hands. More complex flaws and more obscure contingencies might also be attributed to the mysteries of providential purpose. This sort of fatalism or quietism in social and economic matters may be taken as characteristic of Gladstonian Liberalism — despite, or because of, its hyperactivism on another range of political and moral issues.

Hence the state collectivism of the early Fabian era challenged a whole notion of the *agenda* of politics, and did so generally under the name of socialism. To the Fabians, there was nothing more despicable than the Gladstonian politics of morality. Shaw professed himself 'boilingly contemptuous of the common English plan of dealing with social evils by catching a scapegoat, overwhelming him with virtuous indignation, and calling *that* politics'.[8] It was undoubtedly Fabianism, with its bureaucratic and collectivist emphasis on planning and state control, which made the running in discussion of social questions in the 1880s and 1890s. It would be a mistake, however, to draw the conclusion that the New Liberalism was merely a derivation from or imitation of Fabianism. It was rather a revision of it. It represented a

[8] Dan H. Laurence (Ed.), *Bernard Shaw: Collected Letters, 1898–1910* (1972), p. 168.

discovery of the old liberal values in a collectivist context.

The test issue here was the Boer War of 1899–1902. Leading Fabians like Shaw and the Webbs supported imperialism, finding plausible and consistent grounds for so doing. After all, what was imperialism but international collectivism? The need of the hour was to sweep away small states which stood in the way of progress, in the confidence that big was beautiful and that natural history not morality governed these affairs. Hobhouse and Hobson, by contrast, took their stand here as pro-Boers. They mounted a general critique of imperialism as a sectional concern of the plutocracy, not an interest of the nation at large. Hobson's famous book *Imperialism: a study* (1902) claimed that it buttressed conservatism at home by means of a jingoistic distraction from the real domestic issues, and in particular ate up the revenues which were needed for social welfare. More than this, Hobhouse found that the Fabians — with whom new Liberals like himself had previously found so much in common — failed the crucial test. Their attempt to smuggle in socialism via the Big State of the imperialists showed that they had lost sight of what collectivism was *for*. It had become an end in itself, in empty antithesis to the free-market individualism of the nineteenth century. According to Hobhouse, the Fabians' fallacy was to hail every extension of state authority as a triumph for socialism, and to manipulate the system in order to impose socialism from above by experts who knew best. But there was, he insisted, 'all the difference between benevolent officialism setting the world in order from above, and democratic collectivism which seeks not to restrict liberty but to fulfil it'.[9]

Following Hobhouse, it may be useful to distinguish between *moral* and *mechanical* reformists.[10] Thus a moral reformist believes social defects are systematic and structural. The remedy is to reform the system (and this is taken to be possible). But reform must flow from the free will, spontaneous endeavours, and participation of the citizens in a democratic society. The mechanical reformist, on the other hand, is not so optimisitc, possessing little faith in people's capacity to

[9] *Manchester Guardian*, 7 July 1899.
[10] See *Liberals and Social Democrats*, esp. pp. 5, 65.

achieve the necessary reforms. Since, however, he knows what progress ought to be, he seeks to achieve it by substituting manipulation as the means — to do what the people are incapable of doing for themselves. Thus Hobhouse identified the Fabians' fatal flaw as their illegitimate opportunism — their attempt 'to force progress by packing and managing committees instead of winning the popular assent'. This led to an exaltation of efficiency and the expert, whereupon 'all that was human in Socialism vanishes out of it'.[11]

Hobhouse and Hobson were clearly social democrats in their radical wish to use the state to further equality in an interventionist manner. They were also surely liberals in philosophy, each reaffirming the 'enduring' or 'illimitable' value of liberalism. They were Liberals, too, in party commitment up to the First World War and helped set their stamp upon the new Liberalism of that period. The distinguishing characteristics of this new Liberalism can, perhaps, be captured in the following ways. In the first place, it meant the end of *laissez-faire*. The death of the old individualism was pronounced — whatever good it might have done in the nineteenth century. The market was now exposed as neither fair nor expedient in its workings; and in particular the entitlement of the poor to the state's active assistance was explicitly claimed.

Secondly, however, socialism and the class war did not provide an efficacious remedy. This was partly because socialism as a proposal to change the ownership of the means of production simply missed the point. It ignored the efficiency of the market in creating wealth and allowing choice. It was open to objection because it would create a top-heavy bureaucracy. More public ownership might well be an answer but it was hardly *the* answer: it offered no fundamental solution. Liberal socialism certainly had its merits; but an illiberal socialism was just as conceivable. The other part of the objection was that although trade unionism might well be a good thing, none the less in itself it was limited and sectional in outlook. It was in this sense only another vested interest,

[11] See Clarke, *Liberals and Social Democrats* pp. 64-72, quotations at p. 71. The definitive study of Hobhouse's thought is to be found in Stefan Collini, *Liberalism and Sociology* (Cambridge, 1979).

and could not be universally effective as the creator of a new society.

A third proposition followed logically. The *ends* of politics were thus best expressed in terms of social justice, with a variety of means available to further it. The means did not exclude state collectivism and public ownership. Generally, however, the emphasis fell upon fiscal methods. It was necessary to create a structure of taxation which would recoup for the community from functionless wealth, and at the same time provide a system of incentives for useful activities. The aim was thus to use the design of the tax system as a way of harnessing market forces rather than fighting them. Finally, in this general policy there was held to be much common ground with organized Labour, and most of Labour's practicable aspirations could be satisfied within this framework. Partly, no doubt, this claim depended on equating the trade unions with the poor — a proposition more plausible in the first than the last quarter of the twentieth century.

This may serve as a thumb-nail sketch of an ideological position, worked out in detail in such books as Hobson's *Imperialism*, Hobhouse's *Democracy and Reaction* and *Liberalism*, and Hobson's *The Crisis of Liberalism*. The analysis, moreover, exhibited a faith in ideas, coupled with an assertion of the need for hard thinking, and a confidence in the power of persuasion. Although it might be an uphill struggle to effect this persuasion, in face of the entrenched conservatism of vested interests at all levels, there was *no other way*. All short cuts were barren expedients which would negate the democracy in social democracy — they represented illiberal rather than liberal solutions.

The practical significance of the new Liberalism, conversely, may be seen in two salient developments in Edwardian party politics. First there was the reorientation of Liberal policy in this period. Curiously, this may not have been explicit at the time of the party's great electoral landslide victory in 1906, but by the time of the general elections of 1910 a big shift was apparent as compared with the standards of the Gladstonian era. Old-age pensions had been introduced in 1908, Lloyd George had framed his People's Budget to help finance them in 1909, the National Insurance scheme was in train.

In short, we see a legislative programme built around ostensibly redistributive taxation and marking the inception of a welfare state. Secondly, electoral politics was now dominated by what contemporaries called a progressive alliance between Liberals and Labour. The Labour party achieved a hefty measure of parliamentary representation under the terms of an electoral pact with the Liberals — to clear mutual benefit. There was an impressive degree of ideological consensus between the new Liberalism and the bulk of the Labour party, which was seen mainly as a trade-union pressure group within this broader coalition. This led Hobhouse, indeed, to speak feelingly of the artificiality of current party divisions. There was, as he saw it, a real difference within the Labour ranks between doctrinaire socialism and the practical collectivism of the trade unionists. Likewise, Liberals were also divided between the Whiggish elements (or old Liberals) and the rising force of new Liberals. But between new Liberals and ordinary Labour, he maintained, there was 'no division in principle or method'.[12] At a more mundane level, of course, one can see that up to the First World War progressivism was cemented by tactical considerations. It was the bidding of self-interest for Liberals and Labour to hang together rather than the proverbially unwise alternative. The cruelty of the electoral system towards third parties needs no elaboration, and perhaps the Liberals hoped that an awareness of this factor would help keep Labour in check. (Is this the reason why the Liberals did not reform the electoral system while they still had the chance?)

All told, the Edwardian period was a good time for both liberals and social democrats — and best of all for people who were both liberals and social democrats. Never again did ideological and tactical pressures converge so happily. The First World War really saw the divergence in this respect. New tactical imperatives separated Liberals and Labour in a way that left social democrats stranded. There was a

[12] Introduction to 2nd edn. of *Democracy and Reaction* (1909), reprinted ed. P. F. Clarke (Brighton, 1972), p. 271. The ideological significance of this kind of progressive thought is examined in different ways in Michael Freeden, *The New Liberalism* (Oxford, 1978) and H. V. Emy, *Liberals, Radicals and Social Politics, 1892–1914* (Cambridge, 1973).

comprehensive breakdown of the progressive alliance. First there was the fact that the Liberal party lost the political initiative. Then it lost its own unity in a peculiarly damaging way. Liberals could perhaps have made sense of a parting of the ways between left and right; and a numerically decisive breach between a legitimate majority and a mere rump might also have settled the issue cleanly. But the split between Asquith and Lloyd George did not take this shape and proved instead to be a recipe for seven years of internecine factionalism. Finally, then, this gave Labour a unique opportunity to assert a will to power in 1917–18, which manifested itself in a deliberate strengthening of its appeal and organization. Labour had a corresponding success in recruiting people who had previously been spokesmen for the new Liberalism, like Hobson and the Hammonds. And despite Clause IV of the party's new constitution, much of Labour's ideology was in fact progressive or social democratic in tone, notably as conveyed by Hobson's old friend Ramsay MacDonald.

Yet the continued vitality of Liberalism in the 1920s remains impressive, especially after the reunion of the party in 1923. Partly this was a direct result of the impact of Lloyd George — as Charles Masterman put it, 'when Lloyd George came back to the party, ideas came back to the party'.[13] The dominant intellectual influence in the late 1920s was increasingly that of Keynes. Although he was a generation younger than Hobson and Hobhouse, Keynes's essential political outlook was as a social democrat in their sense. At the risk of seeming unduly schematic and procrustean, one can demonstrate that the four salient characteristics of the new Liberalism are all applicable to him — not surprisingly in view of the formative influences working upon him. Thus one can marshal some representative utterances under the same four heads:

First, his attitude to *laissez-faire*. In 1924 he was asserting that 'there is no place or time here for *laissez-faire*',[14] and in 1926 delivered a well-known lecture on 'the End of

---

[13] Lucy Masterman, *C. F. G. Masterman* (1939), p. 346.
[14] *The Collected Writings of John Maynard Keynes* (1971–), vol. xix, Donald Moggridge (ed.) *Activities, 1922–9*, p. 220. (This edition abbreviated below as *JMK* plus volume number.)

Laissez-Faire'. His theme was that Liberals must be ready to attach the industrial problem on new lines. 'Many of those who, without disrespect, I may call the old Liberals, are blind to this new problem', he wrote in 1927, and went on to argue that 'it means that on the economic issues they are Conservatives'.[15] The urgent need as he saw it was for radical rethinking of the economic role of the state.

Secondly, what did he think about socialism and the class war? According to Keynes, Liberals 'are inclined to sympathize with Labour about what is just, but to suspect that in the blind ignorant striving after justice Labour may destroy what is at least as important and is a necessary condition of any social progress at all — namely, efficiency'.[16] There was, he maintained, nothing so irrelevant to Britain's real economic problems as the panacea of nationalization. Keynes acknowledged some of the attractions of Labour, but found difficulties too. 'To begin with, it is a class party, and the class is not my class. If I am going to pursue sectional interests at all, I shall pursue my own . . . I can be influenced by what seems to me to be justice and good sense; but the *class* war will find me on the side of the educated bourgeoisie.'[17] He consistently treated trade unionism with sympathy, and argued against wage cuts as inexpedient and unjust throughout the late 1920s and early 1930s; but he had little faith in the ability of trade-union leaders to master the real problems.

Hence, thirdly, his view of social justice. For Keynes was advocating a different agenda from that of socialism. He looked for 'the development of new methods and new ideas for effecting the transition from the economic anarchy of the individualistic capitalism which rules today in Western Europe towards a regime which will deliberately aim at controlling and directing economic forces in the interests of social justice and social stability. I still have enough optimism to believe that to effect this transition may be the true destiny of the New Liberalism.'[18] Rather than direct intervention in industrial processes and wage-fixing, however, he opted for a policy of high taxes rather than high wages. This would, he suggested, serve to unite the views of liberals

[15] *JMK*, xix, p. 648.
[17] *JMK*, ix, *Essays in Persuasion*, p. 297.
[16] Ibid., p. 639.
[18] *JMK*, xix, 439.

and moderate socialists without squeezing the initiative out
of business.

Finally, how did Keynes view the Labour Party? When
Lloyd George's future hung in the balance in 1926, Keynes
singled out for commendation his 'strivings to work out a
radical policy, his desire to orientate the Liberal Party with
a view to an eventual co-operation with Labour'. Indeed
Keynes made co-operation with Labour a touchstone of good
Liberalism, and professed himself content to settle down to
'working out a new radical programme, from which some day
Labour will be glad to borrow'.[19] This led him to envisage a
tutelary role for Liberals which seems distinctly condescend-
ing: 'It is the task of Liberals, as I conceive it, to guide the
aspirations of the masses for social justice along channels
which will not be inconsistent with social efficiency . . .'.[20]

In passage after passage, one can quote Keynes echoing
the sentiments of new Liberals of the Edwardian period —
citations which do no violence to the structure of his argument nor the pattern of his thought. It is thus not surprising
to find Hobhouse still reiterating the same message about the
politics of the 1920s. He told C. P. Scott in 1924 that 'if we
divided parties by true principles', the extremes of left and
right would flank a division between progressives (comprising
true Liberals and moderate Labour) on the one side, and
conservatives (comprising old Liberals and Tories) on the
other. 'Ordinary Labour' and 'Good Liberal' seemed to him
manifestly one and the same — it was *party* that now got in
the way.[21] For this is the crucial difference made by the
First World War. By the 1920s the ideological convergence
of liberals and social democrats was matched by a tactical
divergence. Alliance between the Liberal and Labour parties
was no longer possible, much to the frustration of those of a
progressive outlook. As Keynes put it in 1930: 'So long as
party organization and personal loyalties cut across the
fundamental differences of opinion, the public life of this
country will continue to suffer from a creeping paralysis.'[22]

As far as Liberals were concerned, there were two obvious

---

[19] Ibid., pp. 539, 541.   [20] Ibid., p. 640.
[21] Clarke, *Liberals and Social Democrats*, p. 237.
[22] *JMK*, xx, *Activities, 1929–31*, p. 474.

impediments to working with or through Labour. One was socialism — ritualistically proclaimed, albeit not dominant in practice. It had the effect, however, of acting as an alibi against taking any radical initiative in economic policy, on the argument that all such initiatives were mere tinkering. The other difficulty was that the Labour party remained shackled to a sacrosanct trade-union viewpoint. 'The Constitution of the Labour Party', Hobhouse explained, 'binds it tight to the Trade Unions and their sectional selfishness, a most serious defect.'[23] Admittedly, trade-union leaders of vision and insight, notably Ernest Bevin, offered a more hopeful prospect; but the problem remained. The biggest obstacle to co-operation, however, lay in the tactical priorities of the party struggle. Labour's prime aim was to finish off the Liberals. The paradox here was that the closer they stood ideologically, the more urgent this task became, as can be seen plainly in the case of MacDonald. Under his leadership, party credibility loomed larger than constructive administration. The Labour Government of 1924, for all the paucity of its legislative achievements, must therefore be accounted successful because in the following general election the Labour vote went up from 30 to 33 per cent, while the Liberal vote declined sharply. In seats, of course, the Liberal collapse was even sharper.

There are two ways of viewing the actions of the Liberal party in the late 1920s. They can be seen as a last despairing effort to cling to major-party status. Or they can be seen as the first constructive attempt to provide an alternative to the class-bound polarity between Conservatism and Labour — setting the pattern for the waves of Liberal revival in the last twenty-five years. There is, in fact, plenty of evidence for both views.[24] The party showed its new face in the attention it gave to policy-making, first in the Liberal Summer Schools and then in the Liberal Industrial Inquiry, which grew out of them. When the talents of Keynes were pooled with those

[23] Clarke, *Liberals and Social Democrats*, p. 237.
[24] Liberal decline is well charted in Trevor Wilson, *The Downfall of the Liberal Party, 1914–35* (1966); Liberal revival in John Campbell, *Lloyd George: the Goat in the Wilderness* (1977). I am also indebted to the perceptive criticisms in Michael Hart, 'The decline of the Liberal party in parliament and in the constituencies, 1914–35', Oxford D.Phil. thesis, 1982.

of Lloyd George, which had a more bankable nature, a well-conceived, well-directed, well-funded think-tank was put at the Liberals' disposal. The so-called Liberal Yellow Book offered an analysis of current economic difficulties in dauntingly impressive detail. For those who found it too academic in tone, the main themes were given political punch in *We Can Conquer Unemployment*, the Liberals' election manifesto in 1929; and given intellectual sparkle in 'Can Lloyd George do it?', the supporting pamphlet produced by Keynes and Hubert Henderson.

The old face of the party, however, also showed itself, and in a less appealing light. Lloyd George was the party's greatest asset and also its greatest liability. His notorious political fund at a stroke removed the acute financial inhibitions which had hampered Liberal activity and removed likewise the incentive and ability to raise money within the party. His espousal of policies of national development lent them the aura of the man who won the war and gave them the taint of the man who lost the peace. If Lloyd George found them good, there were plenty of Asquithians left to draw an opposite inference. The Liberals' electoral base, moreover, was more shaky than it seemed. A few opportune by-election campaigns, financed by the Lloyd George Fund, temporarily masked the suppressed factionalism of the party. The party's poll in 1929 was certainly an improvement upon 1924, but it did not deliver a strong and cohesive body of MPs. Labour had clearly now fulfilled its aim of pushing the Liberals into a minority-party role.

The electoral structure itself clearly reinforced this struggle. There was not really a three-party system in the 1920s but a two-party system with three parties locked inside it. By then it was fairly obvious which two would become dominant. Given the prevailing electoral rules, and the existing shape of the class structure, Labour was able to achieve a *negative* success in this period; that is, the Liberals were destroyed as a credible force. Labour, however, never succeeded in winning more than 38 per cent of the vote in the inter-war period. Its failure to emerge in the 1930s as an adequate replacement for the old Liberal party helps explain movements of 'middle opinion', like the Next Five Years Group, and the proposals for popular fronts of various hues.

Hobson was a supporter of the Labour party, but one with little faith in its strategy here. For example, in 'A British Socialism' in 1936 he pointed to 'the failure of Socialism to make a sufficiently intelligible and equitable impression upon the minds of the mass of the wage-earners on the one hand, and of the salaried, professional and public employees on the other.' He advocated reinstating the liberal approach to measures, like the extension of public ownership to major utilities, which were generally advocated on narrower socialist grounds.[25] Keynes was expressing the same frustration in 1939 about a Labour party blinkered by dogma and unable to mobilize wide support: 'Why cannot they face the fact that they are not sectaries of an outworn creed mumbling moss-grown demi-semi Fabian Marxism, but heirs of eternal liberalism?'[26] This despairing cry might well stand as an epitaph for social democrats within the Labour party.

It was the Second World War which made Labour, almost in spite of itself, a repository for such aspirations. Its *positive* success in breaking through to majority-party status represented a qualitative change, achieved under extraordinary conditions. In round figures, 8 million voted Labour in 1935, compared with 12 million in 1945 (and 14 million in 1951). The premiss for all popular-front arguments was that Labour by itself could not rally sufficient support. In 1945, however, it emerged as a popular front in its own right, drawing upon the wartime consensus for change and prepared to implement the social-democratic programme of a whole generation. The Attlee Government was thus able to fulfil its historic role in carrying out virtually all the party's agreed policies — with the result that there remained outstanding the policies on which there was no agreement. This meant that the real challenge for Labour came after 1951, in seeking to evolve what Crossman called 'a second stage of Socialism'.[27] This involved a rethinking beyond the position worked out in

[25] See 'A British socialism', *New Statesman*, 25 Jan. and 1 Feb. 1936.
[26] *JMK*, xxi, *Activities, 1931-9*, p. 495.
[27] Janet Morgan (ed.), *The Backbench Diaries of Richard Crossman* (1981), p. 503. I have elaborated some views on this theme in 'Crossman and social democracy', *London Review of Books*, vol. 3, no. 7, 16-29 April 1981, pp. 8-10.

the early twentieth century by the sort of thinkers dealt with here.

For socialists, the difficulty appeared less as one of analysis than one of will. What was needed was more socialism; and the curious worship accorded to the Morrisonian public corporation supplied the approved means to this end. For social democrats, on the other hand, the problems were more intractable. In the first place, the confusion over whether they were 'socialists' was in itself unhelpful. Like his old friend Durbin, Gaitskell insisted on describing his sort of revisionism as socialism. This was the label on the bottle, even though what it contained might more accurately have been described as social democracy. At any rate, the Labour party found it unpalatable and Gaitskell's attempts to redefine the party's aims were doomed. Moreover, as social democrats, their practice was not always liberal. The Webbs had left an influential heritage of Fabian social engineering of an élitist and manipulative kind. In rhetoric social democrats were often moral reformists, but in practice mechanical reformists. Furthermore, their reliance on the old Labour Right and on the trade unions to sustain their power-base in the Labour party proved, in the long term, a weakness as well as an inconsistency. The developing instability of this relationship at a number of levels has become apparent in the last twenty years in the loss of control of conference and the party's swing to the left. More fundamentally, the axiomatic identification of the trade-union movement with the poor has become more obviously spurious. In retrospect, the road to Limehouse appears better signposted than anyone noticed at the time.

The language of social democracy was not readily adopted in the Labour party until the late 1970s. Instead the barren disputation about 'good socialists' and 'bad socialists' held the field. In reality, of course, social democrats are not socialists at all in their basic analysis, and have only accepted 'socialism' in a special sense which rendered it compatible with liberal and democratic goals. Likewise their support for trade unionism has been qualified by the wider ends it purports to pursue. In all this there is nothing new — or at least not as new as it seems. Social democrats were always uneasy in their support for Labour, making such support in effect conditional upon Labour *not* being essentially a socialist and trade-union party. Such a party would naturally preach nationalization as the only remedy and the class struggle as the only means of implementing it — claims strongly denied by social democrats. Perhaps they deceived themselves on this score.

At any rate, the circle can be squared no longer. Social democracy is plainly not compatible with the sort of outlook Labour has adopted. Social democrats may now be able to recognize more clearly that the roots of their creed lie in historic liberalism, not socialism. The conception of liberalism invoked here, however, is not that of a rigid set of political principles, established once and for all in the nineteenth century. It was the effort to formulate a new Liberalism that put social democracy on its feet in Britain. It was when liberals and social democrats were able to work together that a real record of success was achieved before the First World War. It was when Labour came nearest to fulfilling social-democratic aspirations in the 1940s that it enjoyed its most satisfying period of office. It was, on the other hand, in the inter-war years, when liberals and social democrats were artificially and factiously divided, that the country languished under governments notably lacking in the spirit of radicalism and generosity in facing up to the real problems.

Where does the present Alliance stand in this historical perspective? Its strength surely derives from its capacity to draw equally upon the legacy of Maynard Keynes and Ernest Bevin. They may stand as symbolic figures, each with authoritative claims to represent a notable tradition. In their own lifetimes, they were separated by differences of class, upbringing, education, and culture, which made it inevitable that they were attached by deep loyalties to different political parties. These differences could not be wholly bridged, therefore, by the mutual respect which they developed, nor by the similar outlook which they brought to the great issues in economic and international affairs of their era. But the erosion of class stereotypes during the last generation has correspondingly undermined the premises on which the conventional sociology of politics was based. The peculiar role of the Liberal intelligentsia and the unique mission of the Labour movement have alike become anachronistic. The old loyalties will no longer bear the weight that once gave them political leverage.

The Alliance has already shown in the local elections of May 1982 that, although not able to harvest a large number of seats during the Falkland gales, it has an impressive ability to break new ground. This can be seen in the total votes polled, in the improvement on past performance where the Liberals had previously been weak, and in the thick slice taken off the already shrunken Labour vote.[28] The Alliance is able to take its message into all kinds of residential districts, with particular success on recently built housing estates, whether council or owner-occupied, and in streets where renovation has brought new patterns of occupation. Virtually every sort of change in the basic habits of life loosens some tie which binds people to the Labour and Conservative parties. As a result, the section of the population open to persuasion by the Alliance is expanding all the time. The sociological opportunity for the Alliance is therefore obvious, as is the electoral imperative in making a concerted effort to seize it. Whether this effort will be forthcoming depends in part on how the SDP and the Liberals regard each other and whether their sense of affinity is more than skin-deep.

Tactical pressures and historic party loyalties have served to keep liberals and social democrats apart for a long time. Although there are rarely simple and unambiguous lessons to be learnt from history, there is surely a clear practical relevance today in recognizing that liberalism and social democracy in Britain spring from a common tradition, characterized by radicalism and openness to new thinking. History does not make a peremptory demand that these distinctive tendencies should be amalgamated; but it certainly permits one to regard their alliance as natural, consistent, and sensible.

[28] See the illunimating analyses of the results, *New Statesman*, 14 May 1982, and *The Economist*, 15-21 May 1982.

3. Survival and Revival

William Wallace

Never before in our history has a political party appeared so finished (we can say that now) and then — fighting on — won back its place in the life of the nation as the Liberal Party is now doing (*Liberal News*, 3 April 1958).

In politics of recent times there has only been one miracle — that is the survival of the Liberal Party (Roger Fulford, *The Liberal Case*, 1959, p. 10).

By all accounts . . . the Liberal Party ought to die. And yet it does not (*The Times*, Leader, 12 May 1964).

For a Liberal revival to be possible in the 1960s and 1970s, the Party had first to survive the long years of decline. There had of course been a series of 'revivals' ever since 1922, culminating in the grand hopes of 1947-9 and the disaster of the 1950 General Election. Between 1950 and 1954 the Liberal Party came very close to extinction. After the 1951 election Winston Churchill made overtures to Clement Davies's tiny parliamentary party, only one of whose six members had been elected against Conservative opposition. Davies's refusal to accept a government post prevented the rump of the independent Liberals following the National Liberals into the Conservative fold.

But it was very much the rump of a once great party. In the 1951 election only 43 Liberal candidates had saved their deposits, out of the 109 who fought; nine of these had been given clear runs by the Conservatives. The Party's finances were thin, dependent upon the loyalty and generosity of a small number of large subscribers. Party membership, after its post-war upsurge, sank to a low point in 1953 of just over 76,000, according to the Party organization's estimates. There was no evident place for the Liberal Party in a British political system dominated by 'Butskellism'; certainly, the Party itself had no clear strategy, no objectives beyond the preservation of the Liberal tradition and of Liberal principles. What those principles should be was the subject of a bitter battle within the Party, which reached its peak at the 1953 and 1954 Assemblies, between the 'radical individualists' who stressed the traditional commitment to free trade, minimum government, and individual liberty, and the Radical Reform Group, a ginger group which espoused the tradition of social liberalism developed by T. H. Green, J. M. Keynes, and William Beveridge. The anti-socialism of the individualist wing led to a slow drift away to the Conservatives; recognition by the social liberals of the achievements of the 1945–50 Labour Government led the Radical Reform Group to dissociate itself from the Liberal Party between 1954 and 1956, and to attempt a negotiation *en bloc* with the Labour Party after the 1955 election, which resulted in the defection of two former MPs (Dingle Foot and Wilfred Roberts) to Labour. In spite of the modest improvement in the Party's vote in the 1955 election, therefore, the Liberal Party of 1955 must to a dispassionate observer have looked rather more like an interesting historical relic than a live political party.

The history of the Party since then divides fairly naturally into five periods. The years from 1955 to 1959 saw the first stirrings of revival, and the first attempts to define a new purpose for the Party. 1959 to 1966 was the period of the first great revival, reaching its peak in the summer of 1962, and ultimately failing after the manœuvrings of Lib–Labbery in the spring and summer of 1965. The years from 1967 to 1971 were ones of uncertainty, financial stringency, and gradual readjustment — overtaken by the unexpected revival of Liberal support in the great surge of by-elections in 1972–3, carrying the second revival through to its peak in February 1974, with its disappointing aftermath in the October 1974 election. The five years from 1974 to 1979 saw another change of leadership, another period of readjustment, with the Party surviving a period of extremely low public support to mount a moderately successful campaign in the 1979 election.

THE BASIS FOR REVIVAL, 1955–9

There were some faint indications of electoral recovery in the winter of 1955-6. Liberal support rose in by-elections at Torquay and Hereford; and there were a few scattered gains in the local elections of May 1956. But the turning-point in Liberal fortunes can be dated fairly precisely to the spring and summer of 1956. In February 1956 the Radical Reform Group formally 'realigned' itself with the Liberal Party, despite the resistance of a minority of its members; in September a number of the leading individualists announced the formation of a 'People's League for the Defence of Freedom', independent of the Party, thus progressively disengaging themselves (and a number of the Party's wealthier subscribers with them) from the Party.[1] At the annual Assembly in September Clement Davies announced his resignation, and the young MP for Orkney and Shetland, Joseph Grimond, became leader. Shortly thereafter the Suez crisis erupted, and after an initial hesitation the Liberal parliamentary party committed itself to opposing the military intervention. The aftermath of Suez, which shattered for many the image of the Conservative Party as the natural inheritor of all that was best in the Liberal tradition, brought back into active politics a number of Liberal sympathizers, and led to an invaluable influx of new recruits. Together with the exit of the leading individualists and the return of the Radical Reform Group, it helped to set the predominantly anti-Conservative tone which marked the Liberal approach to politics in the years which followed. Despite the loss of Carmarthen in the winter of 1956-7, therefore, the Party was beginning to rediscover a sense of purpose and a place in the political spectrum.

Most immediately, the Party needed a political strategy,

[1] Where not otherwise footnoted, information for the 1955-6 period is taken from 'The Liberal Revival: the Liberal Party in Britain, 1955-1966', by William Wallace, Ph.D. thesis, Cornell University, 1968. Information on the RRG came primarily from *Liberal News* and from two of its active members, Desmond Banks and Edward Rushworth. Edward Martell, who had played a leading part in the 1947-9 organizational buildup, was one of the founders of the PLDF, and of its successor body, the National Fellowship. Other individualists and free traders, such as S. W. Alexander and Oliver Smedley, retained for some years active involvements on the fringes of politics, supporting the cause of economic liberalism; some, like Arthur Seldon, worked through the Institute of Economic Affairs to influence the intellectual climate in a way which profoundly affected the Conservative Party.

to justify its presence in British politics and to persuade potential converts. The main impetus towards a reinterpretation of the Party's purpose came from Mr Grimond, representing and redefining the aims of the Party's social-reforming wing. He presented, in a series of articles and speeches from 1953 on, an interpretation of Liberal politics which combined a plausible analysis of British political trends with a persuasive and attractive image of the sort of movement the Liberal Party must become. He asserted, for example, that political issues were more important than interests in politics — which was the fervent wish of all Liberals, clinging to their self-image as a party of ideas and rejecting the 'class politics' of the major parties. But he also suggested that identification with class was likely to decline, bringing with it the decline of the Labour Party, and enabling a realignment of British politics along 'the fundamental division' between progressives and conservatives, between those who welcomed change and those who resisted it.[2] The future of the Liberal Party was therefore bound up with the perceived exhaustion of the Labour Party, unable to reform itself after the completion of its short-term post-war programme.

The cause of the Labour Party's distress is the decay of the very roots of its being . . . But there is a great yearning for a purpose, a yearning for some cause which will appeal to the heart and to the head, a yearning such as is also felt in the Liberal Party. There is a chance that out of the frustration of which . . . Bevanism is a symptom, something new will emerge. If it does emerge, I believe it must be grounded on the freedom of the individual.[3]

The strategy of realignment was thus developed well before the 1959 election suggested that it might be a realistic prospect: it was set out in depth in Mr Grimond's speech to the Southport Assembly in September 1957. It had many weaknesses. Its target voters were seen as the army of 'Liberal-buts', who were only discouraged from supporting the Party by its apparent weaknesses and its poor chances of forming a government. Grimond's Southport speech, for

[2] See, for example, 'The Principles of Liberalism', *Political Quarterly*, July–September 1953, p. 237; and *The Liberal Future*, 1959, pp. 19–21.
[3] J. Grimond, quoted in *Liberal News*, 25 March 1955.

example, was reissued as a pamphlet under the title 'Grimond to those on the touch-line', as if the mass of intelligent fence-sitters could provide the new party with a firm electoral base. There was little attempt to appeal to the traditional Labour vote in industrial areas and little evidence that many within the Party understood their needs. Mr Grimond's preferred image was of a 'new' party, welcoming change and (from 1959 on) modernization. Its initial appeal was to provide 'a constructive protest against Conservatism'. Its place on the political spectrum, as conventionally defined, was thus clearly the centre-left; though under the pressures of the 1959 election campaign the attraction of the image of moderation, reason, and honesty brought out the alternative image of a centre party trying to carve out a space for itself between Macmillanite Conservatism and Gaitskellite Labour.

The Party's tactical approach benefited from a new concentration on by-election campaigning, combined with the luck of by-elections falling in favourable Liberal areas. The Hereford campaign in the winter of 1955-6 saw for the first time a campaign 'team', with a mixture of show business and organizational flair, recapture 36 per cent of the vote in an old Liberal stronghold. Alongside this, constituency Liberals in scattered areas were beginning to use local elections as a means of rebuilding support and strength. At the 1957 local elections the Liberals claimed 31 net gains; not a massive triumph, but after the long years of decline a modest and encouraging success.

But the sense that survival was assured and revival possible really came with the Rochdale and Torrington by-elections in February and March 1958, − both luckily, in areas with a strong Liberal tradition, though neither had been fought in 1955, both fought with nationally known and attractive personalities, with the assistance of a by now experienced by-election team. Ludovic Kennedy gained 35.5 per cent of the vote at Rochdale, to run Labour a good second; Mark Bonham-Carter, a grandson of Asquith, captured Torrington from the Conservatives with 38 per cent. With the Labour Party in disarray and the Conservatives in the doldrums, it looked as if the Party's fortunes were high. But, as so often later, the Party's mid-term buoyancy declined as the general election approached and as the two major parties recovered their internal balance. Three of the six Liberals elected in 1959 had beaten both Conservative and Labour opponents; Bonham-Carter failed to hold Torrington, but the impressive local efforts of Liberals in North Devon, where the Party then claimed several thousand members, provided the base for the election of Jeremy Thorpe.

As important a sign of organizational revival was the Party's ability to fight 212 seats, doubling its share of the national vote. Alongside the reshaping of the Party's strategy and policy from the top, largely by the parliamentary party without much involvement from the national executive or the Party officers, a gradual recovery in membership and activity was taking place in the country. So far it was sporadic, dependent upon individual activists; most of them appear to have been loyalists who had stayed with the Party through thick and thin, or new members brought up within the Liberal tradition who had been spurred into activity by their response to Suez, their distaste for the Labour Party's internal difficulties, or other accidental factors. The incidence of nonconformity was strong; in several constituencies associations were revived by informal contacts through the nonconformist churches. In one Lancashire town in 1971 eight of the nine Liberal councillors were Methodist lay-preachers; half of the Liberal workers in Newcastle-under-Lyme at the beginning of the 1960s were nonconformists, against a quarter of the local population.[4] There was, in addition, a trickle of converts from the other parties, which widened into a stream from 1959 on.

The Party organization, however, was ramshackle and underfinanced. A quarter of the Party's central income in the years 1954–62 came from the annual Assembly appeal alone. The 1958 Assembly at Torquay came close to collapse through bad chairmanship and an over-lengthy agenda, contributing to an image of a party of enthusiastic amateurs without a real sense of power. Part of the key to Grimond's success in reshaping and rebuilding the party was the successful circumvention of the party machine by a small group of

[4] F. Bealey *et al.*, *Constituency Politics*, 1965, pp. 289–90.

efficient operators — legitimized, after the 1959 election, as 'the Organizing Committee' — who supplied the organizational and administrative capacities which Grimond himself lacked. Frank Byers, the Liberal Whip in the 1945 Parliament, now a business man; Richard Wainwright, a Yorkshire accountant with close links to the Rowntree Social Service Trust, who later became MP for Colne Valley; Mark Bonham-Carter; Arthur Holt, Liberal MP for Bolton West and the Party Whip; Jeremy Thorpe, who won North Devon in the 1959 election; these constituted the core of a kitchen cabinet which directed the party throughout its first revival.

There had been little new development in party policy between the 1930s and the mid-1950s, beyond the commitment to 'co-ownership' in industry adopted at the 1948 Assembly. The arguments between the free-traders and the Radical Reform Group echoed those of the pre-war Liberal summer schools. It was one of Grimond's first priorities as Party leader to reshape its policies into a form appropriate to the issues of the next ten years. It is important to emphasize Grimond's individual role in this process, as a politician predominantly interested in policy and ideas, always at his best with a university audience or when teasing a group of policy advisers. He had clearly identified himself with the social-reforming wing of the Party, and set out to reformulate its policies in that image. A series of eighteen articles on party policy appeared in *Liberal News* during the spring of 1957, with the endorsement of the new Party leader. Significantly, the first was in support of European integration, on which there were many doubters within the Party's free-trading wing. Alongside a number of restated Liberal commitments, to common ownership, international co-operation, site-value rating, and parliamentary reform, were such important innovations as the proposal that Britain should abandon its independent deterrent and give up all land-bases east of Suez except Singapore — an approach to defence which Mr Grimond owed largely to Alastair Buchan, one of the many experts on whom he had drawn for informal advice. Later in 1957 'the first full-scale book on the attitudes and policies of British Liberalism since *Britain's Industrial Future* in 1928' was published, with contributions by Mr Grimond and a number of academics.[5] The Liberal Publications Department, of which Arthur Holt MP became chairman in May 1957, began the publication of a series of pamphlets initiated by the parliamentary party. For this not insubstantial effort in policy-making the parliamentary party relied upon the services of two newly recruited assistants, together with those voluntary advisers whom Mr Grimond's charm and concern for new ideas could bring in. The party outside, if one is to take Assembly resolutions as a guide, was some way behind its parliamentary leadership; the 1958 Assembly, for example, carried a resolution reaffirming the Party's commitment to the principle of unilateral free trade, and a resolution on the necessity of support for agriculture was only narrowly carried against free-trading opposition.[6]

THE FIRST REVIVAL, 1959-66

Much of the groundwork for the first upsurge of 1960-2 had thus been laid before the 1959 election. But the opportunity, and the rationale, were provided above all by the internal disarray of Labour, reinforced by sociological analyses of the 'inevitability' of Labour's decline and of the emergence of a 'new political class'. The fortunes of third parties in the British political system are dependent fundamentally on two things: the success or failure of the two major parties in maintaining their grip on substantial sections of the electorate, and the ability of the third party to capitalize upon the opportunities which major-party divisions from time to time present. The successful reshaping of the Party's appeal and policies in the late 1950s, together with the personal standing of its leader, gave the Liberal Party the capacity to seize the opportunity as it passed; but the opportunity was itself created by temporary factors well beyond the Liberals' control.

Looking back, one is struck by how similar the Liberal Party's appeal and approach in 1960-2 were to those of the

---

[5] *The Unservile State*, ed. George Watson, 1957, p. 7.

[6] J. S. Rasmussen, *The Liberal Party*, 1964, contains a full account of policy-making — and of the uproarious character of Assembly debates — during this period.

SDP in 1981-2. Both presented themselves as a 'new' movement — though in neither case was this strictly accurate.
Both claimed for themselves a commitment to reasoned
politics, a concern for issues and for good government, in
contrast to the old and discredited parties. Both identified
their voters with the emergence of a new political class,
optimistically suggesting that 'the working class will disappear
with universal education, television, cars and a middle-class
wage'.[7] Both successfully attracted a substantial group of
newcomers to political activity, predominantly drawn from
the professional and salaried classes, together with the
sympathy and temporary support of large sections of the
electorate. The Liberal revival faltered when Labour recovered,
from 1962 on; the fortunes of the SDP were similarly dependent upon the continuing disunity of the Labour Party.

The Labour Party's vulnerability, particularly between the
conferences of 1960 and 1961, gave the realignment strategy
credibility. It allowed the Liberals to clarify their position
on the political spectrum; no longer a party of 'the extreme
centre', as Mr Grimond had described it on many occasions
between 1956 and 1959, but of the centre left, providing 'a
radical alternative' (or, more ambitiously, *the* radical alternative) to Conservatism when the main opposition appeared
unable to perform that role.

It was a plausible strategy, though its sweeping formulation
disguised a number of unresolved ambiguities. Grimond and
others implied in the years immediately after 1959 that
realignment would come from the grass roots up, following
on the gradual disintegration of the Labour Party — though it
was not until 1962 that the Liberal Party made any concerted
effort to organize safe Labour constituencies and to campaign
for the working-class vote. But there was always a hope that
realignment from the top could provide a short cut, bringing
together the reasonable men within the Labour Party and the
Liberals in a 'radical realignment' of British politics. The
target voters were predominantly the expanding salariat, from
which so many of the Party's new recruits were drawn — a
target justified by reference to the 'embourgeoisement'

---

[7] J. Grimond, quoted in *Liberal News*, 26 June 1958.

thesis, thus enormously overestimating the speed of generational change.[8] The problem with this was that — as with the SDP twenty years later — the Liberals thus found themselves trying to replace the Labour Party by attracting discontented voters from the Conservatives; an approach which could only succeed if the Labour vote continued to crumble of its own accord. As it became evident, from the spring of 1962 on, that this had not happened, the Liberal Party was driven back to a centrist position, subtly altering its appeal to that of a 'radical *non-socialist* alternative' and picking up once again the theme of moderation and reason in politics.

The speed with which the Party grew from the summer of 1959 to the spring of 1963 is remarkable. Estimates of individual membership from the centre were unavoidably impressionistic and inaccurate; but they can provide a rough indication of the development, which is confirmed by scattered studies of local parties during this period. By the end of 1959 party membership had doubled to 150,000. Two years later, in the winter of 1961-2, it stood at 250,000, to touch a brief peak of 350,000 in 1963, before its rapid decline in the two years following. The new members included veterans from past Liberal activity and from other parties, major and minor; six of the Liberal candidates in the 1964 general election who replied to a postal survey carried out by Michael Steed and William Wallace had been active in the Common Wealth Party during the Second World War. The degree of continuity between the old Liberal Party and the new is suggested by the length of experience of 1964 candidates; half of them had been active in the Party before 1957, though many had had periods of inactivity and some had spent time in other parties in the interim.[9] But the bulk of the new recruits were coming into politics for the first time. Many of them were young, even straight out of university; the Young Liberals and the Liberal Students saw an enormous increase in membership and activities in this period. Most of

[8] See, for example, Mark Abrams and Richard Rose, *Must Labour Lose?*, 1960, and Ch. 2 of *The British General Election of 1959*, by D. E. Butler and Richard Rose, 1960.

[9] See William Wallace, *op. cit.*, Ch. 7.

those holding leading positions in the Liberal Party at the end of the 1970s had come into the Liberal Party in this three- or four-year period — an injection of new blood which ensured the survival of the party after the collapse of 1963-6, to take over from the faithful remnant who had kept the Party alive through the lean post-war years.

Tactically, the Liberals remained a conventional political party, differing from Labour and the Conservatives only in their imaginative use of by-elections and in the enthusiastic amateurism of their campaigning at the national level and in the constituencies. During 1960 the Party demonstrated its determination to break out of its fringe position by contesting the Bolton East by-election, thus ending the remaining electoral pacts with the Conservatives, which had given the Liberal Party straight fights with Labour (and so two of its six parliamentary seats) in Bolton West and Huddersfield West since 1950. In 1961, with a former Scottish rugby international as its candidate, it gained over 40 per cent of the vote in Paisley, while building up an impetus in local elections and by-elections which led the Conservative Government to postpone a threatened by-election in Orpington for five months over the winter of 1961-2. The result there, in March 1962, seemed to mark the breakthrough, with Eric Lubbock capturing nearly 53 per cent of the vote and the Labour candidate losing his deposit. Meanwhile, in local elections, the scattered gains of 1960 were reinforced by 192 net gains in the counties, boroughs, and UDCs in 1961, and the astonishing total of 567 net gains in 1962; which, with the more modest 169 net gains of 1963, brought almost a score of councils briefly under Liberal control.[10] For a moment after Orpington the National Opinion Poll put the Liberals ahead of both the Conservative and the Labour Parties (though Gallup never followed that far); it seemed that the breakthrough to major-party status had been made.

But it could not be sustained. The same opinion polls demonstrated the weakness of the Liberal position, in the

---

[10] These statistics were provided by Conservative Central Office. None of the councils controlled by the Liberals was large, and most were urban district councils; the most significant borough, Blackpool, also provided the most sobering lesson of the dangers of a too rapid rise to power.

continuing buoyancy of the Labour vote throughout most of the country. In spite of the enormous improvement in party finance and organizational capacities in the two previous years, there was a limit to how many campaigns could be managed at once. At Derbyshire West and Leicester North-East in June and July 1962 the Liberals managed good second places to Conservatives and Labour respectively, but it was Labour instead of the Liberals which captured Middlesbrough West from the Conservatives. On the more favourable ground of Chippenham in November, the Liberals managed only a third of the vote. The luck of a by-election in the traditionally Liberal territory of Colne Valley provided the Liberals with the rare chance to capture a seat from Labour, and so to give the revival renewed impetus and to reinforce the claim to be an alternative to the Labour Party. But the 40 per cent that Richard Wainwright achieved in a snowbound campaign in March 1963 crushed the Conservative vote without dislodging Labour.

The reformulation of party policy also moved forward at a faster pace in the three years after the 1959 election. With the appointment of Harry Cowie, in September 1959, as director of research, a full research department was established, with four staff researchers and two information officers at its peak, funded with the assistance of the Rowntree Social Service Trust. Advisory panels were created, a regular series of *Current topics* was initiated to promote internal debate, and statements and policies flowed out, on the need for economic modernization, the decentralization of government, partnership in industry, parliamentary and electoral reform, and a redirection of priorities in foreign policy from the Far East to Europe. Alongside this the New Orbits Group, a ginger group on policy which grew out of the Young Liberal movement, and the Unservile State Group which had developed out of the 1957 volume of essays, were contributing a wealth of new ideas. In the political atmosphere of 1960–2 the growth of political satire such as 'Beyond the Fringe' undermined the Conservative image, while the Labour Party was preoccupied with disarmament and Clause 4. The combination of a youthful leader, a set of policies which emphasized the transformation and adaptation of economy, society, and

foreign policy, and the novelty and freshness of the Party
itself contributed to a distinctive and appealing image; its
appeal reinforced by the transatlantic echoes of the Kennedy
revolution, with a new political generation coming into power
with fresh ideas, making Harold Macmillan look like a distinguished figure of the past.

But in the course of 1962–3 much of this distinctive image
was weakened by the shifting policies and attitudes of the
two major parties. The Liberal commitment to Europe had
been overshadowed, from 1961, by Harold Macmillan's
application to join the European Community, in spite of the
evident hesitations within his own party. Conservative
conversion to the idea of indicative planning and industrial
intervention, symbolized by the establishment of the National
Economic Development Council in 1962, borrowed many of
the Liberal clothes in economic policy. With Gaitskell's
unexpected death in January 1963, Harold Wilson's decision
to emphasize industrial innovation as the hallmark of the
Labour appeal (characterized, and caricatured, in his phrase
'the white-hot heat of the technological revolution') imitated
the Liberal appeal as a modernizing and innovating force in a
stagnant society. The Liberals could only reiterate the depth
of their commitment to these reforms, doing their best to
resist the effective two-party squeeze as both Conservatives
and Labour moved over to occupy the ground which the
Liberals had marked out. This was, after all, how classic
two-party systems were supposed to work; their refound
unity, and their willingness to go for the centre ground,
uncovered all the ambiguities of Liberal strategy and the
illusions on which Liberal hopes had been based.

Had the Conservative Government succeeded in taking
Britain into the European Community, politics might have
been very different. There had been a number of unofficial
contacts between Liberals and Gaitskellites since the 1959
election, arguing the respective merits of their paths towards
a realignment of the Left – a common aim, but differing
over the possibilities of reshaping the Labour Party from
within, or of building a new coalition from outside. There
were some highly informal discussions between the pro-
European group of Gaitskellites and the Liberal leadership

in the immediate aftermath of Gaitskell's condemnation of
the Common Market. Had the issue not been killed by de
Gaulle's veto, the strains within Labour between the pro-
European Campaign for Democratic Socialism and the anti-
European stalwarts in the unions and the left wing would
have broken out into renewed faction-fighting — and, as one
or two Labour MPs had discreetly been hinting, a divided
party and a further lost election would have brought them
to the point of leaving the party. But the French veto and the
revival of support for Labour during 1963 stifled such
thoughts, and the vision of realignment from the top receded.

In a pattern which was to be repeated time and time again
in the following fifteen years, Liberal support dropped
steadily from its mid-term high to a low point in the winter
of 1963-4, only to recover again in the course of the election
campaign. In the eight months that followed the 1963
Assembly, the Liberals lost five deposits in nine by-elections;
but in the general election they polled over three million
votes, and made a net gain of two seats.

The Party had also overstretched itself in financial and
organizational terms. After the 1959 election the parliamentary party had, in effect, executed a *coup* on the party
organization, bringing in Frank Byers and Mark Bonham-
Carter to run a growing professional staff with a rapidly
rising income. But with finances dependent upon short-term
appeals and passing enthusiasms, the downturn in income
in 1963-4 left party expenditure high and dry. By the end
of 1965 the party organization, in its comfortable new
headquarters in Smith Square, was £40,000 in debt and
closer to bankruptcy than it had been at the start of the
expansion ten years before. With such a weak organizational
base, and with such poor communication between the centre
and the constituencies, it was even more difficult to hold on
to new members as the Party's standing and morale dipped.
There were defections both to the Conservatives and to the
Labour Party in the year before the 1964 election; the
estimate of the number of seats they would contest dropped
steadily from the high point of 470 to the eventual figure of
365, while in the 1964 local elections many of the gains of
1961 were wiped out.

The result of the 1964 election — as of the October 1974 election — was the worst possible outcome for the Liberals. A Conservative win, however narrow, would have reopened all the wounds within the Labour Party, so recently plastered over, thus reviving the prospect of a realignment of the left. A larger number of Liberal MPs, and a hung parliament, would have offered a position of real influence; though the Liberals had shied away from facing up to the dilemmas of holding the balance of power, as too divisive an issue within the Party, and as raising worrying echoes of past coalitions, from which veteran Liberals retained only bitter memories. With a Labour majority of five, rapidly reduced to three, the Liberals were left in a position of seeking to support a reforming Labour government without receiving any credit for the influence they might exert.

The anti-Conservative bias which the Liberal Party had developed over the previous decade was evident in the initial sympathy which most leading Liberals offered to the Labour Government. The alternative, after all, was a return to Conservatism, turning their backs on their commitment to modernization and reform. This was, as the Party's youngest and newest MP put it soon after his by-election win in Roxburgh in the spring of 1965, 'the best left-wing government we've got. The immediate alternative . . . would be a Conservative government.'[11] Immediately the result was declared, Mr Grimond made it clear that the Liberals were prepared to support the Government on a limited programme, carefully and publicly detailing the policies which the Liberals would back.[12] After the Leyton by-election in January 1965 he returned to the theme, calling for 'some reasonably long-range agreement with the Govenment' to guarantee stability for a programme of reform.[13] Through the spring and early summer he made a number of public invitations for Liberal-Labour co-operation, receiving in return only discreet gestures and hints from Labour.

The evidence suggests that Mr Grimond was still hoping for a short-cut realignment from the top, by regrouping the more

[11] David Steel, MP, in *New Outlook*, October 1965, p. 17.
[12] The *Observer*, 18 October 1964.
[13] *The Times*, 8 March 1965.

moderate elements in Labour with the Liberals in some form
of loose alliance. After the 1964 election, two Labour MPs
proposed the negotiation of an electoral pact, and there were
other gestures and noises — the inclusion of the Liberals in
the honours list for the first time since the war, the dropping
of hints on electoral reform in the summer of 1965 — which
could encourage the optimistic to mistake a swallow for
a summer.

But in reality Labour had no incentive to negotiate with
the Liberals. It was easy for Harold Wilson to take care not
to offend the Liberals too deeply by its initial programme of
legislation, without formal consultation, and to throw back
on to the Liberals the responsibility for its survival or collapse.
Suggestions in the by-elections at East Grinstead (in February
1965) and Roxburgh (March) of a 'grass-roots' movement
towards Lib–Lab voting brought some satisfaction; but there
were many Liberals who were more impressed by the opposite
shift of tactical voting in by-elections where Labour was
starting from a stronger position. The 1965 Liberal Assembly
heard many expressions of unease; and in the following
week, with Labour support reviving in the polls, Harold
Wilson effectively ridiculed the Liberal pretensions to power.
The defection of one of its nine MPs, in effect, through his
acceptance of the deputy chairmanship of Ways and Means
to resolve the further crisis in Labour's position brought
about by the death of the Speaker, dealt another blow to
Liberal unity and morale. By the winter of 1965, the idea of
realignment as the basis for a Liberal strategy was dead, and
the Party was faced with the necessity of finding a new
purpose, a new justification for its existence in British
politics.[14]

Mr Grimond, his vision of a new progressive party in ruins,
began to consider resignation — a prospect which caused
consternation when it was leaked to the press in January
1966. The announcement of another general election at the
end of February rallied the Party again; the campaign revived

[14] The 'Lib–Lab' debate of 1965 was rehearsed in a *Guardian* pamphlet of
that year, *The Liberals and the Government*. The *Guardian*'s role has recently
been outlined, more explicitly, by Alastair Hetherington in *The Guardian Years*
(1981).

spirits and recovered some support, and in spite of a decline in the constituency vote there was a net gain to twelve parliamentary seats. But, more important, the Labour Party had achieved a clear majority. The rationale for the Liberal advance of the previous five years, that Labour must lose, had been decisively destroyed.

READJUSTMENT ON THE SIDELINES, 1967-71

In many ways the Liberal Party did little more than mark time between the 1966 election and the almost spontaneous revival of 1972-3. But in many other ways it was a period of readjustment, much of it painful: financially, organizationally, strategically. In finance and organization, the leading role came more from the party leadership than from the grass roots; but in strategy and, to an extent, in policy the process of adjustment came pushing up from below, often against the leadership's wishes.

The leadership group which had led the first revival played a much smaller role in the Liberal Party in these years. Mr Grimond himself was depressed and exhausted by the failure of his strategy, by Harold Wilson's effective double-cross, by the death of one of his sons, and by the prospect of a full parliament without any significant influence on government. His resignation, in January 1967, was a surprise only in terms of its timing. Arthur Holt, who had played an active role in publications and in organization, had lost his seat in Bolton in the 1964 election, and was preoccupied with the family business. Frank Byers was devoting more attention to his business career, and Mark Bonham-Carter to other political causes. Jeremy Thorpe was now, after Jo Grimond, the longest-serving of the party's twelve MPs, and seemed to be his natural successor as leader. A highly extrovert personality, an excellent and regular performer on television and radio, he was already one of the party's best-known figures. Had there been a leadership election open to the whole party member-ship — as there was on his resignation in 1976 — he would undoubtedly have won by a landslide. But he was less popular among his closer colleagues and among the party organization; only one of the professional staff at headquarters was a

Thorpe supporter at the time of his election. There was an abortive attempt to persuade Richard Wainwright, who had entered Parliament only the previous year, to run against him, as someone who could command the confidence of the party's activists. In an election confined to the twelve MPs, with some informal consultation as to the views of the party outside, Thorpe received six votes and two other candidates (Emlyn Hooson and Eric Lubbock) three each.

Thorpe's strengths were as an organizer, a money-raiser, and a public personality. After his election in 1959 he had retained responsibility for a crucial part of the fund-raising and organizational effort, through his responsibility for the 'special constituencies' which the Liberals hoped to win in the 1964 election. In 1966 he had been elected treasurer, with a mandate to raise the Party's sources of finance — a preoccupation which remained with him throughout his period as leader. In contrast to Jo Grimond, who had preferred to leave organizational details to his colleagues while he concentrated on ideas and objectives. Thorpe was largely uninterested in policy, and not much concerned with strategy.

He had a difficult first year as leader, faced with rising discontent within the national executive and party council at his continued acceptance of a conventional strategy, in which the MPs conscientiously fulfilled their parliamentary duties and their social obligations in London, and in which he continued to assert the moderating reasonable influence of the Liberal Party as a force in British politics. With a party which was rapidly becoming more radical, and more discontented with conventional politics, this led to an unfortunate eruption of public criticism when he was abroad on his honeymoon in May 1968, accompanied by another effort to float an alternative candidate for the leadership. For many in the constituency parties, this outburst of plotting and criticism was puzzling; but Thorpe's strength as a public persona, at its best with large audiences, was not accompanied by an easy manner with small groups, which left him much less support within the party hierarchy than at the grass roots.

The situation was complicated by the radicalization of the Party after 1966, as Liberals searched for a new rationale in spite of the reluctance of their leader to countenance a change. After the failure of the revival, and even more after the collapse of Lib–Labbery in 1965, it had become clear that 'there are no short cuts to a radical future for England. It will be a long grind and very hard work and the plums will not fall into our lap for years. Liberals must just soldier on.'[15] For some this meant a return to the concept of a party of ideas, producing new policies to be taken up in due course by the major parties within the political debate. For others the failure of the 'conventional' approach towards a breakthrough demanded more radical solutions. John Pardoe MP, frustrated at the invisibility of the parliamentary grind, suggested that the parliamentary party should consider whether 'to opt out of Parliament all together, and to stump the country in a great continuous national crusade'.[16] The minority within the Party which had from 1961 on protested about the 'softness' and conventional nature of the Liberal approach to politics gained ground, and the Party's youth movement began to cause consternation among some older members by organizing demonstrations and collaborating with other youth groups like the Young Communist League in several campaigns. The Party's youth movement, indeed, was gaining increasing prominence in a period when dis-illusionment with the Labour government was rising, and when the imitation effect from student activism in the United States and, in 1968, in Continental Europe was sweeping through Britain's universities and colleges. Theirs was a different image of Liberalism from that presented by its reasonable and middle-class MPs; more radical, more raucous, even — in the eyes of the conservative press — revolutionary. Thorpe's reaction, and that of the small group of advisers on whom he depended, was to see the youth movement as a threat to the Party's continued respectability — leading to repeated clashes at assemblies and councils from 1967 to 1971. Others within the party hierarchy, who would have liked to have seen an accommodation between the

---

[15] Revd. Timothy Beaumont, *New Outlook*, November 1964, p. 10.
[16] *New Outlook*, September 1966. *New Outlook*, September 1969, contains an interesting critique of Thorpe's leadership.

leadership and the younger radicals, struggled with intermittent success to prevent a split — which was most directly
threatened at the 1971 Assembly, when Jeremy Thorpe
talked of the possibility of 'throwing people out' of the
Party.[17]

But out of the youth movement, and out of the disillusionment with Labour which also spawned a number of single-
issue groups on aid, housing, child poverty, and social reform,
came an alternative rationale for political activity within a
third party largely excluded from political influence at the
centre. Disillusionment with the Labour Party, reflected by
the rapid decline in Labour membership between 1967 and
1969, was reflected within the Liberal Party by a rejection
of the idea of realignment from the top; reinforced by the
uncomfortable discovery within Parliament that on specific
radical issues, such as the well-publicized stand the Liberal
MPs took against the Kenyan Asian Bill in 1968, their allies
were to be found more often on Labour's left wing than on
its moderate right. Groups of Liberal activists were beginning,
with some success, to establish bridgeheads in the inner cities,
the heartland of the Labour Party's traditional territory;
in many cases moving into specific wards in Leeds, Liverpool,
and Newcastle (in true bed-sit fashion) to attack the Labour
Party from below. Community campaigning was not entirely
new to the Liberal Party — hardly surprising in view of the
strong commitment to participatory democracy. Wallace
Lawler had built up a base in central Birmingham sufficiently
strong to carry him into Parliament in the Ladywood by-
election of 1969. There had been other examples in Leicester,
Lancashire, and Yorkshire; while the politics of Rochdale
had a localist tradition all their own. But the deliberate
articulation of a 'Community Politics' strategy, as a justification for the long march through local activity and local
power to undermine the sovereignty of Westminster, emerged
out of the intellectual ferment within the Young Liberals in

[17] The first proposal that the party should be prepared to consider civil dis-
obedience as a means of drawing attention to its aims and grievances was made,
so far as I am aware, by John Griffiths in *New Outlook*, January 1964, p. 6.

the years before and after 1968.[18] Beyond the control of the
party leadership, impervious to the neglect of the national
press, Liberal activists could thus work to mobilize the
electorate into local activity and to build up pockets of local
strength from which to expand when the opportunity came.
The radical image of the Liberals' youth wing, so worrying
to those who were aiming to attract Conservative voters in
rural and suburban seats, was reinforced by the central role
which such Young Liberals as Peter Hain and Gordon Lishman
played in the Stop the 1970 Tour in the run-up to the 1970
general election.

Aside from its youth wing and from these pockets of new
activity, the Party as a whole drifted slowly downhill. Its
most striking failure was its inability to tap the discontent
with the Labour Government during the mid-term period,
at a point when the Conservative opposition had little to
offer in terms of charismatic leadership or popular policies.
In Scotland, which had supplied five of the Party's twelve
MPs in 1966, the Liberal Party lost out — and lost supporters
and members — to the reviving Scottish Nationalist Party
which regarded the Liberals — fainthearted supporters of
devolution rather than independence — with hostility. In
Wales, too, discontent with Labour swung to the Nationalists
rather than the Liberals, with Plaid Cymru capturing the old
Liberal stronghold of Carmarthen. The overall number of
Liberal councillors of England and Wales continued to
decline, though with some significant shifts in representation
as the first bridgeheads were established in Liverpool and
Leeds. Worst of all, the Party's finances were in a dreadful
state. Over-optimism in attempting to maintain expenditure
without guaranteed income led to an overdraft which touched
£93,000 in the autumn of 1969, after the failure of successive
appeals and fund-raising measures. In 1968 the headquarters
moved from the comfort of Smith Square to an alley off the
Strand, with the headquarters staff shrinking from over 40
in 1966 to around 20 in 1969. On the eve of the election

[18] The invention of the label itself is claimed by Gordon Lishman and Lawrence
Freedman, at one of the YL strategy sessions early in 1969. The parallels with
the revolutionary rhetoric about mass involvement and popular mobilization,
current at that time, are evident.

Mr Thorpe secured a six-figure contribution from Jack Hayward, an expatriate millionaire who had been persuaded by Mr Thorpe to buy Lundy Island for the nation in 1968; but this (at the time) anonymous donation did little more than wipe out the overdraft and provide a small surplus for a modest campaign.

Party policy was developed and consolidated during this period, rather than being launched along radically new lines. The parliamentary party were rather too ready to fall back on a reiteration of the received doctrines of the early 1960s, as proving 'that the Liberals had been right'. The muffled revolt of May 1968 had led, under Young Liberal leadership, to the establishment of a 'Liberal Commission' to review and restate the party programme in coherent form; its report, published in time for the 1969 Assembly, formed the basis for the 1970 manifesto. The Party was most clearly identified with civil-liberty issues, during a period in which the Labour Government seemed at best ambivalent on such concerns. David Steel, successful in the ballot for private members' bills in 1967, pressed through a bill to reform the law on abortion (with the discreet help of the then Labour Home Secretary, Roy Jenkins, so forming a personal link which was to bear fruit years later). On immigration, on police powers, and on government secrecy, the Liberals were distinctive; but they had much less to say on major economic issues.

A last-minute effort before the 1970 election raised the number of Liberal candidates just over the 50 per cent of parliamentary seats necessary to give even the faintest credibility to any long-term claim to represent a potential alternative government. This was far short of the 'broad front' strategy demanded by the party council in 1968, of over 500 candidates, but as much as could be managed in the state of constituency organization and the absence of substantial central subsidies. Mr Thorpe led a campaign which was colourful and energetic, but which failed to attract the serious press or to draw the fire of the two major parties. In the event, he only narrowly retained his own seat in North Devon, returning to lead a parliamentary party reduced once again to six members. The national Liberal vote, at 7.5 per cent, was however not too badly down from 1966, and still well above the 5.9 per cent of 1959. In an election which the Nuffield study described as 'an unpopularity contest' the apparent irrelevance of the Liberals to the central issues of the campaign, compounding their failure to catch the swell of mid-term discontent with Labour, was extremely worrying; but yet the Party in the country was still there, with a gradually shifting local base, which could under different circumstances provide the foundation for another revival.

THE SECOND REVIVAL, 1972-4

The year after the 1970 election was another low point in Liberal fortunes. Jeremy Thorpe suffered the personal catastrophe of the death of his wife, killed in a car crash while returning to London after the campaign. The division between the leadership and the radicals within the Party continued, though moderated a little by the replacement of Louis Eaks by Tony Greaves as Young Liberal chairman in 1970, and by the gradual disengagement from the party of some of the most radical of the Young Liberal leadership during the next two years. The 'Radical Bulletin' group emerged as a counterweight to the orthodoxy of the parliamentary party, as a caucus and a focus for internal debate. The 1970 Assembly passed, against the misgivings of the leadership, a Young Liberal resolution which committed the Party to campaign on a Community level as a major part of its political strategy. But in the 1971 local election Liberals did worse than at any point within the fifteen years previously — though there were some isolated gains of future significance, as in Liverpool.

It is difficult to explain what triggered the spectacular upsurge of 1972-3. One element, clearly, was the lucky incidence of by-elections, in favourable territory, building up a sense of momentum in the public mind. Rochdale, which fell vacant in the late summer of 1972, combined a strong Liberal tradition with the rare 'local son' appeal of Cyril Smith, enabling the Liberals to capture a seat in October from the Labour opposition. A concentration of Liberal campaigning efforts in Sutton and Cheam led to a more remarkable victory in December 1972; though the Liberal failure in Uxbridge, on the same day, which resulted from a deliberate decision to focus efforts in Sutton, emphasized the Liberals' limited capacity in human and financial resources, and the importance of flying columns of Liberal activists in winning new seats. In the 1973 local elections, an unusual opportunity provided by the reorganization of local government, the Liberals made a number of major advances, winning control of Eastbourne, and achieving substantial gains in Labour as well as Conservative areas, in Liverpool, Pendle, and other centres of community campaigning. The peak of the revival came in July, with the capture of two safe Conservative seats on the same day in different parts of the country, in Ripon and the Isle of Ely. With the capture of Berwick in November, the Liberals had gained five by-elections in the course of a single parliament, to come close to doubling their parliamentary strength — a far more impressive and sustained eruption than the single victory of Orpington in 1962.

Part of the explanation was to be found in the greater experience and organizational capacities of the Party. In spite of the Party's straitened finances, and the continuing decline in the size of its professional staff, there now existed a relatively coherent network of experienced campaigners across the country, hardened by their experience in the years since the first naive revival, and reinforced by successive generations of Young Liberal activists throughout the late 1960s. The new recruits which the Party attracted between 1972 and 1974 thus learned the requirements of third-party campaigning quickly. Community Politics as a technique, if not always as a philosophy, was gaining ground rapidly. Trevor Jones, the architect of the Community-Politics approach in Liverpool, won election for president at the 1972 Assembly against the official candidate as the champion of the radical wing; dashing across the country from by-election to by-election, he and others introduced the techniques of pursuing local grievances and regular leafleting to constituency after constituency. Though its membership was not fundamentally different in social background from that of 1961–3, its approach to politics had thus become a great deal more professional.

In contrast to the first revival, there was relatively little novelty value in the Liberals' policy proposals. With only the vestiges of a professional research staff to guide them, the Party had established a new Standing Committee in its revised constitution, to take over from the ineffective National Executive the direction of the Party's voluntary panels on policy. Under John Pardoe's chairmanship, it strengthened the Liberals' commitment to social reform, and spelt out the necessity of a statutory prices and incomes policy; but the other main planks on which the Liberal Party fought the 1974 elections were familiar themes from 1966 and before.

Nor did the Party have any clear strategy, any convincing rationale to guide it through the complexities which were to face it after the 1974 election. The speed of the revival enabled the Party to pass from an unhappy acceptance of minority status to the plausible claim to be a potential majority, without passing through the awkward choices of an intermediate stage. With a Party membership more anti-Conservative than anti-Labour — most clearly among the activists who attended the assemblies and turned up to help at by-election campaigns — the Party retained a parliamentary party overwhelmingly drawn from Conservative seats, and necessarily concerned about the peripheral problems of rural voters rather than the preoccupations of the urban masses. Jeremy Thorpe, as leader, took happily to the renewed claim to be a major force in British politics, without considering in detail how to use that force after the election, or how to carry his Party with him in whatever decision might be made. Two members of the Party's Machinery of Government Panel, Michael Steed and William Wallace, had prepared a paper for discussion at the February 1974 meeting of the Party Council on the choices that would face Liberals in a balance of power situation. This was presented for debate despite the hesitancies of the leadership; immediately on the announcement of the election, Mr Thorpe ordered all copies of the paper to be destroyed. Thorpe fought an excellent campaign, largely from his constituency base in North Devon, in which the rise of the Liberal percentage in the opinion polls as the campaign proceeded became almost its own self-sustaining theme. But his reiteration that 'the Liberal Party is

in this election, first and foremost, to form a government'
left dangerously unclear on what basis the Liberals would,
if they emerged from the election as a substantial but still a
minority force in Parliament, offer support for 'an agreed
package of economic policies put forward by reasonable
men in another party'.[19]

As before, the Liberal Party was only able to take advantage of a situation created by the failings of the major parties.
The reopening of Labour's internal disputes, in the course of
1971-2, the recriminations over their record in government,
and the reversal of policy on the European Community again
deprived the official opposition of the benefit of mid-term
disillusionment. As the Conservative Government reversed
its initial priorities in the course of 1972 disillusioned voters
turned to the Liberals in England — though they turned,
increasingly, to the nationalists in Scotland. The challenge
to the Liberals was to consolidate and to educate this discontented vote, and despite its limited resources, to build a
more positive and permanent basis for a major party role.
Community campaigning seemed to offer the instrument
for consolidating this new-found support; but the sobering
experience of the 1974 election demonstrated that it was not
easy to transfer loyalties gained by local activity into support
at the parliamentary level.

As in 1964, the result of the election was cruelly difficult
for the Liberals. Without an overall majority for any party,
they had enough members to exert influence, but not enough
to hold the balance. Without consulting his unprepared Party,
Jeremy Thorpe accepted Edward Heath's post-election
invitation for consultations at No. 10, and was then forced to
reject the derisory offer of a seat in the cabinet without any
commitments on policy against a background of alarm and
distrust within the Party and misunderstanding in the press
and public. In the months following, the Liberal Party
launched a crash campaign to organize derelict Labour areas,
raising the number of seats fought in the October election
from 517 to 619 — a larger number than the Party had ever
fought before. Mr Thorpe, meanwhile, was developing the

[19] Speech at the 1973 Southport Assembly.

theme of 'a Government of National Unity', a campaign for coalition which was firmly rejected by both major parties and roundly attacked by many within his own camp. The Party Assembly in Brighton, after a day-long Commission debate on strategy, reached an agreed form of words which avoided committing the Party to oppose any prospect of collaboration with the Conservatives after another election; but while David Steel, his Chief Whip, had collaborated with Richard Wainwright as Commission chairman in agreeing a formula acceptable to the Party, Mr Thorpe was reportedly furious at the inadequate support it gave for his own preferred ideas. The October general election thus witnessed a less convincing Liberal campaign, and registered a decline in the vote gained from the six million of February to a little over five million. If the result of the February 1974 election had provided a potential springboard for a breakthrough, then that opportunity had been lost in the six months that followed; the October 1974 election failed to re-establish the dominance of the two major parties, but equally failed to mark out the Liberals as the major alternative within a new parliament where the two Nationalist Parties had fourteen members to the thirteen Liberals.

CONCLUSIONS: THE RETURN TO REALIGNMENT, 1975-81

The importance to the Liberal Party of the hard core of party activists left behind, layer upon layer, by each receding tide of new enthusiasm from 1956 on, was demonstrated in the five years between 1974 and 1979. For much of this period the Party's standing in the opinion polls was abysmal. With only two exceptions, one just before the 1979 election, the Liberals consistently fared worse in by-elections than they had in October 1974. Local-election results in 1976 and 1977 showed severe losses on 1973, though renewed progress was again made in 1978. The Party was battered by the sad and long-drawn-out ending of Thorpe's political career — though its skilful and successful handling of the Party-wide election for his successor in the summer of 1976 increased membership and morale, and brought some welcome and positive publicity.

Both contenders for the leadership were products of the first revival: John Pardoe a convert from Labour, David Steel from among the first generation of student Liberals whom Grimond brought into the Party. Steel, less radical in policy and rhetoric than Pardoe, was both more radical and more determined in his strategic vision. Unconvinced of the viability of the 'long march' approach of the Community campaigners, he made it clear in his first major speech as leader at the 1976 Llandudno Assembly that he was prepared to take the short-cut route to realignment, through collaboration with other parties in government and through a demonstration that the Liberals could exert a positive influence well before they had achieved the nirvana of a breakthrough to major-party status. He resisted severe pressures from some of his parliamentary colleagues to modify the tone of his speech before it was delivered, stating bluntly that he had been democratically elected by the Party, and that they should therefore have no illusions about the path which he wanted to follow.

The road which the Liberals travelled between 1976 and 1979 was as bumpy as Mr Steel had promised. The Lib–Lab Pact, an imaginative gesture when made, pitted the minute resources of the Liberal parliamentary party against the combined weight of the Labour Party and Whitehall, achieving for a too moderate and reasonable Liberal leadership a good deal less than its supporters might have hoped. With the Conservative opposition, and the conservative press, in full cry against this Liberal 'support for socialism', opinion-poll support fell to within single figures, hardly recovering before the 1979 election. Discontent within the Party (extending to a minority of the parliamentary party) led to the convening of a special Assembly in January 1978, which registered its acceptance for a continued pact only until the summer. To Liberal surprise, Callaghan did not call an election in September, thus depriving them of the credit for precipitating the campaign — though, as it turned out, providing a valuable breathing-space for the Liberals to differentiate themselves again from Labour. With a vigorous Conservative opposition putting forward a radically different set of policies to the Labour Government, it was not easy for the Liberals to portray themselves convincingly as the only fresh alternative to the indistinguishable conservatism of the two major parties. The 1979 election, both in its campaign and in its result, thus represented a defensive battle, with the undoubted personal appeal of David Steel as leader, and the professionalism of its largely volunteer campaign staff, to compensate for the Party's indistinct image and uncertain base of support.

Since 1979, with Labour again suffering the divisive agonies of opposition, the strategy of a short cut to realignment through encouraging a split in Labour has been relentlessly pursued. The accumulated achievements of Community Politics and of attempts to organize the Labour areas had, it is true, begun to produce some modest results. Three of the Party's eleven seats in the post-1979 parliament were in the industrial north, captured from Labour, against none of the nine after 1964. There were now Liberal groups, some large, some small, on the Labour-dominated local authorities of all the major English cities outside London. But on the most optimistic assessment it would take another decade of determined campaigning together with the disintegration of the Labour Party, to translate these toe-holds into the basis for a party realignment from the constituencies up. Almost all the seats in which the Liberals did well in 1979 were Conservative-held, raising again the prospect of contradictory impulses between the need to appeal to discontented Conservatives and the Party's commitment to a realignment of the Left. The consistent encouragement given by David Steel and those around him to Roy Jenkins and his associates in their early discussions about a breakaway party formed one of the elements out of which the SDP was shaped. Steel — and here again we are speaking of a level of personal leadership, dragging his party behind, comparable to that exercised by Grimond twenty years before — indicated that they would be welcome recruits to the Liberal Party if the attempts to launch a significant breakaway failed. But his conviction that the Liberal cause would benefit more from the maximum damage to the Labour Party led him to support the political gamble of the launching of a new party, with the expectation that a satisfactory alliance could be forged between that party and the Liberals. The proof of the pudding is yet to come. If it succeeds, it will at last have freed the Liberals from their dependent position upon the ill fortunes of the major parties, with one or two centre-left parties pushing a left-wing Labour Party into a minority position. That was, after all, the Grimondite aim which brought David Steel and his generation into the Liberal Party. Twenty years later, it seemed still to offer the best hope of achieving that aim before Steel's political generation passes on and out of politics.

4. The Electoral Strategy of the Liberal Party

Michael Steed

Elections play a peculiarly central role in the life of the Liberal party. Contesting elections and winning votes is a more important sphere of activity for the typical Liberal than for an equivalent member of any other British political party. For the Conservative and Labour parties a far higher proportion of their collective leadership is in Parliament; and what happens in the House of Commons, or in Downing Street and Whitehall, critically and continuously affects the thinking of the party. Liberal MPs sometimes behave as if the same were (or ought to be) true for the Liberal party, but it is not. When, briefly, during the Lib–Lab Pact this became a much more important scene for it, the change from the normal situation was noticeable throughout the Liberal party.

For other (and smaller) parties within the British system, there are other spheres of activity. Both nationalist parties see their role much more in terms of consciousness-raising, and therefore focus much more on campaigning that is not specifically electoral. In Scotland and Wales, there is a relative scarcity of parliamentary by-elections and larger intervals between local elections; and there are national media, especially in Scotland, in which they can interact in political debate with the local sections of the British parties. For the tiny British parties, elections matter less still and each of them finds its scene of principal activity – the streets for the National Front, or trade unions for much of the Far Left.

But for Liberals, grossly underrepresented in Parliament and consequently underreported in the London-based media which, through the lobby system, focuses political reporting so much on Westminster, and yet committed by history and ideology to representative democracy, elections have long been the party's main scene of activity and impact. There are annual local elections in most of urban provincial England, until recently parliamentary by-elections used to occur almost all the time[1] and there are, of course, always local-government by-elections.

The rhythm of these elections plays a key part for the Liberal party — both the predictable rhythm of county and district elections and the unpredictable occurrence of by-elections. Elections give the party access to the national media on a more equal footing with the major parties — political balance on television tends to mean that when a matter of national political controversy is discussed, Conservative and Labour spokesmen get equal time whilst a Liberal is lucky to get a look-in: but on election-night programmes three party spokesmen are treated as equals. Consequently Liberal electoral performance gets much more attention than Liberal policy. Impact has thus reinforced a certain natural predilection.

Within the Liberal party, electoral performance gives status. In the standing it gives to its small band of MPs for having won seats, the party is perhaps also reflecting its tradition as a parliamentary party and British political habits, despite the haphazard way in which the accident of by-elections has selected most of them. The rising standing of elected councillors, and of their organization the Association of Liberal Councillors (ALC), within the party (one of the key internal changes of the last decade), has been essentially due to their success in winning elections. Controlling local authorities has been less important.[2] Indeed it is the ALC in conjunction with the *New Statesman* which began to give local by-elections national importance in 1981.[3]

[1] Thus in the third year of the 1959 parliament, October 1961–September 1962, the peak year of mid-term Liberal support, there were sixteen British parliamentary by-elections. But in the equivalent period of the 1979 parliament (May 1981–April 1982), there were only four. It does not require much imagination to see how different the 1981–2 period would have been if sixteen by-elections had occurred.

[2] The ALC includes several councillors with experience of balance of power, but there is relatively little input into the party from the one major authority, Liverpool, which has experienced Liberal administration for several years — perhaps because running that city has preoccupied the Liberal councillors there.

[3] Until the summer of 1981, local-government by-elections were hardly reported in the national media (though *Liberal News* published the voting figures in those with a Liberal candidate, and was therefore the most accessible source for them). Since then the *New Statesman*, the BBC Newsnight programme, and the *Guardian* have been reporting them, and have found the ALC office to be a main source of information.

Parliamentary by-election candidates who obtain good votes also acquire standing in the party thereby.

So participation in election campaigns and the impact of their results play very large parts in Liberal thinking, affecting morale, the internal jostling for position between politicans that takes place in any party, and the public attention the party gets. One can conceive of a third party in British politics with a rather different focus — principally concerned to shift public debate towards its ideology, to further a specific interest or policy demand, or to make an impact on government. The Liberal party has those desires; but they do not predominate and hence the party's electoral strategy has been at the core of its whole strategy.

WINNING SEATS IN PARLIAMENT

Yet though the Liberal party sets greater store than the others on local-government victories, and on impressive totals of votes, at constituency or national level, it is fully aware that constituencies must be won to further a political party's national goals. Before considering its strategy for doing so it is worth examining, therefore, how the party has secured MPs.

From 1955[4] until the formation of the Alliance, there were 88 occasions where a Liberal MP was elected, in 27 constituencies.[5] Excluding five victories in three constituencies due to the operation of a local Con–Lib electoral pact,[6] a condition no longer available after 1959, these are analysed in Table 4.1.

Column A shows the number of constituencies, column B the total number of victories (i.e. times a Liberal MP was elected), and column C an estimate of the potential in the

[4] 1955 is chosen as the last general election before the first victory of the revival (Torrington); it is the only general election in history when the party has neither lost nor won a seat, and hence represents a stable base.

[5] Cheadle (1966–70) and Hazel Grove (Feb.–Oct. 1974) are treated as the same constituency. The constituency named Cheadle following the new boundaries in 1974 has significantly less in common with the old Cheadle than does Hazel Grove.

[6] Bolton West (1955 and 1959), Carmarthen (1955), and Huddersfield West (1955 and 1959).

Table 4.1   Liberal victories 1955–79

		(A) Constituencies	(B) Victories	(C) Potential
I	Celtic Fringe	9	39	about 20
II	Rural periphery	14	57	up to 50
III	Traditional support	15	65	up to 100
IV	By-elections	10	27	accidental
V	All by-elections	12	37	accidental
VI	Second place	5	21	variable: ususally under 100
VII	Tactical squeeze on Conservative	2+	9	about 200
VIII	Tactical squeeze on Labour	14	40	about 200
IX	Local government	4	8	over 500
X	All cases	24	83	623
XI	All in II or V	22	78	very limited

For definitions, see text.

form of the number of constituencies where this situation could occur or a strategy based on it be applied.

Most Liberal victories have been in areas of traditional support (row III: defined as constituencies which elected a Liberal MP in the 1929-55 period), and within that group most are in the rural periphery of Britain (row II: the North of Scotland, Wales, the South-West peninsula, and the Anglo-Scottish border) or even the Celtic fringe more properly defined (row I: the Highlands and Islands, Cornwall, rural Wales), which contributed exactly half the total number of victories. The limitations of the potential in these areas are all too evident.

Second places (row VI: defined as cases where the Liberal MP took over a second place, i.e. excluding those where he started third and took second place *en route* to victory)[7]

---

[7] Cardigan, Montgomery, and Orkney & Zetland are excluded as having started from first place before 1955, although when Cardigan was regained in February 1974 the new MP had inherited a second place.

play much less of a role than many have thought. Indeed in nine of the twenty-four constituencies, victory came directly from a third place or occurred where the seat had not been contested at the previous election. Tactical squeezing (rows VII and VIII), however, is evidently important — but far more important with Labour voters in a hopeless situation than with Conservative ones.[8] Community Politics (as measured by cases where Liberals had already won a voting plurality in local-government elections before winning the parliamentary constituency, row IX) has played some role, though a limited one. However, the table brings out the striking importance of by-elections (row IV: cases where the seat was first won at a by-election; row V includes two other cases, Inverness and Colne Valley, where a by-election played some part in the buildup to victory).

The final row illustrates the Liberal problem dramatically. The party has support throughout the country and aspirations both to appeal to the whole community and to achieve an effective role in government. The vast majority of Liberal candidates are not standing in the far-flung corners of Great Britain, and are not fighting a by-election. A strategy which concentrates only on those situations denies their relevance. Yet only two MPs have been elected (Michael Winstanley in Cheadle/Hazel Grove and Stephen Ross in Isle of Wight) without either a by-election or the advantage of the rural periphery. The nature and distribution of Liberal support, together with both the obstacles and opportunities presented by the electoral system, rather than the amount of support, has determined its parliamentary representation. Finding an electoral strategy to suit this situation is not easy.

In examining the evolution of the party's electoral strategy over the past quarter of a century, it is useful to divide it into partly overlapping periods. Different strategies are not mutually exclusive, though at times a party (or different bits of it) may be pursuing incompatible strategies. Figure 4.1

---

[8] In only two constituencies (Edge Hill and Rochdale) was a squeeze on the Conservatives clearly relevant, but the total number of victories includes Cardigan once (October 1974) and Colne Valley twice (1966 and October 1974). In these two constituencies the Conservative vote has proved only temporarily susceptible to a squeeze; in both it recovered dramatically in 1979.

indicates five distinct periods of a particular strategy and a
sixth when a coherent overriding political strategy was absent.

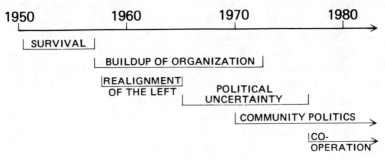

Figure 4.1

SURVIVAL

From the morrow of the disastrous February 1950 election
the party's main concern was to maintain its presence as an
independent political force. At the 1951 and 1955 elections,
three of its six seats in Parliament were held by grace and
favour of the Conservative party and Sir Winston Churchill
tried to entice the then Liberal leader Clement Davies into
his cabinet in 1951. The former Liberal National MPs sitting
inside the Conservative parliamentary party were a reminder
(rubbed in by Conservative references to the Liberal party
as the independent Liberal party) of an alternative strategy
for anti-Socialist Liberals that then seemed more realistic
than it does with hindsight. Other leading Liberals attempted
an arrangement with the Labour party (including three
Liberal MPs in the 1950–1 parliament, Lady Megan Lloyd-
George, Edgar Granville, and Emrys Roberts, the first two
of whom went on to join the Labour party). Most of the
pockets of Liberal strength in local government (mainly
in the North) were dependent on arrangements with local
Conservatives. Apart from constituencies being defended,
there were few seats where the Liberal party was a credible
independent challenger — arguably only one at each of
the 1951 and 1955 elections (North Dorset and Inverness
respectively).

This period saw a singularly sterile debate about fighting general elections on a broad or narrow front. Echoes of it were to be heard around the party right up to January 1974 when the logic of the party's rising popularity created the broadest front since 1929, followed by the broadest front ever undertaken (619 out of 623 British seats) in October 1974. The 'broad fronters' saw a need to strike a claim for credibility by fighting a clear majority of constituencies (enough to form a government) — the purpose of most candidates being to give national credibility to the few who stood a chance of winning. The 'narrow fronters' argued a case for concentrating resources and saw a wide front, with a multitude of lost deposits, as discrediting the party.

In reality there were so few resources either to concentrate or to throw into putting up many candidates that the proportion of seats fought was decided by a much more local and less national process. In both 1951 and 1955 a sixth of the constituencies were contested, selected by local Liberal associations with little political or other logic. The very weakest areas (mining constituencies and Clydeside) had practically no Liberal candidates at all; at the other extreme, there were two areas of local stength (Cornwall and rural Wales) where the party contested a majority of constituencies even in 1951 and 1955. But in the majority of the country the pattern of candidates seemed random — reflecting local decisions which in turn reflected very local factors such as the willingness of a Liberal Club to finance a campaign or the determination of a 1950 election candidate to keep a tattered flag flying. Many constituencies with strong Liberal traditions, often with good votes in 1950 and even second places then, were not fought in either 1951 or 1955 (e.g. Torrington, Ross & Cromarty, Rochdale, and the Isle of Ely, all later to elect Liberal MPs); there was no consistent attempt to maintain a presence where it would more likely have provided a base for subsequent advance. A higher proportion of candidates were standing in areas of relative weakness than was to be the case in the 1960s.

During this period, by-elections were an embarrassment. In the 1950 parliament the Liberal party contested only one out of fourteen British ones and in the 1951 parliament only eight out of forty-four. A deposit was saved only once. Some that were fought were done so against the wishes of the party centrally — by-elections exposed the party's weakness and it was only local obstinacy that ensured that a Liberal 5.3 per cent should be on display in a publicized by-election such as Sunderland South in 1953 (the only seat to switch hands during the period).

Outside the rural Celtic fringe, was there any purpose in fighting elections? Perhaps the best rationalization is that for the Liberal party to maintain its independence it was necessary to enter some candidates in all parts of the country and types of constituency. Sometimes a decision to fight was clearly a declaration of independence where local Liberalism felt itself in danger of being taken over by the Conservatives — e.g. Keighley and Sowerby in 1955. Certainly if the party had only stuck to the handful of rural areas where it did maintain significant local support, thereby saving the many deposits it lost, its own determination to remain in existence as a national political force would have seemed in serious doubt.

This period ended on 15 December 1955, when Peter Bessell raised the Liberal vote from 14.2 per cent to 23.8 per cent in a by-election in Torquay. The Inverness by-election a year earlier had been the first harbinger of change, and some results in the 1955 general election had encouraged the party — but most, like Inverness, were in the Celtic rural fringe. Torquay was the first really good performance in urban Britain and began the first period of Liberal runs of mid-term by-election support which have subsequently become a regular feature of periods of Conservative governments.[9]

BUILDUP OF ORGANIZATION

For the next fifteen years or so, a principal strategic aim was to rebuild the party's organization. This included its central and regional organization, but the main emphasis was on

[9] This dating differs from the statement made in Chapter 3 (p. 45) that 'the turning-point in Liberal fortunes can be dated fairly precisely to the spring and summer of 1956.' The change in electoral fortunes had very clearly preceded Wallace's turning-point, which refers rather to the change in morale, membership, and organization. The electoral turning-point in 1954–5 was thus a spontaneous revival, followed by changes within the Party.

constituency organization. Fighting parliamentary and local elections was seen in this light. During the late fifties the party considered its organization too weak on the ground to tackle a majority of seats either at by-elections or at the 1959 general election, despite the by-election evidence — sometimes dramatic — of increasing support. Associations were advised to fight only if they had the money, the organization, and a candidate. Dodging the broad- versus narrow-front argument, the number of seats fought was thus determined by the state of constituency organization. There was, however, a central decision in 1960 to encourage Liberals to enter local-government elections, and local elections became thereafter increasingly important to the party.

Increases in the numbers of candidates are therefore some measure of the progress of this strategy. At general elections the number of seats fought rose from 110 in 1955 to 216 in 1959 and then to 365 in 1964, levelling off at 311 in 1966 and 332 in 1970. This was neither a broad nor a narrow front, reflecting rather a steady buildup of organization up to 1964 and thereafter a holding operation. As for by-elections, the party contested some two-fifths of those occurring in the 1955 parliament and four-fifths of those in the 1959 parliament. It kept the same ratio of four-fifths during the 1964–70 Labour government, though it was losing ground during much of this period. The contrast between the latter sixties and the late fifties is worth stressing. In the earlier period, the party's by-election performance was an enticement to fight more but it felt unable to take up the opportunity unless it had the necessary organization; in the latter period it had that organization in more constituencies and so fought more by-elections, although the point in doing so was less evident.

The result of deciding which constituencies to fight in this manner was that increasingly Liberal candidates were concentrated in more middle-class (and also more rural) areas and hence, as Table 4.2 shows, in more Conservative constituencies. Conversely, less of the party's effort, as denoted by parliamentary candidatures, went into more industrial areas or more Labour constituencies.

Between 1955 and 1959 the additional 105 British Liberal candidates meant 61 more in the most Conservative seats but

Table 4.2   Liberal candidates

	Least	Middle-Class	Most	All	Least	Conservative	Most
1955	7.8	14.6	30.8	17.8	9.7	17.3	26.0
1959	13.2	33.2	57.7	34.8	13.5	34.6	55.3
1964	23.4	64.9	86.5	58.4	26.9	58.2	88.5
1964–70	8.3	31.7	70.2	36.9	11.5	25.5	72.6

This table shows the percentage of seats in each category with a Liberal candidate at the three general elections and, in the bottom row, the percentage which were fought continuously by Liberals in the 1964, 1966, and 1970 elections. The categories are constructed by dividing the 618 British constituencies into three equal groups according to the proportion of employers and managers among economically active males in the 1966 census, and according to the Conservative share of the two-party vote at the 1964 election. The Middle-Class categories are, respectively, 205 under 8.1%; 205 with 8.1%–12.7%; and 208 with over 12.7%. The Conservative categories are, respectively, 206 under 43.36%; 206 with 43.36% – 56.28%; and 206 over 56.28%. I am indebted to John Curtice for the data on which this table is based.

only 8 more in the most Labour ones. The effect is most striking if we compare the pattern of the 228 British constituencies where a Liberal was continuously present in 1964, 1966, and 1970 with the 215 1959 or 110 1955 candidatures. The consequence of allowing local organizational strength to determine where the Liberal party most consistently sought to win votes was a distinctly greater proportion of effort in middle-class and Conservative areas than in the days when the party had been weaker. The organizational strategy produced a highly significant concentration of resources.

The organizational emphasis of the party's strategy during this period was combinable with a number of political strategies. In so far as it had a logic of its own, it was that there was a substantial pool of potentially Liberal voters who could be persuaded to vote Liberal if the party appeared to be locally effective. As such support built up, so would the general credibility of the party, and therefore its capacity to tap its potential support.

REALIGNMENT OF THE LEFT

For the period of Jo Grimond's leadership, the party had an

overall political strategy: that of a realignment of British parties in which the Liberal party would be at the core of a new radical force opposing the Conservatives. The concept depended on a view of the Labour party's incapacity to win — as Mark Bonham Carter put it: 'Since 1931, with a single interval of six years, this country has been governed by a Conservative, or Conservative-dominated, administration . . . this is how the "two-party" system, of which we hear so much, has worked. It has lead to what is virtually one-party government.'[10]

The implications for electoral strategy were not too clear. There was some talk of a Lib–Lab pact from one Labour MP, Woodrow Wyatt, but the Liberal party, heavily conditioned by its struggle to maintain its independence, showed no real interest. In the increasing number of constituencies in which a Liberal came second and Labour third, Liberals concentrated on trying to get local Labour supporters to vote tactically; the curious habit of investing Liberal second places (almost all in Conservative seats and mostly very safe ones) with special significance and counting and listing them started in this period.

But whilst the tendency for Liberals to be local challengers to Conservatives rather than Labour could be regarded as evidence of the desired realignment taking place at local level,[11]

---

[10] The opening words of the first essay 'Liberals and the Political Future' in George Watson (ed.): *Radical Alternative* (1962).

[11] A notable example of this interpretation was in the reaction to three by-election results on 6 February 1965:

Comparison with October 1964 General Election

	Con.	Lab.	Lib.	General Election Position	
Altrincham & Sale	+3.2	+1.1	−5.8	Lib. third,	21.6% behind Con.
East Grinstead	+1.8	−6.3	+4.5	Lib. second,	28.2% behind Con.
Salisbury	−0.1	+3.0	−4.4	Lib. third,	31.0% behind Con.

This pattern was welcome to some Liberals as showing that second places could be used to the party's advantage, and noted by independent observers; 'It seemed for a time that the radical alliance which had eluded the party at Westminster was being forged spontaneously in the constituencies.' (David Butler and Anthony King, *The British General Election of 1966* (1967), (p. 75). Yet such an attitude meant writing off the vast majority of Liberal contenders in Conservative-held constituencies, including those closer to victory than some in second place (e.g. Altrincham & Sale) and those with a better long-term prospect (e.g. Salisbury, which ten years later had become easily the most winnable of the trio).

it was also evidence that the Liberal party was least able to make an impact where Labour was strongest. From time to time various Liberals would point out the relevance of this failure to the realignment strategy, and urge that resources be put into building up support in industrial areas. But normally the party had no mobile resources at its command; an ambitious expansion plan which aimed to build up strength in Labour areas was adopted in 1966 — but had to be abandoned as the party's financial position worsened.

This was the most serious mismatch of the party's organizational and political strategies. A party committed above all to replacing the Labour party would logically have gone for Labour's own base — or at any rate such parts of it as looked most vulnerable. But the organizational strategy meant building up constituency organization where voluntary labour was most available to provide it — and therefore where the middle class was thicker on the ground, and so in the Conservative party's natural territory. The Labour voter that the Liberal party set out to woo was the Labour voter in a Conservative seat whose vote was not needed by the Labour party. The Labour party's prospects of electoral victory were not therefore threatened by the Liberal party — indeed by threatening to take more Conservative than Labour seats, it actually slightly increased the chance that in a close-fought election Labour would win more seats than the Conservatives, as happened in February 1974.

The realignment strategy gave a coherence to Grimond's leadership. It was a good response to those who doubted the point of reviving what had seemed to be a dying party, and a response which made the party seem more relevant to the future than to its immediate, desolate past. Yet it also echoed nicely the historic Liberal sense of being the natural opponent of Toryism. It made good sense as a rationale to gather in recruits and motivate activists. It might have made immediate political sense if the Labour party had split in 1960 or lost the 1964 election — or even if the Liberals had been able to win the trio of Labour-held seats where they came close to by-election victories (Paisley 1961, Leicester North-East 1962, and Colne Valley 1963).

But it was not used as a rationale for utilizing the party's resources, limited as they were. Nor did it provide a rationale for a general-election campaign (the Labour defeat, upon which the strategy depended, could hardly be advocated by the would-be catalyst of a radical anti-Conservative force). At the 1959, 1964, and 1966 elections, the party had to concentrate on displaying its policies and personalities without a unifying logic. There was some vague talk of moderation and a centre force, and explicit espousal of a constitutional doctrine which flew in the face of nearly a century of British political habits: 'At the general election the votes [sic] do not choose a government, they choose a parliament. The first task is for everyone to vote for a member of parliament, and that member should represent you and your neighbours.'[12] When 44 per cent of the voters did choose a Labour government in 1964, and 48 per cent confirmed their choice in 1966, the realignment strategy was — at any rate temporarily — exhausted.

POLITICAL UNCERTAINTY

For about a dozen years until David Steel's first speech as Liberal leader at the 1976 Llandudno Assembly, the party lacked a defined or agreed strategy for its role in parliament and at elections. Jeremy Thorpe failed to give the sense of political direction that his predecessors and successor did. A variety of strategies were discussed or tried briefly.

Commitment to Grimond's realignment strategy never disappeared; for some Liberals it remained the goal, with the Labour party likely to decline or disintegrate at some distant point in the future. Yet at the 1970 general election, plucking a tactic from the opinion-poll forecasts, Thorpe's final television appeal was for a strong Liberal presence in parliament to moderate the Labour government which he informed the electorate it had decided to elect.[13] At other times, the

[12] 1959 general-election manifesto, published in *The Times House of Commons 1959*, p. 255.

[13] Thorpe's final 1970 message was summarized (David Butler and Michael Pinto-Duschinsky: *The British General Election of 1970* (1971, p. 219), 'Thinks voters decided to return Lab., not because Lab. deserve to win, but Con. deserve to lose. Still question of opposition, vital in democracy. If Tories lose, danger of party civil war. More Libs. needed for constructive opposition . . . Problem of government settled: see there's effective opposition . . .'

party toyed with going for the balance of power. John Pardoe persuaded the 1973 Assembly to discuss the idea, but as the 1974 election was sprung, the party, far from bidding for it, attempted to avoid the question and to suppress debate on it.[14]

Another Pardoe initiative to give some purpose and impact to the party's general-election strategy was his unsuccessful proposal at the 1970 Assembly to commit the party to fighting every constituency — with a view to making a credible bid for power. Earlier in 1970, David Steel had talked publicly of an opposite idea — that the Liberal party should selectively support a few more liberally inclined Conservative and Labour MPs. But the adverse reaction within the Liberal party dissuaded him from pursuing it.[15]

At the following election, February 1974, the opinion-poll surge of support, following the remarkable run of by-election victories in the previous eighteen months, suddenly made a bid for power credible. As William Wallace records (pp. 67–8), Thorpe had talked, at the 1973 Assembly, of Liberal government, when Pardoe was raising the forbidden question of balance of power. Yet the party was utterly unprepared to make such a bid: twenty days before polling, it was talking of 380 candidates[16] — barely more than the 1964–70 period middle-sized fronts. The number exploded to 517 by nomination day (with four more Independent Liberals emerging in constituencies where the party did not get an official candidate in the field) as the party's local and regional levels of organization responded to a mounting demand for Liberal candidates. Thus a credible broad front suddenly arrived

[14] The official briefing to February 1974 candidates suggested the following answer to any questions about the balance of power: 'What happens in this situation is surely a matter for the other two parties. In the light of the suggestions of the other parties the Liberal MPs will have to decide whether to support one particular party in Government or, if such an arrangement is unsatisfactory from the Liberal point of view, whether to vote for every piece of legislation according to its merits.' See also Chapter 3, p. 67.

[15] In a speech whose text was published in *Liberal News*, 9 July 1970. See also *Liberal News*, 23 July 1970 for reports of the 'almost uniformly hostile' reaction to Steel's suggestion.

[16] David Butler and Dennis Kavanagh, *The British General Election of February 1974* (1974), p. 80.

as a result of pressure from below. The campaign, however, had been planned around a leader concerned to preserve a tiny majority in a remote constituency where boundary changes made his hold even more precarious. He stayed there, probably gaining from the distance at which that put him from the two-party fray, but losing the opportunity that many supporters saw, of taking up the opinion-poll bandwagon and stomping the country to offer the voters a Liberal government.

The sense of a chance of a breakthrough thrown away haunted Liberals after February 1974. The opinion polls peaked around the weekend before polling — Marplan announced a 28% figure on 24 February — but fell away thereafter. The actual vote on 28 February was 19.3%, compared with a mean 22.3% predicted by six polling organizations on polling day and a mean 23.4% predicted by five of them in the previous four days. This could be — and was — interpreted as a surge of popular support which, if grasped at the right point, could have been turned into an irresistible flood of votes for a Liberal government.[17] Equally, there were some who felt that the falling-off of support in the last few days of the campaign was because some voters took fright at the prospect of a Liberal government. The only consistent theme that emerged from the Liberal campaign was the successful emphasis on moderation and on a centre ground abandoned by the increasingly extremist and divisive two big parties. The government question was avoided, to the party's cost in the confusion which followed the inconclusive election result.

At other times the party sought to promote itself in a diametrically opposed manner. During the 1966–70 Wilson government a Liberal campaign poster showed the heads of both Harold Wilson and Edward Heath under the slogan 'Which Twin is The Tory?' The argument, in which many Liberals strongly believed, was that the party was the true radical challenger to two increasingly similar establishment parties and should project and build itself up as such. Yet

---

[17] Butler and Kavanagh record that two-fifths of the Liberal candidates who answered a questionnaire from them thought that Thorpe should have played a more national role (February 1974), p. 129.

following February 1974, Liberal MPs played with the idea of all-party or National Unity Government, the very antithesis of this anti-consensus stance.

Thus there was no consistently applied national strategy during this period. Decisions about electoral tactics were reactions to opportunities rather than considered plans. Steel's ironic comment on the 1970 election, 'We had no very clear message except the assumption of innate virtue and superiority in a host of Liberal policies',[18] could be applied also to February 1974 and (except that then the focus was on two key areas of constitutional and economic reform) October 1974.

Thorpe, however, was not without a strategy. He had first risen in the party during the 1950s as the struggle to survive gave way to the emphasis on building up organization. He concentrated on raising funds, under his personal control, to be used to build up organization in key constituencies, on the assumption that such local organization was the key to local victory. Had it proved to be as simple as that, the party could have steadily built up a bridgehead in Parliament, until the number of Liberal MPs there gave it credibility. The 1966 election result, when the Liberal vote dropped from 11.2% to 8.5% but the number of seats won rose from nine to twelve, gave some credence to this view. But February 1974 was in that respect a total disaster: the massive six million vote produced only fourteen MPs. Some other way was needed, other than reliance on the Celtic fringe and the luck of the by-election draw, to turn Liberal votes into seats.

COMMUNITY POLITICS

The evolution and theory of this strategy are dealt with fully by Stuart Mole in Chaper 11 and hence it will receive briefer treatment in this chapter than would otherwise be merited.

As a strategy it has provided a synthesis between electoral objectives, tactics, and techniques on the one hand and broader political goals on the other in a way that no other strategy pursued by the party has. Preparing the artwork for

[18] David Steel, *A House Divided* (1980), p. 10.

a Focus newsletter[19] or dealing with the inadequacy of some municipal service as it affected a particular household were linked to the vision of the promised land, a Liberal society. It thus combined the motivation of activists with the spreading of successful electioneering methods.

But whilst the strategy was, as a coherent whole, new and distinctive and was specifically adopted by the party in response to a movement from below, at the 1970 Assembly, it also happened to grow out of several of the earlier strategies considered in this chapter. It borrowed much from Grimond's thinking aloud about realignment, though it saw this process as occurring at the grass roots and between Liberals and local community groups rather than at the top between Liberal MPs and the failed politicians of the 'old' or 'establishment' parties. In the emphasis on local capacity to campaign effectively as the key to winning elections, it has a clear connection with the organizational strategy — though, again, it eschewed the Thrope approach of disbursing central funds and moving in professional organizers to places with good prospects for victory. It viewed any type of community as a good prospect if the local effort was put in. The party's decision in 1960 to utilize local elections was a precursor of the strategy — as Grimond had put it then, 'Every time a local Liberal councillor gets a bus-stop moved to a better place he strikes a blow for the Liberal party.'[20]

The strategy may also have helped to resolve the perennial problem that dogged earlier strategy discussions — lack of resources, particularly mobile resources and therefore the pointlessness of any national attempt to concentrate effort, whether in winnable constituencies or in a particular type of territory such as industrial areas. The true resources of the Liberal party lie in the unpaid labour of its activists. As the

[19] That most Community Politicans prepare their own artwork is critical to the technique of all-the-year-round communication with their electorates. Without the development of cheap offset printing facilities (which increasingly Liberal associations now own themselves), the costs of Focus newsletters would have been prohibitive. As it is, the free labour given to the preparation of camera-ready copy and to door-to-door distribution means that Community-Politics techniques are highly cost-effective. As one technological change (television) nationalized political communication so the Liberals exploited another technological change in the printing industry to localize it again.

[20] October 1960: quoted in Alan Watkins, *The Liberal Dilemma* (1966), p. 108.

potential of the strategy became apparent, several younger, footloose Liberals have moved into what they saw as fertile ground — particularly in Liverpool and East London. Such self-created resources can be mobile, though on a non-directed voluntary and medium-term basis rather than centrally directed and instantly available. With the introduction of allowances for local councillors, many Community Politicians have found it convenient to have part-time (or badly paid, undemanding full-time) jobs; or even no other income, and live off their allowances — especially if they could get elected to both district and county councils and so draw two sets of allowances. Lacking many national full-time politicians paid by the state, and finding it increasingly difficult to finance professional agents or organizers, the Liberal party has thus been able to compensate by building up a force of professional local politicians.[21] Owing allegiance to their own communities and electorates rather than to the party leadership, the existence of this force has greatly reinforced the decentralist and localist spirit within the party and helped to transfer control of real resources from the centre to the grass roots. In that respect, the Community-Politics strategy has already succeeded in developing the party into an instrument more suited to its objectives.

At least for some of its more committed adherents, the Community-Politics strategy has been linked with a view of the road to national success. Surges of Liberal support have come spontaneously during periods of Conservative government, only to ebb rapidly. If the party used a surge to expand its local bases, and then to hold on to them during the subsequent ebb, it would be much better placed to utilize the next surge. That surge, or the one after next, could then be the breakthrough to national power. The lesson of the fourteen seats for six million votes of February was the danger of expecting parliamentary seats to fall too easily — but the prospect was that the electoral system could

---

[21] To get the fullest picture of how public money affects political activity and is distributed between the parties, MPs' salaries and costs plus councillors' allowances and facilities need to be added to the other subsidies in kind as Michael Pinto-Duschinsky has shown in *British Political Finance 1830–1980* (Washington DC, 1981).

turn round and work for the Liberals if the six million became eight or nine. Intermediate roles, such as a wedge of power for a couple of dozen Liberal MPs, were scorned; Community Politics would produce Liberal MPs committed to Liberalism and unsullied by Westminster politicking. Thus the strategy that, at the local level, involved an initial concentration of effort on target wards was compatible with the broader view of the purpose of a general-election campaign. Curiously, Thorpe, the recent Liberal leader who had probably least natural sympathy with the philosophy of Community Politics, gave most credence to this view with his talk at the 1973 and 1974 Assemblies of Liberal government and total breakthrough.

However, there was a gulf between the anti-consensus view of the Community Politicians and the other tactics pursued by Thorpe in 1974, notably the idea of a government of national unity. There is a similar incompatibility with Steel's co-operation strategy and much of the image and thinking behind the Alliance with the SDP. The weakness of the Community-Politics strategy is that it provides little guide to the role of Liberal MPs in Westminster (as opposed to their constituencies) or to the logic of voting Liberal in national elections when the colour of the next government is at stake — other than a 'plague on both your houses' attitude which perhaps corresponds well with the protest element in Liberal voting. Too many Liberal Community Politicians found it easier to assume that such an attitude would suffice for a posture, and were without an answer or much influence at critical moments in the party's development, as in 1974, 1977, 1978, or 1981. Furthermore, to allow what Liberals saw as the mounting economic, political, and social problems of Britain to wait until the long march brought the party to full power would be for many an abdication of responsibility; any opportunity to influence government should be seized.

In electoral terms, the success of the strategy is problematical. It has certainly had successes. The local-election successes of the late fifties and early sixties were almost all confined to middle-class suburbia or areas of a surviving Liberal tradition (some, such as Greenock, industrial). From the late sixties, Community Politicians have been able to break into literally every type of community. The only two by-elections in the 1974–9 period where the Liberal vote improved were notable triumphs.[22] In the 1982 local elections Liberal candidates won nearly five times as many seats as the SDP, though the two parties had put forward a similar number of candidates and shared the types of territory between them equally. Liberal candidates simply performed better, most notably in the wards where the party had built up its strength.[23] Yet in the 1974 general-elections results, the party's worst performance came in Liverpool where it had done so remarkably well in the 1973 district elections. And in 1979, the party's markedly better performance in many places in the local elections that were held simultaneously with the general election suggested that the party's localist focus was persuading people to distinguish between supporting Liberal candidates in national and local elections rather than switching their allegiance to the Liberal party. If that were to prove generally true, the Community-Politics strategy risks running the party into a dead end so far as its national ambitions are concerned.[24]

CO-OPERATION

The launch of the co-operation strategy can be dated as precisely as Community Politics in 1970 to David Steel's

[22] In Newcastle Central in November 1976 the party's national Community Politics Officer raised the Liberal share of the vote by 17.3 per cent; in Edge Hill, which local-election results from 1973 onwards had demonstrated to be the strongest municipal stronghold in Liverpool, the Liberal share was raised by 36.8 per cent in March 1979. The only other by-election in which the 1974 Liberal share was even maintained was also in a Northern Labour constituency with a Liberal local-government base (Penistone, July 1978); in the remaining twenty-six by-elections of that parliament the Liberal share of the vote dropped, on average, 7.5 per cent.

[23] This is clear in the analysis of the local elections published in *The Economist*, 14 May 1982, and in J. Curtice, C. Payne and R. Waller, *Electoral Studies*, Vol. 2 No. 1 (1983). In table 1, Curtice, Payne and Waller show only 0.3% difference in performance where the 1980 Liberal base was under 15%, but a Liberal improvement around 5% better than the SDP's where the Liberal base was between 15% and 40%.

[24] Such a system with a party strong in one level of government but not at the level above would be totally new in British politics, but has a parallel in the Canadian party system.

1976 speeches. Launching his campaign for the party's internal election for leader, he called for 'the readiness to work with others wherever we see what Jo Grimond has called the break in the clouds — the chance to implement any of our Liberal policies' and in his first speech as leader to the Assembly he went further, proclaiming that at the following election, 'We must be bold enough to deploy the coalition case positively.'[25] Just as the 1970 strategy came from below, so the 1976 one was an act of leadership from above. Though Steel saw his election by the party membership as a mandate to change the party's thinking, the contest between him and John Pardoe had really been one of style and not strategy.

Yet as with Community Politics, the strategy had diverse sources within the party's collective thinking and experience. It, too, built on the idea of realignment, and Steel has been skilful in demonstrating the links between Grimond's ideas and his own. It was also another logical response to the problem of February 1974: to exercise power, the Liberal party had to get the electoral system changed, and could only hope to do this by finding allies who agreed on the need for electoral reform. The growth of the critique of adversary politics outside the Liberal party, and the formation of the National Committee for Electoral Reform made this hope increasingly realistic. As the case for proportional representation came to be stressed, Liberals started to face up to the arguments in favour of the likely consequence in Britain, coalition government.

The co-operation strategy, of course, was put to an immediate test in the 1977-8 Lib-Lab pact, or parliamentary agreement. For a number of reasons, this was initially much more acceptable within the party than perhaps the strategy itself was. The party's anti-Conservative reflexes approved a move to prevent a government led by Mrs Thatcher coming to power and meant that a Steel-Callaghan deal was received very differently from a hypothetical Thorpe-Heath one. The increasing number of Liberal councillors who had had to operate on a council without an overall majority were an

[25] Extensive quotations from these two speeches are contained in Steel (1980), pp. 22-5.

element within the party which accepted the pragmatic logic of such a deal — but which expected results from it. The real conflict within the party in fact came over this expectation rather than the principle. Hoggart and Michie referred to: 'the gap between Steel himself and most of the Liberal party; they wanted tangible achievements, whereas he was more interested in the concept of the agreement itself'.[26] Hence the crisis that came in December 1977 over Steel's failure to put sufficient pressure on the Labour government to get a proportional voting system for the European election.[27]

Yet that crisis in the pact reflected also the party's profound electoralism. The 1977 county-council elections had been disastrous, easily the party's worst local-election results in the 1972-81 decade; there were many Liberal county councillors who, with some justice, felt the pact had lost them their seats. The by-elections during the period of the pact gave the party the same message, and indeed there can be no doubt that in the short term Steel's action stripped the party of a slice of its previous vote.[28]

In a party so concerned with electoral performance, electoral grievance and fear joined the indignation of those who had hoped that the Labour party could have been induced to deliver on the European elections. Liberal MPs were bitterly accused of throwing away the party's real base for an illusion of power. But even among those who accepted the pact and conceded the electoral attractiveness of the idea

[26] Alistair Michie and Simon Hoggart, *The Pact* (1978), p. 97.

[27] In addition to the critics whose local-government experience led them to believe that Steel could and should have been tougher over this issue, several British Liberals had close contacts with leading Continental Liberals well used to inter-party bargaining and hence the party's keenest Europeanists were aware that many leading Continental Liberals thought the British Liberals could and should have extracted proportional representation from the Labour government. The most vocal critic of the Pact among the Liberal MPs, Cyril Smith, was also the only one with experience of local-government inter-party bargaining.

[28] Steel concluded that 'the failure and unpopularity of the Labour government rubbed off on us', the anti-Pact propaganda being 'something I wholly underestimated' (Steel, 1980, p. 153). In the ten by-elections between the making of the Pact and the announcement of its termination, the Liberal share of the vote dropped by an average of 9.5 per cent. In the period before and after the comparable figures were 3.7 per cent and 0.5 per cent: if the wholly exceptional Newcastle Central and Edge Hill by-elections are excluded (see footnote 22), the average drop was 5.8 per cent both before and after.

of co-operation, there was real concern about the longer-term damage that could be done to Liberal support by the pact. It was ended in the summer of 1978 rather than prolonged into 1979 as Steel had originally hoped, partly because Steel had misunderstood his party's acceptance of the tactic, and partly as a response to electoral stimulus.

Prior to the launch of the SDP, the co-operation strategy had obvious implications for the Liberal appeal to be projected at a general election but uncertain ones as to whether constituencies were to be fought and how resources should be used. In the discussions in early 1978 designed for an autumn 1978 general election — there was extensive consultation and careful preparation to a greater extent than the Liberal party had experienced for many years — there was general agreement on the policies and themes to be stressed, with electoral reform taking a logically obvious central place as the mechanism to change the operation of the party system. In 1974 electoral reform had received remarkably little emphasis in the party's election manifesto and when it had been stressed before, it was much more in terms of the abstract arguments for democracy and the representation of voters' desires. The party's economic policy, too, was readily fitted into the thesis of adversary politics and linked to this strategy, as Gamble shows in Chapter 9. In political terms co-operation gave a coherence and thrust to the party's electoral message.

But there were widespread fears inside the Liberal party in early 1978 on two grounds. First it was thought that the Lib–Lab pact and the general message of co-operation between parties would blur the distinctive identity of the party, undermining its capacity to built up longer-term loyalties. Older memories of the struggle for survival and younger commitments to Community Politics joined hands in this concern.

This reinforced the second fear: that the emphasis on getting just a 'wedge of power' was an argument for not voting Liberal, or even not putting up candidates, in the majority of constituencies. Memories of Steel's 1970 initiative and echoes of the old broad-versus narrow-front debate were heard, but by this time the party had become generally convinced of the need to fight on a very broad front.

The intensive discussion of early 1978 produced an internal consensus that a massive popular vote was a primary aim at the coming election. Publicly, this was in order to sustain the case for electoral reform and to give moral authority to the demands on a larger party that would be made by a small number of Liberal MPs holding the balance of power. Amongst the large majority of Liberal candidates, it was to provide a rationale for their role in a campaign which effectively admitted they had no hope of winning. Limited resources, such as Steel's battle bus, were concentrated in a limited number of more winnable seats, though internally it was agreed to call them 'tactical' rather than 'winnable'. And the party agreed explicitly to

aim to secure the election of as many Liberal MPs as possible in order to increase their hold on the balance of power in the next Parliament and achieve electoral and political reform. To this end, we are willing with appropriate safeguards, in principle, to share power with either party in the next Parliament.[29]

Electorally, the strategy can so far be accounted a partial success, like that of Community Politics. The party's support recovered during the 1979 general-election campaign, and opinion polls showed that Steel's stress on parties working together as opposed to one-party government was popular. But it was a limited recovery: the popular vote dropped by 4.5 per cent compared with October 1974 and was only higher than the 1964 vote because over two hundred more candidates were standing. Eleven MPs were returned, exactly the average of the previous five general elections. As a base from which to move forward during the next phase of Conservative government, it was fairly encouraging; as a verdict on Steel's strategy, it was inconclusive.

In one critical detail, the Lib–Lab Pact also produced problematical electoral success. The 1974 surge had brought many Liberal candidates in Conservative-held constituencies into second place, with some of them fairly close to victory. It was hoped that Lib–Lab co-operation in Westminster could lead to a reciprocal co-operation in these constituencies with Labour voters seizing the chance to vote for a party of now

---

[29] Quoted from the official confidential summary record of the discussion of Liberal Strategy on 19 February 1978.

proven anti-Tory credentials. If the Pact led to an increase in the number of MPs despite a fall in the Liberal vote (as had happened in 1966), many Liberals would have accepted it as a successful electoral strategy.

In the event there was more tactical voting by erstwhile Labour supporters in 1979 than there already had been in October 1974, but only a little more. Close examination of the results indicates that it was confined to those constituencies where the Liberal challenger had the credibility of being very close to victory, and absent in most second places; it probably saved just one Liberal MP.[30] As Table 4.1 demonstrated, tactical voting has assisted the election of a number of Liberal MPs, but it has proved not to be generally available to second place Liberal candidates in the way hoped, and only rarely of sufficient assistance outside peripheral Britain or the special drama of a by-election. It could be no more than a marginal contribution to the problem of electorcal strategy.

CONCLUSION

The Alliance between the Liberal and Social Democratic parties has not altered the basic problem. It was anyway likely that a mid-term surge under the Thatcher government would carry the Liberal party to the level of by-election support that it reached in 1981;[31] the dual difficulties of holding sufficient of that support into a general-election campaign and of turning it into seats remain. The political experience and standing in the media of the SDP leadership may well give an Alliance campaign more credibility in a

---

[30] John Curtice and Michael Steed, 'An Analysis of the Voting', in David Butler and Dennis Kavanagh: *The British General Election of 1979* (1980), pp. 406-7.

[31] The level of Alliance support in the Warrington, Crosby, and Croydon North-West by-elections was about 5 per cent above that during the 1972-3 peak of Liberal by-election support; but as the 1972-3 peak had been a similar amount higher than the 1962 (Orpington) peak, which in turn was similarly higher than the 1958 (Torrington) peak, this looks more like a steady progression of mid-term protest than a new level of support. Opinion polls, however, show a clear difference, which may say more about the difference between surveys and actual voting than about any difference between the Alliance impact and that of the Liberal party.

general-election period than the Liberal party could have commanded, and might therefore resolve the first. But the 1982 local elections demonstrated that SDP support was even more evenly distributed than the Liberal vote: the Social Democratic defectors dramatically failed to win over localized pockets of Labour support which might have provided potentially winnable constituencies. Hence, psephological projections of Alliance performance made by the SDP have had to assume that at any level of Alliance support below about a third of the vote, it will be dependent on areas of Liberal strength to win seats.

This problem underlay the well-publicised difficulties into which the negotiations between the two parties for the allocation of seats ran. The determination of the SDP to have some of the limited number of constituencies with strong pockets of Liberal support forced the national Liberal negotiators to concede a number, despite local Liberal opposition, where the party felt, with reason, that it had a better chance of winning than the Social Democrats. Publically, the differences were resolved with a national agreement between the two leaders in September 1982. But local disagreement on the allocation of a few seats remained to remind the Liberal party that the Alliance posed strategic dilemmas for it as well as the obvious strategic opportunity which the party had grasped with near unanimity at its 1981 assembly.

Thus the euphoria of the party's reception of the Alliance and of the Crosby and Croydon North-West by-election victories in 1981 gave way in 1982 to a more realistic and sometimes strained relationship between two parties which are potential competitors as well as natural allies. That relationship has opened a new phase in the evolution of the Liberal party's electoral strategy; how it develops remains to be seen.

5. Liberal Voters and the Alliance: Realignment or Protest?

John Curtice

In 1951 the Liberal Party tottered on the edge of electoral extinction. Fielding just 109 candidates, it polled only 2.5 per cent of the UK poll. Of its six MPs, only one — Jo Grimond in Orkney & Shetland — succeeded in winning his seat against both Conservative and Labour opponents. It appeared that the replacement of the Liberal Party by Labour as the main alternative to Conservatism was about to reach its logical conclusion.

But the Liberal Party did not die. Following some recovery of ground in the late 1950s, it staged a series of revivals during the later stages of Conservative governments in the 1960s and 1970s. On both occasions the Liberals' hopes of breaking through Britain's two-party system were raised, only to be dashed against the rocks of a receding electoral tide in 1964, and the cruel logic of Britain's first-past-the-post electoral system in February 1974. But each peak of Liberal support proved to be higher than the last and the subsequent trough proved less disastrous than before. Then in 1981 the emergence of the Social Democratic Party and the birth of the Alliance between it and the Liberals saw support for Britain's main third-party alternative reach greater heights than ever before.[1] Consequently, the nature of Liberal support is no longer a mere footnote in the electoral sociology of Britain, but rather one of its central components.

This chapter attempts to do three things. First it reviews what is known about the Liberal vote up to and including the 1979 election, establishing who voted Liberal and why.

---

[1] For example, the highest figure recorded by Gallup in their normal voting intention question for Liberal support prior to 1981 was 22½ per cent in August 1973. In December 1981 the Alliance parties between them scored 50½ per cent. D. Butler and A. Sloman, *British Political Facts 1900–79* (1979); Gallup Report, *Daily Telegraph*, 18 December 1981.

It then considers whether the picture has changed with the advent of the Alliance and examines how the character of SDP support compares with that of Liberal support. In the final section this evidence is put into the context of wider trends both in Britain and abroad.

THE CHARACTER OF LIBERAL SUPPORT

Research into the Liberal vote has been heavily influenced by the political circumstances of the time. Following the 'Orpington revival' of the early 1960s, Liberal voters received some attention and, indeed, a chapter of their own in the first edition of Butler and Stokes's pathbreaking study of British voting behaviour. Even so, that attention was focused as much on any differential impact increased Liberal support had upon the Conservative and Labour parties as it was on the character of that support itself. When they came to write their second edition, incorporating surveys conducted in 1969 and 1970, a low point in Liberal fortunes, Butler and Stokes decided to omit the chapter on the Liberals.[2] But the Liberals' surge of support in the February 1974 election reawakened interest. For the first time academic articles appeared whose principal focus was Liberal support and which brought to bear on that subject a considerable amount of survey evidence.[3] More generally, in this period studies of British voting behaviour often included Liberals in their analysis and did not follow Butler and Stokes's habit of omitting them from many of their tables. Consequently, we are now able to paint a reasonably clear picture of the character of Liberal support although inevitably some features remain ill-defined.

The social structural approach to voting behaviour and the development of party systems emphasizes the role of social

[2] D. Butler and D. Stokes, *Political Change in Britain* (1st edition, 1969; 2nd edition, 1974). All page references to the first edition in this chapter are to the paperback version (1971).

[3] Most notably, one number of *Political Studies* contained two such articles. P. Lemieux, 'Political Issues and Liberal Support in the February 1974, British General Election', *Political Studies*, xxv (1977), 323–42; J. Alt, I. Crewe, and B. Särlvik, 'Angels in Plastic: The Liberal Surge in 1974', *Political Studies*, xxv (1977), 343–68.

and political cleavages in society as a determinant of voting behaviour. In Britain this approach has traditionally emphasized
the dominant role of social class in voting behaviour, with the
middle class strongly supporting the Conservative party and
the working class, a little less strongly, the Labour party.

Because it showed that British political loyalties would not
fit completely into a neat dichotomization, Liberal support
by its very existence challenged so simplistic an account. But,
more importantly, the Liberal vote has generally defied
social structural explanation. Liberal support has revealed
some tendency towards concentration amongst the middle
class, that is both among middle class individuals and in the
more middle class constituencies, but each of these relationships is relatively weak (see Table 5.1 for data on individuals).[4]

Table 5.1   Liberal support by social class at recent general elections

Percentage

	All	Middle AB	Lower Middle C1	Skilled Working C2	Unskilled, 'Very Poor' DE
1964	11	15	14	11	9
1966	9	11	11	8	7
1970	8	10	9	7	6
1974 (Feb.)	20	20	25	20	17
1974 (Oct.)	19	22	21	20	16
1979	14	16		15	13

Source: Nuffield election studies for each election, quoting the following opinion polls:– 1964–74 (Feb.), NOP; 1974 (Oct.), Louis Harris;
1979, MORI.

However, with the spread of Liberal candidatures in the
1970s and a consequent reduction in their concentration in
middle-class constituencies, Liberal support has become even
more evenly spread socially. Further, Butler and Stokes's
breakdown of party support by social class and region, using
combined NOP polls undertaken between 1963 and 1966,
showed that in the Liberals' strongest area – the South-West

[4] On the relationship between Liberal voting and the class composition of a
constituency, see W. Miller, *Electoral Dynamics* (1977); M. Steed and J. Curtice,
From Warrington and Croydon to Downing Street (Manchester, 1981).

of England — Liberal support was marginally greater amongst the working class than in the middle class.[5] Liberal support, then, is not clearly organized on class lines. Further, efforts to explain Liberal voting in terms of other social cleavages have proved either indeterminate or fruitless.[6]

This impression that Liberal support has a socially 'rootless' character is confirmed by social psychological explorations of Liberal support. Such approaches to voting behaviour have emphasized the importance of a psychological attachment between voter and party, which is transmitted from one generation to another through family socialization and which ensures that the voter gives consistent support to his favoured party through thick and thin.[7] This attachment, known as 'party identification' (or sometimes, as in Butler and Stokes, 'partisan self-image'), has been shown to be held by lower proportions of Liberal voters than of Conservative and Labour voters. Further, Liberal identifiers are less likely to translate their attachment into a Liberal vote than other identifiers, or to transfer their identification to their offspring.[8]

The weakness of the attachment of most Liberal voters to their party has been amply confirmed by their voting histories. British Election Study data reveal that between 1959 and 1979 on average under a half of those who voted for a Liberal at one election did so again at the following election, compared with nearly three-quarters of Conservative and Labour voters.[9] Even in the short period between February

---

[5] Butler and Stokes, 2nd edition, p. 126. For further figures on the class composition of Liberal support, see R. Rose, *Class Does Not Equal Party* (Glasgow, 1980).

[6] See, for example, Miller's multivariate analysis of social and political alignments in England in 1974. Apart from a tendency for younger voters to vote Liberal, only nonconformity was particularly associated with Liberalism. This latter relationship is clearly a consequence of the long historical link between Liberalism and nonconformism. See W. Miller, *The End of British Politics?* (Oxford, 1981), pp. 140–50.

[7] For a more detailed summary of models of voting behaviour based on party identification, see H. Himmelweit, P. Humphreys, M. Jaeger, and M. Katz, *How Voters Decide* (1981), pp. 6–10.

[8] Ibid., p. 161; A. Mughan, 'Party Identification, Voting Preference and Electoral Outcomes in Britain, 1964–74', *British Journal of Political Science*, ix (1979), 115–28.

[9] I. Crewe, 'Is Britain's Two-Party System Really About to Crumble?', *Electoral Studies* Vol. 1 No. 3 (1982) pp. 280–81.

and October 1974 nearly half of those who voted Liberal in the first election failed to do so in the second.[10] This pattern arises simply because Liberal support contains a higher proportion of defectors (who are in general more likely to switch their vote in future than other voters) than is the case with the Conservative and Labour parties, and not because defectors to the Liberals become disenchanted with their new choice more quickly than defectors to Conservative or Labour.[11] While approximately a quarter of the electorate voted consistently Conservative or Labour in the 1970s, only 2 per cent voted consistently Liberal;[12] these consistent voters represent approximately five-sixths of the overall Conservative and Labour shares of the electorate across the four elections of the 1970s, but only one-sixth in the case of the Liberals. Only a relatively small proportion of this discrepancy is to be accounted for by the failure of the Liberals to fight all the constituencies, especially in 1970.

The obverse of this pattern of weak attachment is widespread sympathy. From their 1974 surveys the British Election Study team showed that for every voter who had voted Liberal at least once between 1966 and October 1974 there was another who could be classified as a 'potential Liberal'; in total, sometimes actual and potential Liberals amounted to 43 per cent of their sample.[13] The existence of this sympathy has repeatedly been tapped by surveys which have asked voters whether they would vote Liberal if they thought the Party had a chance of winning. For example, an ORC poll conducted in September 1968 got a 52 per cent 'yes' response to the question, 'If you thought that the Liberals stood a chance of forming a government would you ever consider voting for them?'[14] Support for the Liberal Party is widely if thinly spread.

---

[10] Alt *et al.*, 'Angels in Plastic', p. 348.

[11] Ibid., p. 347.

[12] Crewe, 'Britain's Two-Party System', p. 281.

[13] Alt *et al.*, 'Angels in Plastic', p. 349.

[14] *Sunday Times*, 22 September 1968, quoted in M. Steed, 'The Liberal Party', in H. Drucker (ed.), *Multi-Party Britain* (1979), p. 84. Gallup have occasionally asked a similar question and acquired a 33 per cent or so 'yes' response. Butler and Stokes, 1st edition, p. 386; Lemieux, 'Liberal Support in February 1974', p. 326.

Given the weakness of the support for the Liberal party among those who actually vote for it, and the thinness of the opposition to it on the part of many of those who do not, it is not surprising to find that tactical considerations play an important role in generating Liberal support. This has been evident in responses to surveys and in election results. Butler and Stokes found that both those with a Liberal Party identification and those without were more likely to vote Liberal if they thought the Liberals had a chance of winning in their constituency.[15] From election results it has been clear that Liberal support tends to be squeezed in seats which are marginal between Conservative and Labour, especially where two elections follow each other in a short period of time. On the other hand, voters for the weaker of the two major parties in a constituency where the Liberals acquire a good second place are often tempted to switch to the Liberals in order to defeat the incumbent of the other major party.[16]

Liberal supporters are, therefore, a constantly shifting group who, in a sense, represent a much larger number of people who at some point in their voting lives have actually voted Liberal or seriously considered doing so. But what is the pattern of their movement? A Liberal vote seems for most electors to be a place of temporary refuge from their normal Conservative or Labour home. Most people who defect to the Liberals turn back again to their original party rather than defect to the other major party.[17] The overall rates of defection from Conservative and Labour at any one election, however, are not necessarily equal but reveal a tendency, though by no means a universal one, to be greater in the case of the major party against which opinion is otherwise moving.[18] But such differences in the rate of defection

[15] Butler and Stokes, 1st edition, pp. 395 and 399. See also D. Butler, A. Stevens, and D. Stokes, 'The Strength of the Liberals under Different Electoral Systems', *Parliamentary Affairs*, xxii (1968/9), 10-15.

[16] For a summary of the evidence on tactical voting, see M. Steed, 'The Results Analysed', in D. Butler and D. Kavanagh, *The British General Election of October 1974* (1975), pp. 341-2.

[17] Butler and Stokes, 2nd edition, pp. 272-4.

[18] Ibid., pp. 253-67; I. Crewe, 'Electoral Volatility in Britain Since 1945' (Paper presented at the ECPR Joint Sessions, University of Lancaster, 1981), Table 6.

do not imply that the Liberals' presence or absence in a constituency necessarily has any influence upon the swing between the two major parties. Butler and Stokes undertook an exhaustive analysis of the second preferences of those who had actually voted Liberal, and of the proportion of those who had actually voted Conservative or Labour but would have voted Liberal if there had been the opportunity, and came to the conclusion that there was no clear systematic effect in either case.[19] Although analysis of the election results in seats where the Liberals withdrew or intervened in the 1950s suggested that Liberal supporters tended to come somewhat disproportionately from those who would otherwise vote Conservative, analyses conducted from 1964 onwards have usually shown no such bias.[20]

We now have a picture of the Liberal voter. He is, above all, a temporary defector from one of the major parties.[21] This suggests, that, in order to discover the motivation for voting Liberal, we should direct our attention to the Liberal voter's evaluation of the major parties as much as to his perception of the Liberal Party itself.

Research has clearly established that those voting Liberal at any one point in time can be distinguished from their major-party counterparts by their attitudes towards one or both of the two major parties. In their original study Butler and Stokes showed that Liberal voters were much more likely to offer a negative evaluation of both major parties.[22] Later work has confirmed that such a stance plays a role in inducing a Liberal vote, but has also suggested that a more widespread dissatisfaction with other aspects of life may also be part of the motivation of the Liberal Party's

---

[19] Butler and Stokes, 1st edition, pp. 399–406. Their figures relate to the 1964 and 1966 elections.

[20] See the various statistical appendices to the Nuffield election studies by David Butler and his co-authors.

[21] Or, as Himmelweit *et al.* describe a Liberal Vote, '*it is a vote signifying departure rather than arrival*'. Himmelweit *et al.*, *How Voters Decide*, p. 159 (italics in original).

[22] Butler and Stokes, 1st edition, p. 389. The importance of joint evaluation of the major parties is given further weight by the lack of relationship between propensity to vote Liberal and weak major party identification. See Miller, *End of British Politics*, pp. 150–1.

temporary supporters and sympathizers.[23] It has also been shown, using a different methodology from Butler and Stokes, that Liberal voters may not necessarily have a negative attitude towards both major parties, but simply a lack of preference between the two.[24]

But while Liberal voting may be induced by a balanced or jointly negative evaluation of the Conservative and Labour parties, it may still be true that the more immediate trigger to a Liberal vote is the voter's evaluation of just one of those parties. In two separate analyses Lemieux has shown that Liberal voters tended to have one or more specific policy disagreements with, in 1964, the major party they had previously supported, and in February 1974, with the major party their social-class position would have led one to expect them to support.[25] It seems probable that the joint negative evaluations of many Liberal voters arise out of a combination of long-standing dislike of the major party they do not normally support plus a more immediately generated dislike of some aspect of their usual party.

A Liberal vote is frequently then a 'retrospective' judgement on the merits of the voter's previously chosen party rather than a positive evaluation of the merits of the Liberal party. Consequently, Liberal voters are not a coherent group in policy terms but consist, for example, of erstwhile Conservative voters who oppose the Common Market and erstwhile Labour voters who favour it. Not surprisingly, discriminant analysis of party choice and issue stance shows a much lower ability to categorize accurately Liberal as opposed to

---

[23] Alt *et al.*, 'Angels in Plastic', pp. 364–7. See also M. Steed, 'My Own By-Election', *Government and Opposition*, ix (1974), 345–58.

[24] Alt *et al.*, 'Angels in Plastic', pp. 362–4. See also Miller, *End of British Politics*, Chap. 6.

[25] Lemieux, 'Liberal Support in February 1974'; P. Lemieux, 'The Liberal Party and British Political Change: 1955–74' (unpublished Ph.D. thesis, Massachusetts Institute of Technology, 1977), Chap. 3. Further interesting light on Liberal voters' evaluation of the major parties and the role of policies in its formation is cast by Alt *et al.* who suggest that Liberal voters are less able to discriminate between the major parties on policy grounds than they are in terms of image; major party supporters were better able to distinguish between Conservative and Labour on policy grounds. J. Alt, B. Särlvik, and I. Crewe, 'Individual Differences Scaling and Group Attitude Structures: British Party Imagery in 1974', *Quality and Quantity*, x (1976), 297–320.

Conservative or Labour voters.[26] In addition, analysis suggests that Liberal voters do not occupy a distinctive 'issue space', i.e. they are not distinguishable by their stance on issues which are of less concern to Conservative and Labour voters.[27] But while the negative character of Liberal support is clearly predominant, the role of positive preferences for Liberal issue positions should not be completely ignored. Alt *et al.* found that having at least one such preference helped distinguish between those who were potential Liberal supporters in 1974 and those who actually voted Liberal.[28]

The Liberal party's ability to act as a repository for the disaffected rests on two features of voters' perceptions of the Liberal Party. Firstly, the Liberal Party is seen by a majority of the electorate as lying in the centre of the left/right spectrum, in between the Conservative and Labour parties.[29] In addtion, analysis of the issues which discriminate between voters according to their partisanship reveals a considerable tendency for them to be arranged along a single left/right spectrum.[30] Accordingly, voters who find themselves disillusioned with aspects of their normal party's policy or record are far more likely to regard a shift to the Liberals as preferable to a shift to the other major party.

Secondly, the Liberal Party has a rather diffuse image amongst the electorate. It tends not to be evaluated on the basis of its policies and thus, if its policies do not attract voters, neither are they an encumbrance in the search for electoral support. Rather, the Party tends to be evaluated on vague aspects of style and there is also some tendency to regard it as having neither one quality nor the other of

[26] Himmelweit *et al., How Voters Decide*, Chap. 5; Crewe, 'Electoral Volatility', p. 30. Interestingly, however, Himmelweit *et al.* found such analysis was better able to distinguish Liberal voters from Conservative voters alone, and Liberal voters from Labour voters alone, lending further weight to Lemieux's view. Himmelweit *et al., How Voters Decide*, pp. 166-70.

[27] Himmelweit *et al., How Voters Decide*, p. 165. Their analysis contradicts a previous finding by Wilson, 'The Liberal Extremists', *New Society*, 1 November 1973, pp. 263-4.

[28] Alt *et al.*, 'Angels in Plastic', pp. 358-60.

[29] Butler and Stokes, 1st edition, p. 390; Lemieux, 'Liberal Party and Political Change', pp. 19-22; Crewe, 'Electoral Volatility', Fig. 1.

[30] See the cognitive maps in Himmelweit *et al., How Voters Decide*, pp. 142-8 and 255.

two polar extremes.[31] However, even these two rather minimal qualities are apparently not essential for all Liberal 'protest' voters. Election results have shown a willingness of some voters to vote National Front or for an extreme left-wing candidate if they do not have the opportunity to vote Liberal.[32]

One final important aspect of the Liberal vote is its geographical spread. While, as noted above, there is some tendency for the Liberal vote to be concentrated in more middle-class constituencies, and in addition it tends to be higher the more rural a constituency, its most distinctive geographical characteristic in comparison with the Conservative and Labour parties is its evenness of spread.[33] This characteristic, which can be seen as arising out of the even sociological spread of its support amongst individuals, places the party at a severe disadvantage in attempting to win seats under the first-past-the-post electoral system until it reaches a certain 'threshold' of support at around 30 per cent or more of the vote.[34] The seats that the Liberal Party has won in recent years have been those where the party has established a distinctively local basis of support built upon either the retention (e.g. Celtic Fringe) or acquisition (e.g. Orpington, Sutton & Cheam) of a distinctive image[35] which may well be bolstered by unusually high levels of local political activity and/or the propitious timing of a by-election.

There is one rider that should be added to our analysis. We have seen that the core of constant Liberal supporters constitutes a rather small proportion of the total Liberal

[31] Alt *et al.*, 'Angels in Plastic', pp. 356–7 and 359.

[32] Steed, 'Liberal Party', p. 90. This behaviour, however, was not evident in 1979. See J. Curtice and M. Steed, 'An Analysis of The Voting', in D. Butler and D. Kavanagh, *The British General Election of 1979* (1980), p. 392.

[33] For example, in October 1974 the standard deviation of the Conservative share of the poll was 12.1 and the Labour share, 15.2, but the Liberal share, only 8.3.

[34] For further details, see G. Gudgin and P. Taylor, *Seats, Votes, and The Spatial Organisation of Elections* (1979), Chaps. 4 and 5; M. Oakshott, *The Road from Limehouse to Westminster* (1981).

[35] For interesting examples of these two phenomena, see E. Meehan, 'Working Class Liberalism: A Study of Working Class Liberals in Roxburghshire, Selkirkshire and Peebleshire' (unpublished BA thesis, University of Sussex, 1976) and B. Donoughue, 'Finchley', in D. Butler and A. King, *The British General Election of 1964* (1965), pp. 241–53.

vote at any one time. Consequently, any analysis of the Liberal vote in general will be dominated by the attitudes and attributes of its temporary supporters who may differ markedly in various respects from core supporters. Because of the small numbers of committed Liberals, no general survey of the British electorate will contain sufficient such Liberals for detailed analysis to be undertaken of them. Alt *et al.*'s study did attempt to examine the core Liberal support and found it to be more middle class than Liberal support in general,[36] and also, apparently, to be associated with a distinctive set of issue priorities and attitudes distinguished by a high degree of radicalism on political and civic though not on economic matters.[37] But the character of core Liberal support, and indeed of the activists upon which it relies for organizational continuity, are still subjects that have been largely unexplored.

THE LIBERAL/SDP ALLIANCE

As suggested earlier, the emergence of the Liberal/Social Democratic Alliance in 1981 transformed the immediate prospects for a change in Britain's party system. The combined evidence of opinion polls and local and parliamentary by-elections suggested that the Alliance had the support of a plurality of the electorate during the first twelve months of its existence, with its support for most of that time being at least around the 40 per cent mark. The Liberals had never previously achieved such a position on their own.[38] Any analysis of modern Liberal voting clearly has to take account of this most recent phase in its history. Did the

[36] Though to some extent this may be a consequence of the pattern of continuous Liberal candidatures which occurred more frequently in middle-class constituencies. See Alt *et al.*, 'Angels in Plastic', p. 352, and Steed, 'Liberal Party', p. 85.

[37] Alt *et al.*, 'Angels in Plastic', pp. 353–4.

[38] Gallup had never previously placed the Liberals in the lead (see also footnote 1). The performance of the Alliance in its early life has also been much more consistent than that of the Liberals during their previous revivals. For example, in 1972, on the day that the Liberals won a by-election in Sutton and Cheam they lost their deposit in Uxbridge; in 1981/2 the Alliance won three parliamentary by-elections in succession – Croydon North West, Crosby, and Glasgow Hillhead.

transformation of the Liberals' electoral strength in collaboration with the SDP show signs of being accompanied by a
change in the character of Liberal support into a more stable
and coherent political base?

At the time of writing no academic survey has been
conducted which would enable one to study support for the
Alliance in rigorous depth. But a considerable amount of
material has been collected by the opinion-poll organizations,
and this enables us at least to supply a reasonable descriptive
picture of Alliance support which can be matched against the
one we have painted of the pre-1981 Liberal vote. If the two
pictures look similar, we can reasonably infer that little has
changed in the fundamental character of Liberal support.

The emergence of the SDP in alliance with the Liberal
Party could have a number of implications for the electoral
fortunes of the Liberal Party. Firstly, the SDP could carve
out for itself a distinctive corner in the political market-
place, acquiring a pattern of support distinguishable from
that for the Liberal Party. Thus, as a consequence of the
Alliance the Liberal party's electoral prospects might be
improved either through the ability of the SDP to win seats
the Liberals could not win or because the SDP's distinctive
body of support becomes available to Liberal candidates
where they are the standard-bearers for the Alliance. Alternatively, while the post-Alliance patterns of support for the
Liberals and SDP might be indistinguishable, their support
might in each case be markedly different from that for the
Liberal Party alone prior to the Alliance. These two processes
could also operate in tandem — SDP support might be
distinguishable from Liberal support, but the support of both
of them within the Alliance be different from that of the
pre-Alliance Liberal party.

The evidence, however, primarily suggests that none of
these processes have operated to any great extent during
the first year or so of the Alliance's existence. As we shall
see, while there are a few apparent differences in the pattern
of Liberal and SDP support, the formation of the Alliance
does not appear to have provided a stable, coherent body
of mass support for the principal alternative to the Conservative and Labour parties.

Table 5.2 Alliance support by age, sex, and class, Jan.–May 1982

Percentage

	All	Male	Female	AB	C1	C2	DE
Liberal	14	11	17	14	14	14	14
SDP	16	19	14	16	18	18	13
Alliance	31	32	32	32	33	33	28

	18-24	25-34	35-44	45-54	55-64	65+	
Liberal	12	15	14	13	15	17	(1,060)
SDP	18	20	17	18	14	10	(1,216)
Alliance	31	37	32	32	30	29	(2,381)

Source: MORI combined ombibus polls, Jan.–May 1982. Total N with voting intention = 7,578.

Table 5.2 presents a simple breakdown of the support for the Alliance as recorded in MORI's omnibus polls from January to May 1982.[39] While some subtle differences exist within the table, the overwhelming impression remains that the pattern of support for the Alliance, and for the Liberal party within it, is evenly spread across the population. The sharpest distinction between the two parties lies in their differential ability to appeal to the sexes; this pattern has been found in most surveys since the formation of the Alliance, and cannot be explained away as a spurious relationship caused by the impact of other attributes upon the two parties' support which are unequally distributed between the sexes. But the significance of this finding in understanding the appeal of the two parties is unclear.

The pattern of support for the Alliance across the classes looks very similar to that of the pre-Alliance Liberal Party — broadly spread but somewhat weaker in the lowest social

[39] I am extremely grateful to MORI, and to Brian Gosschalk in particular, for their generous co-operation in granting me access to their detailed breakdowns of this and other data used in this chapter. The total number of respondents giving a voting intention in the combined polls was 7,578, including 1,060 Liberal supporters, 1,216 SDP, and a total of 2,381 Alliance. (Some Alliance supporters were unable to classify themselves as Liberal or SDP.)

category. Examination of the pattern of support across other social categories such as housing tenure or trade unionization, and across various combinations of social categories equally fails to show any particular concentration of Alliance support. The social-class data do, however, have two interesting features. Firstly, evidence from MORI polls taken in 1981 suggests that a shift occurred in the pattern of SDP support towards the end of that year, from being one which revealed a gentle tendency to be stronger amongst the middle class (thereby tilting Alliance support in general in that direction) to one which was more evenly spread with a slight concentration in the two middle categories. This change must remind us that the Alliance's pattern of support may not have been fixed in its first months of existence and should temper our evaluation of the future of the Alliance.[40] The second interesting feature is that the pattern of Liberal support has become even more of a microcosm of the electorate than it had been previously, being equally as strong amongst the working class as the middle class (compare Table 5.1).

The cross-tabulation by age reveals some further points of interest. Alliance support is somewhat stronger amongst younger age groups; this is a pattern which is common amongst 'new' parties and is similar to that of the Liberals at the time of their 1974 resurgence. But within that pattern support is not particularly strong in the youngest age group, while it is noticeably so in the next youngest. This latter group contains those people who first voted in a general election in 1974 and thus contains an unusually large number of people who would have used that opportunity to vote for the Liberals; they may now be displaying a particular propensity to return to that party. Amongst the oldest age groups, SDP support tails off quite sharply but that for the Liberals is above average; for these people the longer established Liberal Party is a greater attraction than the SDP.

Despite these interesting differences, however, these data

---

[40] This change helps to account for the failure of the analysis reported here to identify a concentration of SDP support amongst the younger middle classes such as was found by Crewe in his analysis of Gallup data for October 1981. Crewe, 'Britain's Two-Party System', p. 295. In most other respects the findings here agree with those of Crewe.

show that the Alliance has not carved out a distinctive socio-economic section of the electorate. However, while the social origins of the two parties appear broadly similar to each other and to that of the pre-Alliance Liberal Party, the two parties do appear to differ in their ability to appeal to ex-Conservative and ex-Labour voters. The same MORI polls as those analysed above reveal that the Liberals drew their support evenly from Conservative and Labour — just over 7 per cent of their 1979 vote apiece,[41] but that the SDP were more likely to attract Labour supporters, winning the support of 11 per cent of 1979 Conservatives but 17 per cent of 1979 Labour supporters. The 1982 local elections, the first nation-wide elections to be fought by the SDP, also suggested that the SDP was slightly more attractive to former Labour supporters.[42]

If, however, we turn to the motivation of Alliance supporters we again find that they bear a striking resemblance to pre-Alliance Liberal supporters. Support for the Alliance's policy positions appears not to be an important part of its appeal. In a poll conducted by MORI in November 1981 respondents were asked who they thought had the best policies on a range of issue areas. While the mean percentage of Conservatives who named their own party was 71, and that of Labour supporters, 75, the equivalent figure for supporters of the Alliance was 37.[43] In their March 1982 omnibus survey MORI asked respondents whether a range of statements could be applied to each of the political parties. Fifty-one per cent of Conservative supporters felt their party

[41] These data are based on a recall of the voter's 1979 vote. Such recall data is known not to be very accurate and, in particular, respondents have a tendency to make their past voting behaviour consistent with their current preference. See H. Himmelweit, M. Jaeger, and J. Stockdale, 'Memory for Past Vote: Implications of a Study of Bias in Recall', *British Journal of Political Science*, viii (1978), 365–76. But while this may mean that our data do not accurately represent the level of movement between 1979 and 1982, they should still be a reasonable indicator of the relative magnitude of different types of movement, which is the use to which it is put here.

[42] J. Curtice, C. Payne, and R. Waller, 'The Alliance's First Nationwide Test: Lessons of the 1982 English Local Elections', *Electoral Studies*, Vol. 2. No. 1 (1983).

[43] MORI poll on the economy conducted for *The Sunday Times* in November 1981. Total N = 894. The issue areas were unemployment, inflation, local government spending, managing the economy generally, and defence.

had 'good policies to deal with inflation', and 52 per cent of Labour supporters that their party had 'good policies to deal with unemployment'. But the better of the two scores on these statements for the Liberals and the SDP was only 27 per cent (on inflation) in the case of the Liberals and 23 per cent (on unemployment) in the case of the SDP.[44]

Like the pre-Alliance Liberal Party the Alliance has also failed to carve out a distinctive 'issue space' for itself. Surveys have consistently shown that when respondents are asked whether they are for or against certain policies, the proportion of affirmative responses from Alliance supporters has lain between the equivalent proportions of Conservative and Labour supporters.[45] But even more interestingly this positioning between the two major parties does not appear necessarily to represent a clear preference for 'centrist' solutions amongst Alliance supporters. In August 1981 MORI asked respondents not only whether they favoured a proposal but also to what extent they did so; respondents could place themselves in one of five categories ranging from strongly in favour to strongly against. If those categories are turned into scores from one to five the mean position of Alliance supporters on the six issues covered can be shown to have lain between that of Conservative and Labour supporters.[46] However, the proportion of Alliance supporters opting for one of the three middle categories was not noticeably higher than in the case of Conservative and Labour supporters — Alliance supporters were simply more evenly divided between the

[44] MORI March 1982 omnibus survey. Total N = 1,521.

[45] See, for example, October 1981 and January 1982 MORI omnibus polls and *The Sunday Times* economy poll noted above. The only policies on which Alliance supporters were keener than both Conservative and Labour supporters in these surveys were the introduction of proportional representation, incomes policy, and import controls. 1974 Liberals also proved (not surprisingly) to be particularly keen on proportional representation. Himmelweit *et al.*, *How Voters Decide*, p. 148.

[46] MORI August 1981 omnibus survey. Total N = 1,774. The six issues covered were election to the House of Lords, reintroduction of the death penalty, withdrawal from the EEC, withdrawal of troops from Northern Ireland, stronger laws to protect coloured people from discrimination, and unilateral abandonment of nuclear weapons. The mean score of each party's supporters across all six issues, giving the lower scores for the more right-wing policy in each case, was Con., 2.19; Lab., 3.31; Lib., 2.89; SDP, 2.76. This ordering was replicated on five of the six issues separately. See also Crewe, 'Britain's Two-Party System', pp. 304–5.

two extreme alternatives of support or opposition.[47]

The suspicion aroused by this pattern of replies — that the Alliance vote is very much a protest vote — has been confirmed by a number of polls taken on the occasion of by-elections successfully contested by one of its candidates. At Crosby 42 per cent of Alliance supporters indicated they were voting against other parties' policies rather than in favour of their own and a further 17 per cent indicated a mixture of both motives. At Croydon North West and Glasgow Hillhead a slightly different question suggested that 58 per cent and 51 per cent respectively of Alliance supporters were voting predominantly for negative reasons.[48] The Alliance's success in the first twelve months of its life was clearly based on an ability to act as an even more effective vehicle of protest than the Liberal Party ever could, not on the creation of a new coherent political majority.

Alliance support evidently retains other features of the old Liberal vote. Opinion polls and local election results indicate that it is geographically very evenly spread; indeed a tendency for the Alliance to do best in areas of past Liberal weakness in the 1982 local elections suggests that it may be even more so.[49] The Alliance also retains the Liberals' position as everyone else's second preference; in November

[47] The mean percentage of each party's supporters taking the middle three options was Con., 51; Lab., 51; Lib., 56; SDP, 55. Such difference as exists is almost entirely explained by a slightly greater preference of Alliance supporters for centrist positions on one particular issue — the abandonment of nuclear weapons.

[48] The question asked at Crosby was, 'Are you voting for that party mainly because you approve of its policies, or mainly to protest against any other party or policies?.' The proportion of Conservative and Labour supporters indicating the latter option was 12 and 16 per cent respectively. NOP, *Political, Social, Economic Review*, No. 34. At Croydon North West and Glasgow Hillhead voters were asked, 'What would you say is the stronger, your like of the — party, or your dislike of the other parties?' The Conservative and Labour dislike figures were 41 and 39 per cent respectively at Croydon North West and 33 per cent (in both cases) at Glasgow Hillhead. Gallup Reports, *Daily Telegraph*, 22 October 1981 and 24 March 1982. At Hillhead and Crosby MORI gave Alliance supporters a range of reasons as to why they were voting for its candidate. At Hillhead positive reasons constituted 38 per cent of all mentions, and negative reasons 54 per cent. At Crosby the equivalent figures were 32 per cent and 61 per cent. MORI, Hillhead Poll No. 1 (Total Alliance supporters = 229); MORI, Crosby Poll No. 3 (Total Alliance supporters = 412).

[49] Curtice *et al.*, 'Alliance's First Nationwide Test.'

1981 41 per cent of Conservatives and 43 per cent of Labour supporters named the Alliance as their second preference, representing 78 and 79 per cent respectively of each party's supporters who were prepared to name any second preference.[50] When we come, therefore, to evaluate the wider significance of support for the Liberal Party and the Alliance in general, together with their prospects for the future, we can still reasonably refer to the academic research into the Liberal vote undertaken prior to 1981.

THE SIGNIFICANCE OF LIBERAL SUPPORT

The Liberal Party has made discernible progress in expanding the size of its electoral support over the last thirty years. The early life of the Alliance suggested a continuation of that process. We have so far in this chapter assessed the phenomenon of Liberal support in Britain by examining its character in isolation. But in order to assess the significance of Liberal support and its apparent long-term tendency to increase we need to place this understanding in a wider context. How does what we know about Liberal support fit into our understanding of recent developments in British electoral sociology? And can any comparisons be made with electoral developments in other countries which can help inform our understanding?

Recent research into British electoral sociology has been dominated by two main themes. Firstly, class has become a less powerful predictor of individual voting behaviour, and, furthermore, there has been a noticeable decline in the strength of party identification across the electorate as a whole.[51] Secondly, in contrast to earlier work, it has been increasingly suggested that an individual's issue stance does

---

[50] MORI, November 1981 omnibus poll, Total N = 977.

[51] See especially, I. Crewe, B. Särlvik, and J. Alt, 'Partisan Dealignment in Britain 1964–1974', *British Journal of Political Science*, vii (1977), 129–90; Crewe, 'Electoral Volatility'; Rose, *Class Does Not Equal Party*. The continuing predictive ability of class at aggregate level is shown in Miller, *Electoral Dynamics*; W. Miller, 'Social Class and Party Choice in England: A New Analysis', *British Journal of Political Science*, viii (1978), 257–84; W. Miller, 'Class, Region and Strata at the British General Election of 1979', *Parliamentary Affairs*, xxxii (1979), 376–82.

play a significant role in determining for whom he votes.[52]
Increasing Liberal support fits more immediately with the
first than with the second development. We have seen that
Liberal supporters tend to be drawn evenly from all classes
and lack a strong identification with their party. The decline
in the importance of these two factors look likely to have
assisted in the Liberals' electoral progress. In addition, if the
lack of sociological identity to its vote were to be regarded
as an impediment to success, the relative disadvantage of the
Liberal party, as compared with its major rivals, has declined
in the last twenty years.

But we have also seen that the Liberal Party tends not to
be evaluated by the electorate according to its policy stances
and indeed that it tends to be regarded weakly on this score.
Further, Liberal voters cannot easily be distinguished from
other voters according to their attitudes on issues. The development of Liberal strength in an age of issue voting appears
possible only because, as Lemieux has shown, disagreement
with a voter's previous party's issue position can influence
his or her decision as well as positive evaluation of the alternatives. Indeed, general dissatisfaction with the previous Labour
government has been shown to have been an important factor
in the decision of many recruits to the Conservative party
in 1979.[53] The Liberals' electoral support reminds us then of
the importance of retrospective as well as future evaluation
in the voting decision; indeed, the ability to register such
dissatisfaction, particularly with the government of the day,
might be seen as essential to the health of a democracy.

Turning our eyes abroad enables us to consider whether
the Liberals' electoral progress in Britain fits into any wider

---

[52] J. Alt, B. Särlvik, and I. Crewe, 'Partisanship and Policy Choice: Issue
Preferences in the British Electorate, February 1974', *British Journal of Political
Science*, vi (1976), 273–90; Himmelweit *et al.*, *How Voters Decide*. It is not clear,
however, whether issues have come to play a greater real role in British electoral
behaviour, or whether academics have just come to realize their significance. The
inference can be drawn that the former is true from the facts that (a) levels of
party identification have fallen, (b) an individual's issue stance is more important
in determining his vote, the lower his party identification (see Alt *et al.*).

[53] I. Crewe, 'Why The Conservatives Won', in H. Penniman (ed.), *Britain At
The Polls, 1979* (Washington DC, 1981), p. 296. Note also that the Conservative
and Labour dislike figures at footnote 48, although lower than those for the
Alliance, are still quite high.

pattern of advance in the Liberal cause, or into other relevant electoral trends in democratic party systems. European Liberal parties are a heterogeneous group, forming the least coherent party group in the European Parliament.[54] Their support tends to be more clearly structured by social cleavages than in the case of the British Liberal Party, usually having a middle class and/or secular/Protestant bias in their pattern of support.[55] In those Scandinavian countries where they face an agrarian party there also tends to be an urban bias to their support. But even if we ignore those difficulties in making realistic comparisons between the fortunes of the British and other European Liberal parties, there is no clear evidence that the British Party's improvement in its electoral position over the last thirty years is part of any general return towards liberalism in Europe. Some Liberal parties in Europe have succeeded in advancing their electoral position. In Belgium the party (here regarding its Flemish and Walloon versions as one party) moved from a nadir of 8.9 per cent in 1946 to 21.6 per cent in 1965, and was still polling 21.5 per cent in 1981. In The Netherlands the Liberals have steadily advanced to 23.1 per cent of the poll (in 1982). But in other countries there has been a clear secular decline in Liberal fortunes. In Sweden the Liberals won 22.7 per cent of the poll in 1948, but had fallen to 5.2 per cent by 1982; in Norway support had dropped away to 3.9 per cent by 1981. International comparison thus provides little evidence to suggest that democratic political systems are experiencing a general increase in support for liberalism.

However, when we turn to the perception of the nature of Liberal support in Britain that we have developed in our earlier analysis — as a volatile protest vote — we find that international comparison does provide some evidence of parallels. In their review of post-war developments in European

---

[54] For a brief review of the Liberal group in the European Parliament, see G. and P. Pridham, 'Transnational Parties in the European Community I: The Party Groups in the European Parliament', in S. Henig (ed.), *Political Parties in the European Community* (1977), pp. 258–61.

[55] For a simple overview, see R. Rose and D. Urwin, 'Resistance and Change in Western Party Systems since 1945', *Political Studies*, xviii (1970), 287–319, pp. 314–19. For further details on a number of countries, see R. Rose (ed.), *Electoral Behaviour* (New York, 1974).

party systems up to 1969, Rose and Urwin, following Lipset and Rokkan, were able to claim that there were no discernible systematic patterns with regard to either volatility or secular trends, and that the number and structure of parties in a country were still largely determined by long-standing social cleavages.[56] However, in a more recent analysis Pedersen showed that while there were no uniform trends across all of Western Europe, there was some tendency for volatility to increase in the 1970s compared with the 1960s and 1950s.[57] This volatility has been particularly noticeable in Scandinavia where a number of new parties achieved considerable electoral success in the early 1970s, and where there has been a discernible decline in the importance of class as a determinant of voting behaviour.[58]

The rise of relatively successful new or third parties has also occurred in some Anglo-American democracies where the party system is more similar to Britain's. In Australia, the Australian Democrats won 9.4 per cent of the poll in their first election in 1978, though they fell back to 6.6 per cent in 1980. Their success, while concentrated amongst the tertiary educated, crossed class boundaries to a considerable extent, and occurred against the background of a decline in the intensity of the class cleavage and a small but perceptible fall in the strength of party identification.[59] But perhaps the closest parallel to Liberal and Alliance success has been the recent performance of Social Credit in New Zealand, which more than doubled its share of the poll to 16.3 per cent in 1978 and advanced further to 20.7 per cent in 1981. The background to Social Credit's success and its pattern of

---

[56] Rose and Urwin, 'Resistance and Change'; S. Lipset and S. Rokkan, 'Cleavage Structures, Party Systems and Voter Alignments: An Introduction', in Lipset and Rokkan (eds.), *Party Systems and Voter Alignments: Cross-National Perspectives* (New York, 1967), pp. 1–64.

[57] M. Pedersen, 'The Dynamics of Party Systems: Changing Patterns of Electoral Volatility', *European Journal of Political Research*, vii (1979), 1–26, esp. Table 1.

[58] S. Berglund and U. Lindström, 'The Scandinavian Party System(s) in Transition(?): A Macro-Level Analysis', *European Journal of Political Research*, vii (1979), 187–204. They have not all, however, succeeded in retaining their early support. Perhaps the most startlingly successful newcomer — the Progress Party in Denmark — which won 15.9 per cent of the poll in 1973, had seen its support fall away to 8.9 per cent by 1981.

[59] D. Kemp, *Society and Electoral Behaviour in Australia* (St. Lucia, Queensland, 1978), esp. Chap. 3 and pp. 361–3.

support contain a number of factors akin to the Liberal past. The 1978 breakthrough occurred after both major parties had undergone a rather unsuccessful period in office. While concentrated amongst small farmers and business men, its vote to a considerable extent crosses the class divide.[60] Only a small proportion of this vote consists of committed core voters expressing support for Major Douglas's monetary ideas; its support is composed largely of a protest vote based on a negative evaluation of both parties. It also shares the geographical evenness of the Liberal vote and suffers similarly from the lack of reward that the first-past-the-post electoral system gives to such third parties.[61]

Recent experience abroad suggests that a party whose support is based on a negative protest vote can anticipate considerable success in the face of a decline in the power of traditional social cleavages and of social psychological identification with the established parties, especially if those parties have had a bad record while in recent occupation of office. Indeed, both the Liberal revivals of the 1960s and 1970s, and the Alliance surge in 1981 occurred when the government was encountering difficulties in office and the opposition had either recently been in the same position and/or was currently rendering itself unfit for office through internal squabbling.[62] Our analysis of the Liberal vote does not then pre-ordain the party to electoral failure; if the right circumstances pertained at a general election a tide of disillusion with Conservative and Labour combined with broad sympathy for the Liberal Party/Alliance could propel the party into a strong position in the House of Commons.

What, however, must remain in doubt are the Party's long-term prospects given the current nature of its support. The essential dilemma for any party which gains power on the basis of a volatile protest vote is whether it can hope to retain that support once it is laden with a measure of responsibility for the state of the nation. Evaluation of its own

[60] S. Levine and A. Robinson, *The New Zealand Voter* (Wellington, 1976), p. 139.

[61] On these points, see C. James, 'Social Credit and the Values Party', in H. Penniman (ed.), *New Zealand At The Polls* (Washington DC, 1980).

[62] The onset of the Falklands crisis in April 1982 apparently removed the first condition and was followed by a reduction in Alliance support.

policies and performance could be expected to reckon more highly in the electorate's mind than before, to its disadvantage.[63] This softness of its support, combined with the particular dangers that the first-past-the-post electoral system holds for it so long as its vote is distributed so evenly, provide the party with a strong impetus to ensure that it secures proportional representation before the end of its period of office. If that aim were achieved not only would the Liberals be equipped with a safety net against an unpopular future, but it might also be able to carve out a new role for itself in Britain's party system. It might, for example, play the kind of pivotal role undertaken by the West German FDP, acting as a counterbalance to extremism; then, perhaps it could build for itself a more stable constituency of support based on those who identify with the party's centrist persuasion on left/right economic issues.

It would seem that, should the Liberal/SDP Alliance make an electoral breakthrough, its future and with it that of Britain's party system will depend crucially upon whether proportional representation is achieved or not. That in turn will no doubt depend upon the tactical skill of its parliamentary leaders in a situation where no one party has an overall majority in the Commons. It will be a heavy responsibility for David Steel and his successors to bear.

---

[63] This problem has been highlighted in miniature in certain areas where the Liberal Party has achieved power at local government level. The party's subsequent fortunes in such places have not always been good. See M. Steed, 'The Results Analysed', in D. Butler and D. Kavanagh, *The British General Election of February 1974* (1974), pp. 333-4. It should of course be acknowledged that to the extent that both major parties' support has become more volatile in recent years, and negative evaluation of the party in office more common, the Liberal Party's difficulties in this regard have become less unique. But it still seems significantly more acute than in the case of the Conservative and Labour parties.

6. Organization and Power in the Liberal Party*

Dennis Kavanagh

Students of structure and organization in British political parties will be aware that this subject is neither trivial nor a matter of indifference to participants. For a long time the organization of the Liberal party has hardly mattered to anyone outside the party. But, given the emergence of a substantial number of Liberal SDP-Alliance MPs or Liberal participation in a government, the questions of party structure and party democracy could assume a new importance. The rehearsals for power politics involved in the debates about whether the Liberals would enter a coalition in 1974 and the operation of the Lib-Lab pact in 1977 severely strained the party. The experience confirmed that coalitions are invariably closer at the top than at the grass roots.

This paper examines three issues raised by the Liberal party's structure. First, it describes the party's complicated set of institutions and assesses its political consequences. Second, it considers the party's claims to be a decentralized party; this feature is one that many Liberals believe makes their party distinctive, compared to the other parties. Third, it assesses the accuracy of the claim that the distribution of power in the party is the same as that in the Conservative, and, till 1981, Labour parties, i.e. the parliamentary party is quite autonomous of the extra-parliamentary machine in policy matters.

I
THE STRUCTURE

The complexity of the main constitutional organs of the party partly reflects the fact that in the nineteenth century the Liberal party developed around a number of separate bodies.

* For comments on an earlier version of this paper I am grateful to Hugh Jones, PeterKnowlson, Michael Steed, and William Wallace.

The original central party organization, the Liberal Central Association (founded 1860), still survives but mainly to channel state financial aid to MPs. Over the years many other organs have been established and the structure has been subject to various reorganizations. The present structure was created at a Constitutional Conference in 1969. The most important organs are:

The '*Liberal Party Organization*' (LPO) refers to the party headquarters.[1] It emerged from the old National Liberal Federation in the new party constitution of 1936. In common with the headquarters of the other major parties it services and advises the party in Parliament and the constituency parties. In 1982 it had a small (relative to Labour and Conservative parties) paid staff of seventeen and its head is a Secretary-General. LPO has divisions responsible for organization, policy, finance and fund-raising, press and *Liberal News*, and a Liberal Publications Department.

The National Executive Committee reports to the Council and, according to the constitution, 'directs the work of the party'. Its fifty to sixty members consist of representatives from the regional and national parties, recognized bodies, the senior officers of the party, and eight elected representatives elected by Council. It meets eight times a year and 'directs the work of the party.' It may claim to be the governing organ of the party, though it no longer has responsibility for policy.

The Finance and Administration Board (FAB) was set up in 1969. It has 8 members including 4 who are elected by the party's National Executive, the Secretary-General of LPO, a Treasurer (or Joint Treasurer) who is elected by the Assembly, and 2 more who are elected by the Staff Association. It is supposed to direct 'the administration of the party' and the work of headquarters, through the Secretary-General of the LPO, and raise and administer the party finances.

The *Council* consists of 275 representatives drawn from

[1] The term LPO is also used loosely to refer to the party's central organization or headquarters, but some Scottish Liberals use it to refer to the English Liberal Party.

various sections of the party. It meets quarterly, appoints an Assembly Committee to organize the Assembly, and pronounces on party policy between Assemblies. The resolutions of the Council, together with those of the Assembly, are official Liberal policy. Its membership overlaps with that of other organs, e.g. it includes all members of the Standing Committee and the NEC (all of whom are also Council members).

The *Assembly*, like the Labour party Conference, is regarded as the Parliament of the party. It meets annually and has 2,000 or so representatives from the constituencies, regional parties, recognized bodies, as well as MPs, peers, prospective and immediate-past parliamentary candidates, and party officers. In contrast with the Labour Conference there are no indirect (e.g. trade-union affilitated) members, and no block votes. The Assembly elects various party officers, receives reports, and considers policy resolutions. According to the party constitution the Assembly decides Liberal policy but there is no formal theory of intra-party democracy which makes the resolutions binding on Liberal MPs.

The Standing Committee meets monthly and has about thirty-five members who are drawn from three constituencies; MPs, adopted candidates, and the Council to which it reports. In theory it is a meeting-ground of the Parliamentarians and activists and, under the constitution, an MP is chairman. It expresses the party's views on matters which arise between Councils, oversees the development of party policy, and, subject to the party leader's responsibility, it prepares the manifesto.

Finally, there are twelve *English Regional* and the *National* Scottish, Ulster, and Welsh parties, which are federations of the constituency parties in their areas. The Scottish Liberal (SLP) formally declared its independence from LPO in 1946. Though the SLP participates in the annual Assembly and the election of the leader, it tends to regard the above institutions as being English rather than British.[2] The federal structure and the autonomy of the smaller national parties reflect the pluralist origins of the party.

[2] For an informed commentary on this aspect, see M. Steed: 'The Liberal Party' in H. Drucker (ed.), *Multi-Party Politics in Britain* (London, 1981).

There is no doubt that this structure is cumbersome, fragmented, and poses problems for co-ordinated and speedy decision-taking. Some degree of informal linkage is achieved through people being members of more than one body or having served on them at different periods in the past. Complaints frequently centre on the proliferation of bodies, overlapping jurisdictions between them, and lack of clear lines of responsibility. For example, the Assembly Committee is responsible to the Council and the Assembly, but it may also 'report to' the FAB, NEC, and Standing Committee on matters which fall within their jurisdictions.

There are also various other *ad hoc* committees; indeed, improvisation is an essential feature of the organization. In 1976 a Steering Committee was created to co-ordinate the organization, but gradually faded out and then a powerful General Election Committee was set up in 1977. This contained nominees of the party leader and of the Executive respectively and continued up to the general election. Most dissatisfaction is voiced with the NEC for being, allegedly, too large and unwieldy, poorly attended, particularly by MPs, and suffering too much turnover of members. Many of the reforms have been designed to bypass the Executive. In 1980 an attempt to streamline the Party organization by amending the constitution to create a smaller more influential Executive was rejected by the Assembly. The main problem is not only a matter of failures of central–local co-ordination — which affects other parties also — but the fragmentation at the centre between the organs. Over the years problems have centred on alleged waste of resources and the need to save money to stave off bankruptcy, financial scandals about 'private funds', the cavalier treatment by the MPs, particularly Jeremy Thorpe, of the extra-parliamentary organs, and the demands by local activists to provide effective policy input to MPs. The last two complaints, reflecting tensions between the parliamentary and extra-parliamentary wings, gathered force in the 1970s as the party's growth was more marked outside Parliament — in terms of electoral support — than in Parliament.

There have been numerous attempts to move to a more co-ordinated structure; for political reasons the results were usually 'fudged' and left the various structures intact while creating new institutions to do broadly similar functions. The existence of so many bodies, which, over time, have acquired their own interests, makes rationalization difficult. (Attempted rationalizations of the Labour party have similarly foundered on the position of the affiliated trade unions.) In 1944, a 'Liberal Party Committee' was established to oversee the party. It had equal numbers elected by the party and appointed by the leader. It soon became redundant as party leaders, particularly Jo Grimond and Jeremy Thorpe, simply failed to convene it. A Constitutional Review reported to the Assembly in 1969 and led to the new structure. The FAB and Standing Committee were set up in that year. But the Committee has never proved to be as effective a link as hoped because the party leader so rarely attends it. An inquiry chaired by Richard Wainwright (MP for Colne Valley) in 1975 implicitly abandoned the hope of reforming LPO and proposed a shift of resources and power to the regional offices. This was defeated by the casting vote of the chairman of the NEC in 1975. Perhaps the most important change, the election of the party leader by the party's mass membership, was accomplished in 1976.

Linkages between Parliament and party organization are partly formal, e.g. an MP is chairman of Standing Committee and the Chief Whip is Chairman of the Candidates' Committee, and partly informal, e.g. the leader may be on close personal terms with leading party officers. For various reasons Thorpe often found himself at odds with party officers. Mutual suspicion between the personalities as much as organizational shortcomings led to many of the disagreements.

There are three points to make about such a structure and the labyrinthine process of decision-making which it encourages. The first is that the party leadership is understandably tempted to go its own way and then put up with any negative reactions to any initiative it takes. This clearly happened when Thorpe accepted Edward Heath's invitation to talks about possible coalition in March 1974, and when David Steel floated the idea of Liberal involvement in a coalition to a surprised party in a party political broadcast in June 1974. Four days later a suspicious NEC rejected the idea. The MPs' decision to enter a pact with the Labour government in 1977 was preceded by informal consultation with regional chairmen and party influentials but lack of time precluded discussion with formal party organs. The Council subsequently endorsed the pact.

Second, the structure is demanding of the dozen MPs which the party has returned on average at the last four general elections. They combine a parliamentary role in Wesminster, a constituency one in what are usually marginal and far-flung seats, national speaking tours, and attendance at the extra-parliamentary bodies. It is understandable if their attendance at, and interest in, meetings of the various party institutions pales by comparison with the commitment of activists.

Third, the traditional strength of the Liberal mass party in terms of voters, members, and local councillors is largely urban, particularly in the south-east, the northern conurbations, and, to a lesser extent, in the south-west, while many MPs have recently sat for seats on the Celtic fringe or periphery. This has led to disagreement over policy priorities. Some Liberal constituency leaders who are active in local-government or community politics have less sympathy for the Westminster orientations of the MPs and discussions of pacts and coalitions have little resonance (as was seen in 1974). Many Liberal councillors and community politicians regard local elections as the path of political advancement. Conversely, MPs feel that many Liberal activists are impractical idealists, removed from what is involved in practical parliamentary politics.[3]

Any discussion of party structure and organization has to take into account the subtle distinctions between the formal and informal structure. How the party works depends in part on the nature of the issues, personalities, and circumstances at any one time. But there is a recognizable leadership group, consisting of people who sit on various central bodies and others who have status but not office in the party. Many of them have been near the centre of the party's affairs for twenty years or so and are well known to one another. Their

[3] The 1979 Assembly approved a resolution on party strategy which called on the party to place greater emphasis on local government.

ability to keep in touch offsets the tendency to inertia induced by the plurality of bodies, checks and balances, and passion for consultation found in the party. As a party publication tactfully puts it: 'For this reason an informal network of individuals who know and respect one another is essential for the effective operation of the Party.'[4] A mark of the *ad-hoccery* in the party is that many Liberal 'insiders' would now identify the most important bodies on strategy as the Campaigns and Elections Committee and the eight-man national team which negotiated the share-out of seats with the SDP.

II
CENTRALIZATION – DECENTRALIZATION

The Liberal party prides itself not only on its commitment to a decentralization of government from Westminster and Whitehall but also on decentralization in the party. The structures of other British parties, including that of the SDP, reflect a 'top down' model of authority, i.e. the role of the party outside is to support the parliamentary party.[5] According to a recent party publication, 'Liberals believe in representative democracy · with genuine self-government, and have consistently opposed concentrations of power and autocratic institutions. This belief is reflected in the present party structure which is decentralized, democratically representative, and limits the powers of central committees.'

One indication of local autonomy is the selection of candidates for Parliament. This is left to the constituencies in all the main political parties, but the Liberals have differed in two crucial respects. Effective central control depends on having a large number of applicants and being able to control the distribution of resources. The traditional shortage of suitable Liberal candidates for Parliament has meant that the reality in the constituencies was less one of making selections than of taking what was on offer. In turn this has meant that the scrutiny of candidates for approval has

---

[4] *Structure and Organization of the Liberal Party*, 1981, p. 1.
[5] But the recent constitutional changes in the Labour party make this point no longer true for that party.

often been perfunctory. In the Labour and Conservative parties central influence, in the form of maintaining a list of 'approved' candidates and a rule that the candidate's adoption is subject to approval from the centre, is an important constraint. The Liberal party has a list of 'approved' candidates but no requirement that the adoption be confirmed. Candidates can be adopted before headquarters has given approval and only occasionally is approval withheld. In more electorally promising seats and/or in very active Liberal associations in Devon or the Home Counties there is more competition for selection. But in many inner-city or hopeless seats, a person willing to stand and put up his own deposit stood a good chance of gaining nomination. The constituency's ability to choose depends to a large extent on the competitiveness of the seat.

In 1950 the party was committed to fighting on a broad front and contested 475 seats; it also forfeited a record number of 319 deposits. In the next three elections the party leadership was more cautious and frequently discouraged local associations from fighting seats in the general elections. The numbers of Liberal candidates were 109, 110, and 216. In these elections there was more central control over the selection and the Secretary of the Liberal Central Association was able to interview most candidates personally. The centre was also able to channel funds to selected seats. Ability to deny even modest financial aid to a poor association could be an important sanction. Conversely, the funds generated by local Liberal clubs could strengthen the association's independence.

The improving electoral prospects for the party since 1970 have certainly encouraged a flow of more suitable aspirants, so that many constituency parties are now able to choose from a short list. Yet even for the first 1974 general election some 150 of the total 517 Liberal candidates were selected only during the first two weeks of February and the screening process was much relaxed. The situation improved for the October 1974 election, when the party ran almost a full slate of candidates, though there was last-minute drafting of virtual strangers in a few seats in the West Midlands and Scotland. A telling example of the pitfalls which attend the 'parachuting' of an outsider (particularly one who has his own funds) was the deliberate last-minute withdrawal of the Liberal candidate in Cardiff South East in 1979, and his appeal to Liberals to vote Conservative as a way of unseating Mr Callaghan. In practice, however, the commitment to field a full slate of candidates has strained the ability of the centre and the constituencies to 'control' the selection of candidates.

Today much of the central/local discussion about the desirability of the party contesting a seat is conducted through the regional parties, as is the decision to 'approve' a candidate. Decisions not to fight are as much an indication of a weak regional office as of a weak constituency party. Strong regional offices ensured that all seats in the North-East and Yorkshire were contested in the 1979 election. Among those not fought, three were in the West Midlands, three in the Manchester region, and 28 of the 71 in Scotland and 8 of the 36 in Wales.[6]

The emergence of the SDP/Liberal Alliance may affect the autonomy of the constituencies. The SDP operates with an Area Structure of between one or two, and seven constituencies. It is inevitable that the SDP areas have so far had an input at least as much from the centre as from the constituencies. The Liberal equivalent for negotiations about the share-out of seats has been a mix of regional and 'county' parties. The reduction in the number of centrally approved Liberal candidates at the next general election from $c.600$ to $c.300$ is likely to enhance:-

(a) the ability of the constituencies to *select* candidates in the fewer but more electorally attractive seats.
(b) the ability of the regions and centre to scrutinize more rigorously the quality of candidates.
(c) the role of the regions as they negotiate with the SDP 'areas' over the share-out of constituencies.

One can never present a complete list of a party's organizational resources. What is clear, however, is that, in terms of members, full-time staff, and funds, the Liberals compare badly with the other two main parties. Three hundred Liberal

---

[6] In 1981 only Scotland, and the Home Countries had a full-time professional organizer and a secretary; four regions had either a full-time organizer or secretary: two had part-time staff, and five English regions and Wales had no staff at all.

associations at most have had a continuous existence for the past ten years; that is they fought the seat in all general elections between 1970 and 1979 and paid the annual affiliation fee to party headquarters. The Houghton report on political parties estimated that the average membership per Liberal constituency party was 300, giving a total of 190,000 for Great Britain. Some strong seats have very substantial memberships and compare favourably with any in the country. For many years, North Cornwall, North Devon, and Bodmin have had 3,000 or more members. In some city areas also, e.g. Liverpool, activity is linked to careers in local politics and is vigorous. But in many other seats a local party is centred on a small group or an enterprising individual and may come to life only every few years with the calling of a general election.

In recent general elections Liberals have operated with less than thirty paid full-time and part-time agents. In the 1979 general election only 15 paid agents were employed in the constituencies, compared to 80 Labour and 335 Conservatives. A similar imbalance appears in the level of staffing at the three party headquarters. The 20 LPO full-time staff compared with 63 in Labour headquarters and 92 in the Conservative Central office in 1979.[7] The LPO payroll included 17 of the 46 employees of the central party (Table 6.1), though LPO also provides limited financial help to the regional parties and some of the parliamentary and regional employees are part-time.[8] Complaints about organizational inefficiency, overworked officers, and underfinancing apply, of course, to all British political parties, but they are perhaps even more applicable to the Liberals than to the Conservative and Labour organizations. It is worth noting, however, that the Liberals, with about one-sixth of the total Labour staff and one-fourteenth of the Conservative total, are still able to garner nearly half as many votes as their opponents. Operating on a shoe-string has its disadvantages but one wonders if Liberals would know what to do with the resources of the Labour party let alone those of the Conservatives.

[7] R. Rose, *Politics in England Today* (London, 1980), p. 255. The figures exclude clerical and ancillary staff.

[8] The following discussion of Liberal party finance draws heavily on M. Pinto-Duschinsky's masterly *British Political Finance* (London, 1982).

Table 6.1 Liberal Party central staff, July 1979

On LPO Payroll	17
LPO staff independently financed	3
Employed by Liberal leader and MPs	8 (including 2 part time)
Employed by Scottish and Welsh parties and by regional federations	18 (including 8 part time)
Total	46 (including 10 part time)

From Pinto-Duschinsky, p. 202.

The complexity of the party's finances has been fully reported elsewhere by Michael Pinto-Duschinsky. The Liberals certainly lack the regular source of money that companies and trade unions provide for the other two parties. As a consequence they are less able to make long-term commitments. LPO has been beset by periodic threats of bankruptcy and has been unable to provide a career structure for party workers. The Wainwright report (1975) commented that the structure of the organization was such that it was a disincentive to raising money. LPO survived the damning recommendations of the report, but future Rowntree fundings were diverted to various special funds.

Various Liberal organizations have their own funds. The so-called 'Short-money', state funding for the political opposition in Parliament, is handled by the Liberal Central Association on behalf of the MPs. Before then, the Association had for long maintained a 'secret fund' which was controlled by the Chief Whip for the use of candidates and MPs. There was also a Direct Aid Fund which channelled money to Liberal-held seats and other seats considered winnable. The English regional federations and the Scottish and Welsh parties are separate bodies and control their own money. There is also the party leader's fund which is devoted to parliamentary and other purposes. Finally there has been Rowntree money which, as mentioned, has been steered away from LPO and into other party causes. LPO, though the party headquarters, does not receive the bulk of the money raised for the party. Pinto-Duschinsky notes that none of these various 'other' funds is presented in LPO accounts. The comparison with the other parties is interesting.

According to Pinto-Duschinsky the Liberals in the 1970s raised and spent approximately one-tenth to one-eighth as much as the Conservatives and about one-fifth as much as Labour on routine finance. In recent elections, the ratio of Liberal:Labour:Conservative central spending seems to have been 1:6:8 in 1970, 1:3:5 in the elections of 1974, and 1:7:12 in 1979.

The division of fund-raising responsibilities is certainly confusing and it may have weakened the party's ability to raise money. Recent steps have been taken to unify the structure but until 1982 the Rowntree grants still bypassed the party Treasurer. Indeed the grants are given on condition that they are not spent on the central apparatus. The relative financial weakness of the centre is reflected firstly in the party's pattern of expenditure. Pinto-Duschinsky notes that local spending over the last Parliament amounted to 75 per cent of total Liberal spending compared to 57 per cent for Labour and 65 per cent for Conservatives. Moreover, LPO's financial base has weakened considerably over the 1960s and 1970s. Secondly, constituency contributions to head-quarters have increased from over £1,000 (1970) to over £39,000 (1979). If anything this flow of funds may indicate the centre's financial dependence on the constituencies between elections. During election campaigns help from the centre is directed to winnable constituencies and to guaranteeing the deposits in a score or so of hopeless seats. Something like 40 per cent of total Liberal pre-campaign and campaign expenditure in 1978-9 was in the form of grants and guarantees to constituencies.[9] In 1979 about forty seats received financial assistance, usually sums of less than £100.

A plausible conclusion is that in terms of resources and candidate selection, the party is decentralized. But this is largely a consequence of (a) the weakness at the centre and (b) the weakness of most of the regions and constituencies, in lacking even one full-time officer who is able to receive, let alone comply with, communications from the centre.

---

[9] Pinto-Duschinsky, p. 202.

III
POWER IN THE PARTY

Robert McKenzie claimed that strict intra-party democracy is in practice incompatible with parliamentary democracy. The thesis was originally stated in terms of the impracticability of extra-parliamentary bodies instructing the party in government given our system of Parliament and Cabinet. For McKenzie the most important factor making for the autonomy of the parliamentary leader and his front-bench colleagues was that they are in government or are prospective office-holders. His assessment was that the distribution of power in the Liberal Party 'is the same as the other (Labour and Conservative) parties',[10] i.e. the MPs and the leader are autonomous. It is ironic that Ostrogorski's thesis about 'caucus rule' was developed in the context of the thrust for power over Liberal policy and even the election of party leader by the National Liberal Federation in the 1890s. His fear was that partisans outside Parliament would be an extremist influence. He observed in 1895 that Liberal constituency activists were 'more Radical than the mass of the party' and the MPs. Over eighty years later one might expect the Liberal extra-parliamentary organs, particularly the 'sovereign' Assembly, to have more influence than its counterparts in the other two parties, because:

(a) there have been so few Liberal MPs in post-war Parliaments — an average of 11 per general election since 1945, and
(b) the party has been so remote in time and prospects from office; hence the resources, prestige, and influence associated with being in government are lacking.

Rasmussen's study of the party's power structure up to 1964 also concluded that the extra-parliamentary machine was not influential.[11] On issues of political strategy and declaring party policy, the parliamentary leaders have made decisions independent of the party outside. It had long been recognized that the parliamentary and the mass parties are separate bodies, and that one cannot 'instruct' the other. Yet the post-war reorganization committee on the

[10] *British Political Parties* (London, 1964), p. 592.
[11] J. Rasmussen, *The Liberal Party* (London, 1965).

party spoke of the Assembly being 'sovereign' on policy, and 'The Assembly is the final voice on matters of policy.'[12] It seems clear that, in the absence of a theory of intra-party democracy, Assembly resolutions declare *party* policy but they do not commit the MPs.

One can only satisfactorily test questions about the location of power in the party if we have the MPs lined up on one side of an issue and the Assembly on the other, and the issue is then decided. Unfortunately there are no such clear-cut cases and on many issues both activists and MPs may be divided. Within the party the constitutional impli-cation of such a clash has not yet been posed. In 1926, an attempt by the party leader, Asquith, and other leading figures to expel Lloyd George was frustrated by the oppostion of the Candidates' Association and the National Liberal Federation. In the end it was Asquith who resigned. Another case of successful extra-parliamentary pressure occured in 1932 when the National government relaxed collective Cabinet responsibility over the adoption of Protection. Liberal ministers were allowed to voice their support for Free Trade and remain in the Cabinet. But the party activists pressed successfully for their resignations. In 1933, the NLF passed a motion criticizing the MPs and soon afterwards the Liberal MPs moved to the opposition benches.

Perhaps the issue would have been forced had Thorpe accepted Edward Heath's invitation to form a coalition on 1 March 1974. Even before the two party leaders met, Liberal activists bombarded headquarters with telegrams and phone calls of protest. In the next six months, the MPs tried to maintain a firm hand on the question of coalition, in advance of knowing the result of the next general election. The activists pushed for, and the Assembly voted for, a motion stating that the party would not enter a coalition with either of the two main parties under their existing leaders. It was also arranged that in the event of a hung Parliament the MPs would meet on the Saturday following the election, and the Council on the following Sunday. Although it was understood that the final decision would

[12] Quoted in Rasmussen, p. 64.

rest with the MPs, the event showed the pervasive grass-roots distrust of the MPs, particularly of Thorpe. In the event, Labour gained an overall majority and the issue was not raised. In 1981 the Assembly voted against the stationing of Cruise missiles in Britain, against the views of most MPs. Although MPs who dissented from the vote made it clear that they would go their own way, there was no constitutional crisis.

The party leader, particularly Grimond and Steel, has had the greatest influence on the choice of strategy. Yet the former's support for community politics and the latter's willingness to enter a pact with Labour in 1977 and now to form a Lib–SDP Alliance were backed in many other sections of the party. Liberal activists have been sorely tried by some of Steel's actions — not breaking off the Lib–Lab pact in December 1977 after so many Labour MPs rejected PR for the European elections, the share-out of seats with the Alliance, and his apparent willingness to cede the leadership of the Alliance to the SDP's Roy Jenkins. David Steel's strengths have been that he has presented a strategy to which there was apparently no alternative and, under the new electoral system, is clearly a popular choice as leader. In relation to parliamentary colleagues and extra-parliamentary bodies his influence has been at least comparable with that of most Labour and Conservative party leaders in opposition. One may argue about the extent to which Steel has been pushing at a relatively open door, and about the influence of his personal views. But to a remarkable extent he has managed to impress his own views about strategy on the party. The contrast with Thorpe is marked and reminds one of the importance of a determined leader's values and personality in affecting the character of a (relatively small) party.

Yet the party outside is not without influence. Strategic decisions have been taken at Assemblies — e.g. community politics (Eastbourne, 1970), the future of the Lib–Lab pact (Special Assembly, Blackpool, January 1978), the balance of power and electoral reform (Southport, 1978), and support for the Alliance (Llandudno, 1981).

In 1977, David Steel and the MPs had to make a decision quickly about supporting the minority Labour government on a motion of no confidence. During the first weekend of March extensive telephoning, on the leader's behalf, to party officers and influentials found broad support for a pact. Disillusion with it gradually set in not only among many activists but also among some MPs. David Steel renewed the pact in the summer after minimal consultation with people outside Parliament, an action that provoked widespread criticism. The failure of the majority of Labour MPs to support PR for the direct elections to the European Parliament in December 1977 forged an alliance of pro-PR, pro-EEC, and anti-pact Liberals to work for an end to the pact. In contrast to David Steel, many influential figures in Standing Committee and Council demanded and got a Special Assembly because they regarded the PR vote as an important test of the credibility of the pact. Steel seems originally to have wanted the pact to operate for the lifetime of Parliament and did not want the Assembly to meet. By the time the Special Assembly was convened in January 1978 the vote to terminate the pact, if better terms could not be negotiated in the summer, was acceptable to most MPs. At the Assembly in 1981 support for the Alliance with the SDP was carried overwhelmingly; the contacts of Liberal-party workers with voters made them aware of the appeal of the SDP, and the advantages of co-operation with it. Steel was careful to attend the Standing Committee and discuss the details of the motion to be put to the 1981 Assembly. His original plan was for a short statement welcoming the Alliance; the final motion, which included a reaffirmation of Liberal principles and procedures for the development of the Alliance, reflected the concessions he made.

The experience of the pact, and the formation of the Alliance, certainly suggests that the parliamentarians are more influential — particularly when united — largely because the power of initiative in a developing situation lies with them. In both cases the MPs managed to get their own way, but within the limits of what was acceptable to supporters. Had Thorpe made a pact with Heath in March 1974 he would probably have split the party. The Assembly, therefore, is important as a ratifying body, and as a forum for testing the mood of the party. The initiative, however, lies elsewhere .

Resolutions of the Assembly differ in status from those of the Conservative Conference in that they do decide what official party policy is; they differ from that of the Labour party in that they are not binding on MPs. Although Assembly delegates pay tribute to the authority of Assembly resolutions, the question of power and authority simply cannot be posed in Labour-party terms. Were the Liberals to be in government and the actions of Liberal MPs to have more concrete outcomes then advocates of Assembly sovereignty might become bolder. Perhaps the new system of electing the leader might encourage a Lord Randolph Churchill or a Tony Benn to link his leadership aspirations to the mass party.

There has also emerged a greater degree of Assembly management. In reaction to an ill-organized Assembly in Torquay in 1958, the Agenda (later Assembly) Committee began to play a more directive role. The introduction of television coverage of Assembly debates has encouraged a determination to achieve 'a good Conference', one that is lively, topical but not bitterly divided, and enhances the party image. In the 1950s motions were sent out to constituency ballots the results of which guided the Assembly Committee in compiling the agenda. Since 1969 the Committee has effectively controlled the selection of motions and amendments for debate and compositing of resolutions. This procedure was abandoned in 1976; it was time-consuming and the Committee appeared to be taking less notice of the results. The present method of consultation is to ballot the constituencies for choice of subjects rather than motions. The Committee is able to select amendments and settle the wording of resolutions. Because resolutions have to be submitted before the end of May and amendments before the end of June, the Committee's ability to introduce topical resolutions may help to keep the agenda up to date and 'balanced' in terms of issues. Finally, Assembly Standing Orders give considerable powers to the Committee and chairman of debates, making it difficult for delegates to change the order of business.

But the Assembly is not a passive body. Sufficient pressure from constituencies will ensure that a topic is debated. The motion which excluded incomes policy in 1976, the no-growth motion in 1979, and the Cruise-missiles motion in 1981 were all carried against the wishes of most MPs. Party leaders may be able to 'manage' the Assembly on one big issue, but only at the cost of having to neglect other issues. It seems that Assembly resolutions, if pushed frequently and hard enough, and if they enjoy the support of some MPs, are important in influencing policy decisions of the party in Parliament. Activists may also be able to persuade the Council to summon a Special Assembly as they did in 1978, against the wishes of David Steel.

Two areas in which the extra-parliamentary party has managed to assert itself have been in the election of the leader and the formulation of the manifesto. Neither change occasioned the identity crisis that has overtaken the Labour party. In 1976 a Special Assembly agreed to a new system under which candidates for the leadership had to be MPs, be nominated by at least five other MPs or a fifth of the total, and be elected by constituency members whose electoral weight was related to Liberal support at the previous general election. In 1981 the system was changed to one member, one vote. An annual election can be forced on the initiative of at least fifty associations. Defenders of the role of the MPs might emphasize that the leader not only has to be an MP but has to be nominated by at least a fifth of their number. But this was a shift in the distribution of influence between the parliamentary and extra-parliamentary organs.

Before 1976, the election manifesto was largely left to the party leader. Under its Chairmen, John Pardoe and Richard Wainwright, the Standing Committee gradually came to play a more political party role. In 1979 the party leader provided a personal introduction but the substance of the manifesto was done by the Standing Committee. The party constitution was amended in 1979 to acknowledge the Committee's responsibility for preparing and co-ordinating the manifesto and to provide for consultation with MPs, candidates, and policy panels, while giving the leader final authority over its contents.

An alternative and more appropriate model for describing power in the party at present is one of power-sharing. If the Assembly and other party organs have not managed to instruct the MPs (and the problems which have attended similar claims within the Labour party have not been a recommendation), then the parliamentary leadership has lacked control over candidate selection and the share-out of seats with the SDP. The party leader lacks important sanctions and incentives; he has to accommodate and make concessions because he needs the support of members and local leaders who have their own bases of support. As a voluntary organization the Liberal party is characterized by the features of such associations, namely the 'sparsity of activists, voluntary nature of recruitment for party work, limited rewards available to activists and the irregularity of their loyalty'.[13]

One can only speculate about how the party may change if and when it moves nearer to office. Observation of the internal behaviour of the Conservative and Labour parties as they move from opposition to government suggests that they become more dominated by parliamentarians. The traditions of secrecy and collective responsibility in Cabinet, the need to take governmental decisions, the continuous exposure to the civil service and interest groups (and, perhaps, a coalition partner) all weaken the links with the party outside Parliament. Many Liberal bodies would have difficulty in adjusting to a large parliamentary party. Yet the lack of a tradition of intra-party democracy and the rejection of 'mandates' for MPs already provide room for a large degree of autonomy for the MPs.

The cadre model of the SDP may become more relevant if the SDP/Liberal Alliance moved to a formal merger of the two parties. But changes may take place within the SDP. The SDP as a mass movement was largely invoked by four experienced parliamentarians who were determined to avoid many of the pitfalls of Labour-party 'democracy'. In the draft constitution, for instance, the area parties' objects are defined as 'to promote and support the policies and interests of the party in the area'; they do not make policy. The annual conference is called a Consultative Assembly and cannot mandate the MPs. Policy is formulated by an MP-dominated

---

[13] S. Eldersveld, *Political Parties* (Chicago, 1964), p. 10.

Policy Sub-Committee of the national committee and 'discussed' by the Assembly. The Sub-Committee vets all motions
and amendments before they are considered by the Council
for Social Democracy. Overall, the intention is clearly to
keep power in the hands of the parliamentary leaders. Yet
there are pressures for more activist participation. At the
Constitutional Convention in February 1982, the Steering
Committee was defeated on eight occasions on issues affecting
the party constitution. And the choice of party leader was
decided by a direct ballot of party members. Both parties'
structures are likely to change over time and in response
to being in government, if the opportunity arises. However,
given the commitment of so many Liberals to participation,
accountability, and community politics it is most unlikely
that these values will be absent in any new Liberal Party
structure.

7. The Liberal Party in Parliament

Philip Norton

The House of Commons, in its formal rules, has no cognizance
of political parties. In practice, it operates on the basis of
the existence of two large, opposing parties: one providing
the personnel of government and a majority to support
that government, the other forming the alternative government. Third parties are, for all intents and purposes, an
embarrassment. They do not fit in with the normal adversary
relationship between the two largest parties and the
organization and behaviour with which it is associated.
The size of the Liberal Parliamentary Party in the House
since 1945 – ranging from six Members returned in four
general elections (1951, 1955, 1959, and 1964) to fifteen
for part of the short 1974 Parliament (see Table 7.1) – has
exacerbated the isolation of Liberal MPs in parliamentary
life. The small band of Liberals, as Michael Steed has noted,
has 'never found a natural role'.[1] It is not surprising that there
are distinct differences between the Liberal Parliamentary
Party and the larger parliamentary parties in terms of organization, behaviour, and parliamentary (as well as party)
influence.

ORGANIZATION

The decline in the size of Liberal representation in the House
of Commons coincided with the development of more highly
organized parliamentary parties. The small number of Liberal
MPs precluded the growth of the developed infrastructure
witnessed by both the Parliamentary Labour Party and the
Conservative 1922 Committee.[2] In particular, the Liberal
Parliamentary Party (LPP) was and remains too small to sustain

---

[1] M. Steed, 'The Liberal Party', in H. M. Drucker (ed.), *Multi-Party Britain*
(1979), p. 79.
[2] P. Norton, 'The Organization of Parliamentary Parties', in S. A. Walkland
(ed.), *The House of Commons in the Twentieth Century* (Oxford, 1979).

·Table 7.1   Number of Liberal MPs returned to Parliament 1945–82

Parliament:	Number of Liberal MPs Returned:	
	At general election	*During Parliament (at by-elections or by crossing the Floor of the House)**
1945–50	12	0
1950–51	9	0
1951–55	6	0
1955–59	6	1**
1959–64	6	1
1964–66	9	1
1966–70	12	1
1970–74	6	5
1974	14	1
1974–79	13	1
1979–	11	1***

*The one MP to cross the Floor of the House to the Liberal bench was Christopher Mayhew (Lab.) in July 1974.

**During the Parliament, one Liberal seat was also lost.

***As at June 1982.

a series of subject committees, committees which constitute an important element of the two largest parties.[3] Whereas for Labour and Conservative Members much party activity constitutes parliamentary-party activity, for Liberal MPs it constitutes involvement in the national-party organization outside Parliament.

The formal organization of the LPP is essentially a simple and straightforward one. It comprises two officers (the Leader and Chief Whip) and a weekly meeting when the House is sitting. In addition, each Liberal MP serves as the official spokesman on a designated subject or subjects. Whereas the new Social Democratic Party has a sufficient number of MPs to have both official spokesmen and back-benchers, the number of Liberal Members precludes such a dichotomy.

The Leader of the parliamentary party is Leader of the party as a whole. The practice of electing the Leader is a twentieth-century phenomenon. Only after the First World

[3] See P. Norton, 'Party Committees in the House of Commons', *Parliamentary Affairs*, 36, 1983.

War did the LPP introduce election as a standard practice and even then it was only to elect a chairman, a post that existed for some time concurrently with that of Leader. It was not until 1935 that the practice of electing a Leader upon the retirement of the incumbent appears to have been established, and then only after a certain amount of confusion.[4] This power to elect the Leader remained with the parliamentary party until 1976, when it was transferred to the party as a whole. Liberal MPs alone can nominate, and be nominated for, election. None the less, the change of electorate removed from them the only elective power that they had.

The power of appointment rests with the Leader. He appoints both the Chief Whip and the official spokesmen. (In 1935, the Chief Whip had been elected by the parliamentary party, but the practice was not continued.) The pool of talent from which the Leader may draw in appointing spokesmen is not confined to Liberal MPs: he can and does appoint Liberal peers as the party's principal spokesmen on certain subjects. Lady Seear, for example, speaks for the party on prices and consumer affairs and Lord Avebury does so on immigration and race relations.

In the House, the Leader speaks for the party in major debates, primarily those in which the Prime Minister and the Leader of the Opposition are the principal participants.[5] It appears to be the practice now for the Prime Minister to recommend that the Leader of the Liberal Party be sworn as a member of the Privy Council. This is done in order that he may on occasion receive confidential material, though it serves also to reinforce or rather protect his capacity to catch the Speaker's eye on the floor of the House. It also enhances or, more often, confirms his position as a senior parliamentarian.

As for the Liberal Chief Whip, his functions, unlike his Conservative and Labour counterparts, are not purely parliamentary. He has certain responsibilities for party organization, including liaising with local Liberal associations, done usually

---

[4] See J. Rasmussen, *The Liberal Party* (1965), especially p. 40.
[5] Though for some of the problems associated with this from the Leader's perspective, see J. Grimond, *Memoirs* (1979), p. 228.

through the Liberal Party Organization, and chairing the party's Candidates Committee; he serves also on a variety of party committees in an ex-officio capacity. His parliamentary duties are those normally associated with the position. He has responsibility for keeping abreast of parliamentary developments and of advising his colleagues of forthcoming business. He issues a weekly written whip. This is distinguished from Labour and Conservative whips by the use of asterisks instead of underlining. One asterisk is used to denote a vote to which Members' attention should be drawn, two denote a vote in which it is hoped that all Liberal Members will take part unless they have advised the whips office that they will be unable to be present, and three signify a vote at which the attendance of every Liberal MP is expected. The decision as to how many asterisks to allocate to an item is taken by the Chief Whip after consultation with the relevant spokesman. The whip does not carry the formal sentence to the effect that 'Your attendance is requested', which appears on Government and Opposition whips.

The tasks of the Chief Whip may be considered onerous, though given the small number of Liberal MPs the task of two-way communication between leaders and led is comparatively less demanding compared to his Conservative and Labour opposite numbers. Within the wider context of parliamentary organization, the Chief Whip constitutes part of the 'Usual Channels' (the euphemism for contact between the Government's business managers and the whips' offices of opposition parties) and the current Chief Whip, Alan Beith, serves as a member of the House of Commons Commission, appointed after consultation with minority parties in the House.

The relationship between the positions of Leader and Chief Whip was summed up in characteristic form by Cyril Smith: 'The Leader, rightly, gets the glory. The chief whip gets the work.'[6] The perks of the post, if such they can be called, are few: by virtue of his position, the Chief Whip has two adjoining rooms just off the Members' Lobby; he has the right (recently reclaimed) to the use of a franking machine,

---

[6] C. Smith, *Big Cyril* (1978), p. 178.

which imprints his signature, when sending out the weekly whip; and he has the use of research assistance made possible by the grants to opposition parties to enable them to fulfil their parliamentary duties.[7]

When the House is sitting, the LPP meets each Wednesday at 6.00 p.m. Each meeting normally lasts for about ninety minutes. In addition to the MPs, those attending include representatives of the Liberal peers, the peers who serve as principal parliamentary spokesmen for the party, and the President, Chairman, and Secretary-General of the Party; three members of the research staff also sit in, contributing only when invited to do so. About twenty people are usually present. The chair is taken by the Leader. In his absence, it is taken by the Chief Whip. The agenda encompasses forth-coming parliamentary business — deciding, for example, the line to be taken and whether or not to table an amendment — as well as topics of importance to those present: for instance, a pending or just-held by-election and policy initiatives by spokesmen: on occasion, a spokesman will be invited to prepare a paper for discussion. In the meetings, the contri-butions of the Leader and Chief Whip will carry weight. The Leader will normally seek to proceed by consensus, summing up the views of the meeting and occasionally taking straw polls. Meetings, in the words of one attender, are 'not terribly formal' and votes are rare. Indeed, Cyril Smith once referred to them as pleasant, think-tank sessions, conducted against 'a background of gentle banter'.[8]

In addition to the weekly meeting of the LPP, there are now regular meetings with the Social Democrats in the House. Every Thursday the Leader and Chief Whip meet with their SDP counterparts, joined by the relevant spokesmen for the matters to be discussed. The meetings serve a co-ordinating rather than a decision-making function (those attending are unable to commit their respective parliamentary parties), seeking to maintain a degree of unity between the two Alliance partners. Over and above this, there is frequent

[7] The decisions as to the allocation of the grant to the Liberals is made by the LPP on the basis of a budget prepared by the Chief Whip.

[8] Smith, p. 195.

contact between Alan Beith and his SDP counterpart —
sometimes several times a day — and between the two
parliamentary leaders.

The introduction of grants from public funds to enable
opposition parties to carry out their parliamentary duties
has enabled the LPP to acquire research and support facilities
superior to those which it previously enjoyed. In the present
Parliament, the Leader has two assistants (one concerned
primarily with policy, the other with administrative duties)
and the Chief Whip has one; in addition, there is a research
assistant serving the LPP as a whole. Over and above this,
the Leader has a second secretary as does the Chief Whip,
financed by funds raised outside the House; the Chief Whip's
second secretary serves also the press officer, another post
funded largely by external sources.

The Liberal organization in Parliament is not confined to
the House of Commons. Indeed, the number of Liberals in
the House of Lords is greater than in the Commons and the
party organization in the Upper House somewhat more
extensive.

There are forty-two peers in the House of Lords who are in
receipt of the Liberal whip. Though most of these hold
hereditary peerages, Liberal activity has benefitted in recent
years from the addition of a number of life peers, for example
Lords Winstanley, Hooson, Mayhew, Tordoff, and Banks. Of
those in receipt of the whip, it has been estimated that all
bar ten are regular attenders.[9]

The party organization in the Lords comprises no less than
five officers as well as a weekly meeting when the House is
sitting. The officers comprise a Leader (currently Lord Byers),
a Deputy Leader, a Chief Whip, a Deputy Whip, and an
Assistant Whip. In addition, a number of peers serve as
spokesmen on particular subjects. The number of Liberal
peers is such as to allow for the existence of spokesmen and
back-benchers, a distinction not possible in the Commons.

The weekly meeting of Liberal peers takes place on Thurs-
days at 2.15 p.m. and discusses matters similar to its Commons

[9] Estimate of N. Baldwin, research assistant in the Liberal Whips Office in the
House of Lords 1981/2. Much of the material in this chapter on Liberal organization
in the Lords has been supplied by Baldwin.

counterpart: forthcoming business is discussed, the party line is decided (as in the Commons, a written whip is issued), and duty peers are appointed for each of the working days of the following week, thus ensuring a continuous presence in the chamber. The Liberal peers also enjoy the support now of an administrative secretary and a research assistant, both of whom attend the weekly meeting. The Liberal Chief Whip in the Commons is also entitled to attend the meeting, but has not recently done so.

Though representatives of the Liberal peers attend the weekly LPP meetings, meetings between all Liberal parliamentarians are rare. There is an annual dinner at the time of the Queen's Speech and this is the only regular meeting at which the MPs and peers come together.

In its relationship to the party outside Parliament, the LPP is autonomous. (The same is the case with the Liberal peers.) That this should be so is not surprising. It is a feature it shares in common with the Conservative Parliamentary Party. Both predate the formation of the mass party organizations. The Parliamentary Labour Party, by contrast, is the child of the extra-parliamentary party.

Given its autonomy, then, it is possible for the LPP to pursue a line in the House which is not formally Liberal Party policy. On occasion this possibility has been realized. In 1976, the Party Assembly deleted reference in a motion to a statutory prices and incomes policy, a policy which the LPP continued to advocate. The Party Council has variously expressed its support for the 1967 Abortion Act and opposition to two Abortion (Amendment) Bills; the LPP, by contrast, has never expressed a collective view on the issue, preferring to leave the matter to the conscience of individual Members.[10] There is presently disagreement between the LPP and the extra-parliamentary party on the issue of the siting of Cruise missiles in Britain. Some resentment at the autonomy enjoyed by the parliamentary party, and the apparent aloofness of its leadership especially but not exclusively during Jeremy Thorpe's tenure as Leader, has

[10] D. Marsh and J. Chambers, *Abortion Politics* (1981), pp. 67–8.

also surfaced on occasion among party activists, leading to calls for a process of greater democracy within the party. This helped fuel the pressure which led to the widening of the franchise for the election of the Leader as well as a review of the party's consititutional structure.[11]

Occasions of disagreement on policy issues none the less remain rare. Various linkages exist between the LPP and the extra-parliamentary party in the formulation of party policy. The Party Assembly has responsibility for the determination of policy; in between its annual meetings, policy is determined by the Party Council. In terms of policy initiation, however, the most important body is the party's Standing Committee. It is here that Liberal Members have the most direct impact. The chairman is an MP elected by the LPP and the Leader and Chief Whip serve as members ex officio. John Pardoe, who was chairman until 1976, was reported to have provided especially energetic leadership.[12] Since then, the office has been held successively by Richard Wainwright, David Alton, Stephen Ross, and the current holder, Clement Freud. The input of the LPP into the Committee is greater than the attendance of its members would suggest. On occasion, only one MP is present.[13]

The LPP enjoys also a clear if not always quantifiable influence on the party's election manifesto. The content of the manifesto is the responsibility of the Leader. The Leader, of course, is drawn from the LPP, and Liberal Members exert an influence upon him by virtue of his need for their support in his parliamentary activities and, quite simply, by virtue of sheer proximity. Liberal Members may thus seek to influence the party through its policy-making organs and through contact with the Leader.

BEHAVIOUR

In terms of parliamentary behaviour, two related points — not necessarily criticisms — have been made about the LPP in the Commons. One is that it has limited impact upon

---

[11] Steed, pp. 95–7.
[12] D. Butler and D. Kavanagh, *The British General Election of 1979* (1980), p. 93.   [13] Liberal MP to author.

parliamentary life. This is attributed to the attitude of Liberal Members and to their inability, given their limited numbers, to maintain a continuous and significant presence in the Chamber. The other is that Liberal Members have little opportunity in their voting to convey clearly a distinct Liberal approach to issues. They are faced with the choice of voting for or against motions introduced by the Government or, to a lesser extent, the Opposition. The opportunities for playing an initiating role are few. Both points are important though in need of some qualification.

The small number of Liberal MPs necessarily limits the impact of the LPP in the House of Commons. Government whips can call on more than three-hundred Members to maintain a modest presence in the House. Opposition whips can call on more than two-hundred. Alan Beith, in 1982, can call upon but twelve MPs, including himself. (In an interview with the author, Mr Beith referred to the number as thirteen. He then corrected himself, explaining 'I sometimes have these delusions of grandeur!') Liberal Members suffer from two additional handicaps. One is that, with the exception of William Pitt, they represent constituencies which are not close to London. The second is that they do not enjoy the 'pairing' facilities available to Government and Opposition Members. Pairing with Government Members, though frowned upon by the Government Chief Whip, was possible in the 1950s and 1960s, but was more actively discouraged in the 1970s.[14] It is now non-existent. When Cyril Smith managed to arrange a pair for Alan Beith with a Labour Member for a division in the last Parliament, the Conservative Chief Whip actually suspended all pairing arrangements for three weeks. Indeed, one may forgive Liberal MPs for looking upon the newly formed Social Democratic parliamentary party with some envy: not only are there more SDP MPs (more than double the number of Liberal Members) but there are also more privy councillors sitting on the SDP benches (following the Glasgow Hillhead by-election, five to the Liberals' two) and SDP Members have generally been able to maintain

[14] Lord Wade, *Behind the Speaker's Chair* (Leeds, 1979), pp. 76 and 81.

their former pairing arrangements with Conservative Members.[15]

The difficulty of maintaining a noticeable presence on the Liberal bench has led on occasion to criticisms of poor attendance. As Chief Whips, both Donald Wade and Cyril Smith had to respond to accusations of Liberal absenteeism.[16] Such accusations have often not been well founded. Given the small number of Liberal Members, their record of voting in divisions has not been an unworthy one. The most recent figures available, those for the 1980/1 session, reveal that the Liberal voting record is not much dissimilar to that of the Labour Party and is much superior to that of Ulster Unionist Members and the new Social Democratic Members (Table 7.2). Like the majority of Conservative and Labour Members, most

Table 7.2   MPs voting record by party 1980–1

Voting	Con.	Lab.	Lib.	SDP*	U.U.**	Others
(number of divisions	(N= 333)	(N= 245)	(N= 11)	(N= 21)	(N= 9)	(N= 5)
(maximum possible 317)	%	%	%	%	%	%
Less than 50	0	0	0	0	44.4	0
50–99	1.8	2.5	9.1	33.3	33.3	20.0
100–149	13.2	23.3	18.2	42.9	22.2	20.0
150–199	31.5	53.5	45.4	23.8	0	60.0
200–249	35.7	16.7	27.3	0	0	0
250–299	16.8	4.1	0	0	0	0
300 or more	0.9	0	0	0	0	0
TOTAL:	99.9	100.1	100.0	100.0	99.9	100.0

(Totals do not always add up to 100% due to rounding)

Excluded from calculation: Mr Speaker, his Deputies, by-election returnees, and Members who died during the Session.

*Members who joined the SDP during the course of the session.
**Ulster Unionists: all varieties.

Source: Figures calculated from *The Political Companion*, 32, Spring 1982, pp. 96–125.

[15] P. G. Richards, 'The SDP in Parliament', *Parliamentary Affairs*, 35 (2), 1982, p. 139. Confirmed to the author by a leading Liberal MP.

[16] Smith, pp. 181–2. D. Wade, letter in the *Sunday Telegraph*, 10 Dec. 1961.

Liberals voted in more than 150 out of a possible 317 divisions in the session. Of Members voting in more than 200 divisions, the Liberal figure is bettered only by that of the Conservatives.[17] (However, given the small number of Liberal MPs, the comparative percentages must be treated with caution.) In the first session of the current Parliament, that of 1979/80, there were 500 divisions: one or more Liberal MPs voted in all bar eleven of them, those eleven constituting 2.2 per cent of the total; in 1980/1, the proportion of divisions from which all Liberal Members were absent was 4.4 per cent (fourteen out of 317); and in the 1981/2 session, up to the Easter recess, the proportion was 7.4 per cent (nine out of 122).[18] Of the divisions which witnessed the participation of no Liberal Members, a number were held during late-night sittings; some absences were the product of predetermined abstention. The proportion of divisions in which only one Liberal Member participated was, respectively for the three sessions, 5 per cent, 5.4 per cent, and 4.1 per cent. Of the total of 939 divisions held in the Parliament up to Easter 1982, two or more Liberals voted in more than 91 per cent of them. Overall, the Liberal participation is thus not discreditable.

The accusation that Liberal Members have a limited impact in the House because of an unwillingness to be disruptive[19] is more well founded. The LPP finds itself in the incongruous position of working within a political system which works to its disadvantage and which it wishes to change. None the less, it has proved willing to abide by parliamentary conventions. Cyril Smith in his autobiography recounted the occasion in 1975 when he recommended that Liberal MPs wear T-shirts emblazoned with the words 'Electoral Reform Now' when going to listen to the Queen's Speech and after the Speech to chant the words that appeared on the shirts. His suggestion was met with 'a barely muffled gasp of horror whistled through tight-stretched lips'.[20] From that day on, Smith

---

[17] Figures calculated from the raw data in *The Political Companion*, 32, 1982, pp. 96–125.
[18] Author's research of the division lists, April 1979–May 1982.
[19] See, for example, A. Watkins, *The Liberal Dilemma* (1966), p. 14.
[20] Smith, p. 182.

recorded, 'I think I lost hope that the Liberal Party could ever be stirred into the kind of action which I believe is essential if it is ever to break through as the major radical force in this country.'[21] Yet the behaviour recommended, a publicity stunt as Smith conceded, was not necessarily the best way of achieving Liberal goals. Disrupting the procedure of the House by incessant interruption or swarming noisily in front of the Table, engaged in occasionally by a number of Members, attracts publicity but is often counter-productive: it fails to affect the passage of the measure involved and often attracts the ill will of other Members. When David Owen barged his way to near the head of the procession to hear the Queen's speech in 1981 the main outcome was not a symbolic victory for the Liberal/SDP Alliance but an apology from the SDP Chief Whip for his leader's behaviour. The effective way to use parliamentary procedure to delay or interrupt the passage of legislation is to engage in a process of filibustering and on occasion to use points of order. Liberal MPs are insufficient in number and somewhat lacking in the requisite experience to sustain filibusters and do not have among their number Members whose reputations derive from doting on Erskine May. The only other outlets for the expression of Liberal views are the traditional and formally permissible ones of speeches, votes, and the tabling of motions and amendments. Speeches and votes have limited impact by virtue of the small number of Liberal Members. The ability to achieve discussion of motions and amendments is limited by the rules of the House. In its operations, as we have observed, the House of Commons does not shine with favour upon third parties.

The second claim we noted was that in their voting behaviour Liberal Members fail to convey a clear Liberal approach to issues. This, as we have mentioned, has been attributed to the fact that, in Peter Richards's words, 'minor parties cannot control the basis on which votes are taken':[22] Liberals are faced with voting for or against motions tabled by the Government or the Opposition. A further contributory

---

[21] Ibid., p. 183.   [22] Richards, p. 139.

factor has been presumed to be that Liberal Members, responsive to local demands and relying heavily upon their own efforts to achieve election, have looked more like a band of independent Members than a cohesive party.[23] Neither assumption is wholly borne out by the voting data for the current Parliament.

Indeed, the LPP can make a claim to be a cohesive body. Of the divisions held in the present Parliament, up to the Easter 1982 recess, in which two or more Liberals voted (excluding free votes, a category which includes divisions on private as well as private members' legislation) the Liberal Members were united in more than 92 per cent of them. The proportion of the divisions in which Liberal Members were divided, entering both the Aye and the No lobbies, was 9.4 per cent in the 1979/80 session, 6.8 per cent in the 1980/1 session, and but 2.0 per cent in the 1981/2 session. Even in free votes, Liberal Members voted together in the same lobby in 61 per cent of them. (This is a feature not peculiar to the Liberals: Conservative and Labour Members tend to vote along party lines in free votes.)[24] The proportion of the divisions witnessing Liberal unity compare favourably to that for the Conservative and Labour Parties (at least in comparison with the figures for preceding Parliaments)[25] but such comparisons must be treated with great caution given the disparity in size between the parliamentary parties: persuading more than 300 MPs to enter the same lobby creates greater problems than persuading twelve MPs to do so. This disparity in size also explains the fact that when Liberals enter separate lobbies in a division, the split, proportionately, is more serious than that normally witnessed by the larger parties: one Liberal Member constitutes nearly 10 per cent of his parliamentary party whereas one Conservative constitutes but little more than 0.3 per cent of his.

In terms of both numbers and the seriousness of the split, there are three main topics on which Liberal Members have

---

[23] This assumption appears to be implied by Steed, p. 79. See also Butler and Kavanagh, pp. 86-7.

[24] P. Norton, *The Commons in Perspective* (Oxford, 1981), p. 27.

[25] See P. Norton, *Dissension in the House of Commons 1974–1979* (Oxford, 1980), table 1, p. 428.

divided in the present Parliament: Budget Resolutions and Finance Bill amendments, Northern Ireland or Northern Ireland-related legislation, and, to a lesser extent, Employment Bill amendments. In July 1979, the LPP divided six to three in favour of an amendment to the Finance Bill to exclude work on or repair of buildings from being subject to a proposed increase in Value Added Tax, subsequently dividing nine to one in support of an amendment to exclude laundry services from the increase. In 1981, the parliamentary party divided six to two in favour of the Budget tobacco-increase resolution, then dividing eight to two against the capital transfer tax resolution. On the 1980 Employment Bill, four Liberals voted for and two voted against a backbench Conservative amendment to grant workers the right to demand a ballot before industrial action was taken; there was then a three to two division in support of an amendment to allow those already in a closed shop to demand a ballot on whether to remain one.

The most serious split has been on Northern Ireland and the related Representation of the People Bill. After supporting throughout the 1970s the continuation order for emergency provisions in Northern Ireland, the party divided three to one in favour of the order in 1979. In 1981 it divided five to two in favour of the Government motion approving the proposal to continue the provisions of the Emergency Provisions Act, then dividing two to one against the continuation order itself. The Liberal in the van of opposition to the emergency provisions was David Alton, joined in 1981 by Geraint Howells. The 1981 Representation of the People Bill, designed to prevent a repetition of the occasion when an IRA prison inmate (Bobby Sands) was able to stand for election to Parliament, created the most serious rift: the LPP divided five to three against the Second Reading of the Bill (David Alton leading four colleagues into the No lobby, Messrs Steel, Beith, and Ross voting in the Aye lobby), entered separate lobbies on three amendments to the measure, and then split four to three against the Third Reading. Such divisions are exceptional.

Possibly of as much interest have been some of the free votes on which Liberal Members have been divided. In 1979, two Liberals, Cyril Smith and Stephen Ross, voted for the restoration of capital punishment; nine voted against it. In the same year, one Liberal, Geraint Howells, voted against the Second Reading of the Abortion (Amendment) Bill; four Liberals voted for it. In 1980, five Liberals supported the proposal to boycott the Olympic Games; three voted against it.

The claim that Liberal Members have difficulty in conveying a clear Liberal approach to issues because of Government control of the timetable is well founded but in need of qualification. Though members of minor parties are faced normally with the choice of voting for or against motions tabled by the Government or Opposition, it is not altogether correct to assert that they cannot control the basis on which votes are taken. In terms of procedures and rhetoric the House of Commons can be understood in terms of the adversary model of politics. In terms of Government and Opposition approaches to the substance of measures, and their voting thereon, such a model is less applicable. Indeed, as empirical research has indicated, a consensual model is more applicable.[26] The importance of this for our purposes is that the Opposition does not, as a matter of course, divide against Government measures; indeed, it does so only in a minority of cases.[27] This leaves minority parties and dissenting back-benchers with the opportunity to carve out a distinctive stance by dividing the House. It is an opportunity variously utilized by the Liberals. In more than one hundred divisions in the present Parliament (up to Easter 1982), more than 10 per cent of the total, Liberal Members have either divided the House themselves or, more frequently, entered a back-bench dissenting lobby. Such voting, coupled with the tabling of amendments and contributions to debate, including on private members' legislation, has enabled the LPP on occasion to pursue a distinctive stand, especially on issues in which it takes a special interest.

Most notable among the issues on which the Liberals have shaped a distinctive stance — one recognized as such by other Members of the House and by interested bodies outside —

[26] I. Burton and G. Drewry, *Legislation and Public Policy* (1981). R. Rose, *Do Parties Make a Difference?* (1980).   [27] Rose, ch. 5.

have been those which may be subsumed under the rubric of constitutional issues. The LPP favours reform of the electoral system, a corner-stone now of the Liberal/SDP Alliance, and has sought to achieve a form of proportional representation not only for parliamentary elections but also, in the 1974–9 Parliament, for elections to the European Parliament and the proposed devolved Assemblies in Scotland and Wales. It favours also a new Bill of Rights, one that incorporates wholly or largely the European Convention on Human Rights. In the Lords, Lord Wade has achieved the passage of such a Bill in successive sessions; in the Commons, Alan Beith introduced the measure as a private member's bill.[28] (On devolution, the Liberals have not or rather did not achieve such a clear and differentiated position.)[29] The LPP can make a claim also to have been a consistent supporter of British membership of the European Communities, though its approach has not been greatly dissimilar to that of the Conservatives, especially during Mr Heath's period of leadership.

The LPP can make a modest claim to have pursued a recognizably distinct approach also on the issues of the economy, immigration, and, arguably, worker participation in industry. Unlike the Liberal Party Assembly, the parliamentary party has been a consistent advocate of a prices and incomes policy, enforceable at law. In July 1980, Liberal Members were alone in supporting a motion calling for such a policy.[30] Throughout the past decade, Liberal Members have also regularly voted (though not always spoken) against cuts in public expenditure.[31] Opposition to legislation which is discriminatory against immigrants has led to consistent

[28] See *HL Deb.* 402, c. 999–1071, *HL Deb.* 403, c. 287–311, 502–9, *HC Deb.* sixth series, 4, c. 419–57, and Lord Wade, 'A Bill of Rights for the United Kingdom', *The Parliamentarian*, 61, 1980, pp. 65–71.

[29] In the somewhat confused devolution debate of 1976–9 in which many extraneous factors attracted attention, the LPP was but one of several participants and was itself divided on certain key votes, notably the guillotine motion for the Scotland and Wales Bill.   [30] *HC Deb.* 987, c. 1439–40.

[31] In 1976, the Liberal economic spokesman, John Pardoe, had argued the need to cut expenditure. However, he and his colleagues then voted against the Government when the Chancellor of the Exchequer announced public-expenditure cuts and a request for an IMF Loan.

opposition by the LPP to the immigration bills of successive governments, such opposition extending to the present Government's British Nationality Bill. To a less notable extent, the Liberal belief in greater worker participation and profit-sharing in industry has found expression in debate and, on occasion, through voting support for amendments to particular measures, for example the 1975 Industry Bill and the Aircraft and Shipbuilding Industries Bill of the following year; the Lib–Lab Pact also provided the opportunity to achieve some tangible advances in support of the policy. The Liberals would claim also to have hewn out a distinct position on other issues, education for instance, but such a claim might not be conceded by the other parliamentary parties.

The opportunities to adopt a distinctive approach remain exceptional rather than the norm. The generalization that the Liberals are faced with voting for or against motions tabled by the Government or Opposition remains a valid one. Given that the Government is not a Liberal one, then it is not surprising that Liberal Members will tend to vote against it. This has been a marked feature of the present Parliament. In divisions in which the Government entered one lobby and the Opposition the other, the LPP has been found predominantly in the Opposition lobby: of 612 such divisions up to the 1982 Easter recess in which Liberal Members participated, the Government obtained Liberal support in less than a quarter (131) of them. (A similar anti-Government voting pattern is apparent among Liberal peers in the Lords;[32] it is also apparent in the voting behaviour of SDP MPs in the Commons.[33]) Of legislative measures introduced by the

---

[32] Analysis by N. Baldwin of divisions in the House of Lords in the period 6 October to 29 October 1981. Liberal peers opposed the Government in twenty-four out of twenty-six divisions, supporting it in only one.

[33] Following the formation of the SDP on 26 March 1981, SDP MPs voted predominantly in the Opposition lobby. For the remainder of the 1980/1 session, SDP Members voted in the Opposition lobby (the Government being in the other lobby) on 113 occasions, entering the Government lobby (the Opposition being in the other lobby) on only eight occasions. In the 1981/2 session, up to the Easter recess, SDP Members voted on 73 occasions with the Opposition against the Government and only on ten occasions with the Government against the Opposition. In the latter session, there was an extremely close correlation with

Government, the LPP has voted against more than twice as many on Second Reading as it has voted for. It has opposed consistently the Government's economic policy and has voted against the Government on votes of confidence, doing so as early as February 1980. This has tended to reinforce earlier Conservative perceptions of the LPP as having a greater anti-Conservative than an anti-Labour bias.[34]

In summary, the LPP is essentially, by force of circumstance, a reactive body and in reacting to Government proposals will normally not be supportive, preferring instead its own proposals; the opportunity to divide in favour of those proposals is rare, and hence the LPP will be found usually in the No lobby. However, given that the adversary relationship between Government and Opposition does not always find expression in the division lobbies, the LPP enjoys an ability to carve out a voting pattern somewhat independent of the Opposition. This, coupled with the opportunity to participate in debate (the Liberal spokesman will usually be called, albeit on the same basis as Conservative and Labour back-benchers), allows a limited, a very limited, capacity to the LPP to demonstrate a distinct Liberal approach to issues, more so on some issues than others.

Are there any other generalizations that can be made? An analysis of the voting behaviour of MPs on a range of issues, usually ones on which free votes were allowed, reveals further significant points about Liberal Members' voting compared with that of Conservative and Labour Members.

The period from 1964 to 1970 witnessed the introduction of a number of important private members' measures covering social issues and which Members could decide on the basis of their own consciences rather than by the dictates of the party whips. Most notable among the measures were those covering capital punishment, divorce, homosexuality, and abortion. It could fairly be assumed that most Liberal Members would favour the abolition of capital punishment and a liberalization of the law concerning the latter three subjects.

Liberal voting: SDP MPs voted in the same lobby as the Liberals on ninety-two occasions, and voted in the other lobby on only one occasion.

[34] See Conservative Research Department, *Campaign Guide 1977* (1977), pp. 710–12.

(Indeed, as is well known, it was a Liberal Member, David Steel, who introduced the Abortion Bill.) Such an assumption is borne out by the analyses of Peter Richards and George Moyser.[35] However, Liberal Members' support for the various changes proposed was not significantly different to that of Labour Members. Expressed in terms of the proportion of a parliamentary party voting for or against a measure, Liberal Members emerged as marginally more 'liberal' than Labour Members.[36] When a more sophisticated analysis is employed, incorporating the influence of other independent variables, Labour Members emerge as marginally more liberal than Liberal Members.[37] The differences, though, are not great. If such issues can be viewed in terms of a liberal–conservative continuum, then one may categorize Liberal and Labour Members as taking a liberal line, Conservative Members tending to be conservative (but not as heavily conservative as Liberal and Labour Members are liberal), and Ulster Unionists being heavily conservative.

A not dissimilar picture emerges when the category is widened from one of issues of conscience to the broader but possibly more clearly definable area of civil rights. *Rights*, the journal of the National Council for Civil Liberties, analysed the position taken by MPs in the present Parliament on thirteen issues on which the NCCL had a policy.[38] The issues encompassed both those of conscience (abortion, homosexual rights) and those on which the parties had taken a clear, whipped stance (the Employment Bill, for example, and Imprisonment [Temporary Provisions] Bill). Given that the Government's position was opposed to that of the NCCL on the whipped issues, and the correlation establishment already on issues of conscience, the differences between the two main parties detected by the survey are not surprising. Labour MPs tended to support NCCL policy: 195 Labour Members

---

[35] P. G. Richards, *Parliament and Conscience* (1970). G. Moyser, 'Voting Patterns on "Moral" Issues in the British House of Commons 1964–1969', Paper presented to the Political Studies Association Conference, Exeter, 1980.

[36] Richards, *Parliament and Conscience*, table 2, p. 180. Moyser, table 7, col. 1.   [37] Moyser, table 7, col. 2, and p. 12.

[38] 'Are Social Democrats Civil Libertarians?', *Rights*, 6 (2), Nov.–Dec. 1981, pp. 4–5.

did not vote against NCCL policy on any of the thirteen issues. Conservative Members, by contrast, tended to oppose it: 202 Conservatives failed to support NCCL policy on any of the thirteen issues. Members with the highest record of support for NCCL policies were overwhelmingly Labour; those with the lowest record of support were exclusively Conservative. Though not all falling among the Members most supportive of NCCL policy, Liberal Members supported that policy, on average, on six of the thirteen issues. The average for Labour Members was five. However, Liberal Members voted against NCCL policy on average on two occasions, an average higher than that for SDP and Labour Members. The overall picture that emerges is one of medium to strong support by both Liberal and Labour Members for NCCL policy on the issues selected.

A somewhat different relationship emerges when one looks at the Liberal voting pattern in the first two sessions of the Parliament on issues of individual choice, as defined by the Adam Smith Institute. The Institute considers the distinction between left and right to be not terribly helpful, viewing as more relevant the division between those who believe the individual should be largely responsible for himself or herself, free to take the decisions whose outcomes determine priorities, work, and life, and those who believe that the state must play an active role in caring for people, providing for them and if necessary protecting them from the results of their own actions. The Institute is committed strongly to a belief in the former. Taking a leaf from the book of American organizations which issue ratings of Congressmen on the basis of their voting on certain key issues, the Institute recently compiled its own rating of MPs. Taking forty divisions held in the 1979/80 and 1980/1 sessions, in each of which it considered the issue to be one 'which separates individual choice from corporate care', the Institute allocated a negative mark for a vote cast in favour of more government inter-vention, a positive mark for a vote cast in favour of individual choice, and a neutral mark for absence. (Hence, for example, voting for the compulsory wearing of seat-belts in cars scored a negative mark, voting for a Bill to outlaw the closed shop scored a positive mark.) A rating for each MP was then calculated, ranging from a possible 0 to 100, with a score of fifty denoting neutrality towards individual choice. Given that a number of the issues chosen were economic ones, and the fact that government intervention may be considered necessary to secure some civil rights, then it is not surprising that a different pattern emerges to that of the preceding analyses. Most Conservative MPs scored a rating of 50 or more (the highest scores were achieved by Michael Brotherton and Michael Brown, each with a score of 79); only fifteen Conservatives had a score lower than fifty – the lowest scorer was Peter Bottomley with 40. All Labour Members scored less than fifty, the majority falling in the 29 to 39 range (lowest scorers were Terence Davis and William Hamilton, each with a score of 11). Liberal MPs, by contrast, neatly straddled the median line: ratings ranged from a high of 62.5 (Jo Grimond) to a low of 36 (Richard Wainwright). Six Liberals fell in the 45–54 category.[39] In so far as it is possible to generalize on the basis of these figures, the Liberals may be categorized as falling basically between the position of the two main parties.

From these limited data, it may be possible tentatively to summarize the Liberal position thus: the state has a role to play in protecting vulnerable individuals and groups deemed in need of protection from others, though in terms of the relationship of the individual to the state there should be some balance (where this balance lies is not necessarily clearly agreed to, as for example in the sphere of industrial relations); and that the state should not intervene in cases where individual activity is believed to cause no harm to others (for example, consenting homosexual relationships). This distinguishes Liberal Members from Labour MPs, who appear willing to concede a more interventionist role to government where economic relationships especially are concerned, and from Conservative Members, who favour minimal state intervention, though being willing to utilize the law to preserve order and to prescribe certain moral norms. There is some overlap between the parties – not all

[39] M. Loveday (ed.), *The Adam Smith Institute Index: Sessions 1979–81* (1982).

Members fit in with the foregoing categorization — but the generalization appears to be a useful one. The position of Liberal MPs is none the less not a distinctive one in terms of voting clearly differentiated from the other parties. Nor is it one that has had much impact within the House of Commons.

INFLUENCE

The LPP can make a claim to be somewhat more active than some critics have suggested and to have delineated a clear Liberal approach on a number of issues. But what influence, if any, can it claim to have exerted in the taking of executive actions or in the passage of legislation? On the whole, and to some extent through no fault of its own, the answer is 'very little'.

As a Member of Parliament, each Liberal MP pursues complaints made by constituents against government. In common with other Members, this is the area in which he is likely to have greatest success. There is no evidence that the degree of success is greater for Liberal Members than for other Members. There are some factors which suggest that it may, if anything, be marginally less. Government back-benchers by virtue of their affinity or friendship with Ministers may achieve a marginal advantage (but no more) over Members of opposition parties. Also, at least one Liberal Member affects adversely his chances of a favourable ministerial response to constituency cases by publicizing the complaints before communicating privately with the relevant Minister.[40] Against this, Liberal Members could make the claim that, by force of circumstance, they are attentive constituency Members, a claim that cannot always be maintained with justice by all Members of the House. None the less, the point to be made here is that in pursuing constituency cases each Member of Parliament is acting almost always as a Member of Parliament and not as a Conservative, Labour, or Liberal Member. Attempts to exploit party links in pursuing

---

[40] D. Samuels, 'The Member's Representation of his Constituent's Interests', third-year undergraduate dissertation, Hull University Politics Department, 1981.

constituency matters are, as Alan Beith observed, the exception and not the general rule.[41]

Collectively, the impact of Liberal Members upon parliamentary business is marginal. This is not especially the fault of Members themselves. Indeed, given their position, they would claim that they have to work harder than the average Conservative or Labour back-bencher. They contribute to debate; as we have seen, they participate in divisions and they maintain a high level of unity in so doing. In so far as they are able, they serve on standing and select committees (party strength on committees is proportional to party strength in the House). Indeed, given that not all minority parties take up their representation on committees and Liberal Members are prepared to fill the vacancies, they are slightly over-represented. On occasion they achieve a Supply Day or half-day debate, courtesy of the Opposition, and sometimes a Liberal amendment is selected by the Speaker for debate. Despite this, the Liberal impact upon the House and the business that it transacts is minimal. In the House, the Government — and the Opposition — pay little heed. Why?

The reasons for the lack of Liberal impact are twofold. One is the small size of the LPP. The other is the geographic distribution of Liberal Members' constituencies. Governments listen to other parties in the House if they need them to achieve their goals. The Opposition, for example, has some leverage because the Government needs it to acquiesce in the passage of measures. The Government may also heed a minority party if that party derives its strength from one particular region or, indeed, country; that party's MPs may make a claim to represent or speak on behalf of that area — the Government in effect seeking their seal of approval — and/or the party may be perceived by the Government as an electoral threat. The LPP scores on neither count.

As a rule, the Government does not need the LPP. (The exception of the Lib–Lab Pact we shall consider shortly.) Alan Beith has an input into business management through the Usual Channels, but the acquiescence of the LPP is not

[41] A. Beith, 'The MP as a Grievance Chaser', *Public Administration Bulletin*, 21, August 1976.

important in achieving the smooth passage of measures. Business is largely carved up within the confines of the mutually understood relationship that exists between Government and Opposition; in that relationship, both sides tend to view minority parties as unwanted guests.

The Government needs the LPP neither to achieve the smooth passage of business nor to determine the outcome of that business. As long as it has a parliamentary majority that holds firm, there is no threat to the Government in the division lobbies. Any threat would emanate from dissenting back-benchers and only if they were prepared to enter an Opposition lobby would the Government's majority be in jeopardy. A Liberal lobby, by itself, may serve to distinguish the Liberal approach on a particular issue — it has no impact upon the outcome of the division.

The lack of impact because of its size is something which the LPP shares in common with other minority parties in the House. However, its lack of impact is exacerbated by its geographic dispersion of seats. The Ulster Unionists and, now to a lesser extent than hitherto (because of reduced numbers), SNP Members have been able to exploit their regional concentration. In the 1974-9 period, the Labour Government was wary of Scottish National Members, viewing the SNP as a threat to Labour's electoral position in Scotland. It sought the acquiescence of Ulster Unionist MPs in its policy for Northern Ireland. It sought for a period Liberal support for reasons only of parliamentary arithmetic. The LPP had and has no leverage derived from the geographic distribution of Liberal constituencies.

Having little immediate influence upon the measures before the House, the LPP seeks to make its presence felt by developing a distinct Liberal approach on certain issues. As we have seen, it has to some extent been able to achieve this. None the less, the mere fact of achieving a distinct approach is itself, certainly in the short term, a self-defeating act. It is distinct because it lacks the support of the larger parties. Once it has been embraced by the Government or Opposition party, it ceases to be a distinctive Liberal approach; and the other parties are not noted for acknowledging their debts to political rivals.

Are there any exceptions to the foregoing? There have been two occasions in recent years when the Government of the day has needed Liberal support. The first was in 1974 when, following the indecisive result of the February general election, Mr Heath sought a formal alliance with the LPP. Not wishing to enter into a formal coalition and not satisfied with Mr Heath's response on the issue of electoral reform, the Liberal Members rejected the idea.[42] Thus, in terms of influencing policy, the impact of the LPP was non-existent; it rejected the opportunity to have a say in government. The second occasion was in 1977 when the Labour Government was vulnerable to defeat on a confidence motion. The Prime Minister, Mr Callaghan, sought the support, through David Steel, of the LPP. On this occasion, support was forthcoming and the Lib–Lab Pact was agreed to.[43] From the Pact the LPP derived the opportunity to be involved in the process of government. Liberal spokesmen met with their Ministerial counterparts and a consultative body was established (comprising two senior Ministers and the Government Chief Whip on the one side and Messrs Pardoe, Hooson, and Beith on the other) to resolve any differences of opinion. In concrete terms, it provided also the opportunity to influence the passage of certain measures; and, in some instances, to prevent the passage of others. Compared with what the Liberals had been able to achieve in any other year in post-war history, the year of the Pact witnessed unprecedented success. However, in terms of what was being offered (the maintenance of the Government in office) the returns may be seen as being rather meagre. A number of the policies the Liberals wished to be implemented had already been decided upon by the Government (devolution and direct elections to the European Parliament, for example); others were already being pressed upon the Government by other influential sources. Despite the Pact, the Government could not ensure a majority for the introduction of proportional representation for elections to the European Parliament nor for elections to the proposed devolved Assemblies in Scotland and Wales. (Indeed, there

---

[42] See D. Steel, *A House Divided* (1980), pp. 14–15, and Smith, pp. 162–8.
[43] See A. Michie and S. Hoggart, *The Pact* (1978).

was a majority of 183 against PR for the Scottish Assembly and one of 97 against PR for the European Parliament elections.) There was little the Liberals could do about it. As David Steel in effect made clear to his colleagues, the issue was not one on which to force an election: it meant little or nothing to the voters.[44] What the LPP did achieve was a substantive move in the 1978 Budget in favour of profit-sharing, tax concessions for small businesses, some concessions for farmers, and a small number of minor changes to various measures and policies.[45]

In negotiations, Ministers seemed to get the better of Liberal spokesmen.[46] At the end of the day, the LPP was unwilling to precipitate an election. 'Some Labour Ministers expressed their surprise that the Liberals had allowed themselves to be bought off so easily.'[47] In return for their modest gains, the LPP had not only sustained the Government in office, it has also created a rift within the ranks of the Liberal Party and it had, to some extent, compromised its independence by its association with a Labour Government. Liberal Members may be forgiven for wondering whether it was all worth it. After all, the Ulster Unionists managed to obtain Government support for one of their main goals — an increase in the number of Northern Ireland MPs at Westminster — without entering into any formal agreement with the Government; and more important changes in Government policy had been achieved by sheer parliamentary arithmetic and by the dissent of Labour back-benchers, (for example, Jeff Rooker and Audrey Wise on the 1977 Finance Bill, or George Cunningham who engineered a number of government defeats during the 1974-9 Parliament, most notably in securing the 40 per cent rule on devolution) than by the Liberals through the medium of the Pact. Liberal Members, in a straw poll, decided to continue the Pact in December 1977 by a vote of six to four; in August 1978 the Pact was dissolved. Perhaps the most measured statement on the Pact was that emanating from Jo Grimond, the one Member who had opposed the

[44] Michie and Hoggart, p. 155.   [45] Ibid., pp. 181-2.
[46] Note the recollections of Grimond, p. 252.
[47] Butler and Kavanagh, p. 94.

idea from the beginning. 'It certainly seemed to me then, and it still seems to me now', he wrote, 'a dubious arrangement.'[49]

As a generalization, it would thus be fair to conclude that the impact upon the organization and substance of parliamentary business by the collectivity of Liberal Members *qua* Liberal Members has not been great. It has not been non-existent. On occasion, Liberal amendments have been accepted. Sometimes Liberal votes have mattered, and not just during the period of the Lib–Lab Pact: the Liberal Members helped provide a majority for the European Communities Bill in 1972. Yet the impact of the small band of Liberal Members has probably been no greater (possibly even less) than that achieved by the equivalent number of determined back-benchers on the Conservative or Labour benches; indeed, certain individual Members could probably claim to have had as much impact upon government decisions, and been a greater parliamentary nuisance to the Treasury bench, than the whole of the LPP.[50] Given this, can the LPP make any positive claim as to its influence and its role within the House of Commons? The answer, it can claim with some plausibility, is in the affirmative.

Though not necessarily having much tangible and quantifiable impact upon immediate parliamentary business, the LPP can make a claim to have had a more general influence upon attitudes within the House and to have served at least some purpose as a body of Liberal Members. The point was put well by Jo Grimond: 'Many Members and groups', he wrote, 'I would include the Liberal Party, appear to have been weaving sand for decades yet their toe-hold on the political process has given them influence. Had there been no Liberal Party, in the wings at least, and spasmodically making some impact from the stage, the Tory and Labour Parties would, I believe, have been different.'[51] Merely by virtue of being in the House, he argues, Liberals can utilize their position as a platform for reaching the wider public.

---

[48] See Norton, *Dissension*, appendix, and J. Barnett, *Inside the Treasury* (1982), pp. 119-20.   [49] Grimond, p. 251.

[50] The most obvious example would be George Cunningham. See 'Ministers examine wreckage after fateful vote', *The Times*, 27 Jan. 1978.

[51] Grimond, p. 156.

And, both within and outside the House, they can put across the Liberal message. That message may not find immediate acceptance, but over time Liberal ideas may gain ground; they may serve to temper the approach taken by the larger parties; they may serve to remind others of the Liberal alternative if the main parties take an extremist path. In time, certain Liberal policies may actually find acceptance.

Such assertions, of course, cannot easily be proven. Even if a government adopts a policy which has been advocated by the Liberals, it does not necessarily follow that the Liberals have been responsible for its adoption; devolution serves as a useful illustration of this point. None the less, there is some plausibility in the argument. If there were no Liberal MPs, Liberal ideas and policies would lack a useful platform. On certain issues, Liberals have been in the van of a growing and influential movement favouring change. Electoral reform is one such issue. Though having little success in achieving its implementation in the 1970s, Liberal Members can claim to have helped ensure that it was an issue that remained on the political agenda; and during the period support for reform grew, extending beyond the small band of Liberal Members to a much broader body of parliamentarians. A Bill of Rights has been another such issue, especially so in the House of Lords. And, by their participation in the Lib–Lab Pact, the Members of the LPP can make some claim to have been important not so much for what was done but rather for what they prevented being done;[52] of helping, if only for a short period, to have moderated the approach of the Labour Government — providing, in Cyril Smith's words, a 'balancing effect against the doctrinaire demands of the fringes of the Labour Party'[53] — and for preventing a period of greater economic and political instability. It is a point emphasized by David Steel.[54] It is not necessarily a point that would be conceded by the other parliamentary parties.

As for the future, the LPP displays a greater degree of hope and optimism than has been the case in past years. In the 1981/2 session, it acquired an ally in the Social Democratic

---

[52] See point 5 of David Steel's letter to Mr Callaghan, reproduced in Steel, p. 37.
[53] Smith, p. 271.   [54] Steel, ch. 11.

Party: in alliance the two boast more than forty MPs. However, in the House, the Alliance has not had a notable impact upon business. There is also potential for friction between the two partners. None the less, the two appear to have achieved a degree of amity, more so than their party activists in the country. And, for the Liberals, the Alliance holds out the hope of the two things which they most wish to achieve. One is a place in government, be it in an Alliance or a coalition (Alliance plus another party) Government. The other is electoral reform. Proportional representation is perceived as the means, the just means in Liberal eyes, for ensuring a significant and enduring place for the LPP in the parliamentary sun.

Achieving these aims remains a daunting task: political opponents, this author among them, will seek strenuously to prevent their realization. If achieved, though, the implications for the LPP, and indeed the House of Commons, are profound. The organization, behaviour, and influence which we have examined in this chapter have been those of a handful of Liberal Members. The emergence of the LPP as a major parliamentary party would produce radical changes in all three.

8. The Liberal Party and Constitutional Reform

Vernon Bogdanor

I

Constitutional reform is now a central concern for Liberals, as it was before 1914. Russell and Bright fought for the extension of the franchise. Gladstone devoted his last two ministeries to the crusade for Irish Home Rule. Asquith fought to limit the power of the Lords. Today, the Liberal Party, joined by the Social Democrats, is distinctive in the priority which it has given to electoral reform, to a written constitution, and to the reconstruction of the United Kingdom as a federal state. It has sought, indeed, not merely con-stitutional reform, but a new constitutional settlement. Whereas the Labour and Conservative Parties see the remedies for the nation's ills in socio-economic prescriptions, Liberals continue obstinately to ascribe Britain's decline to political factors; and it is in the political kingdom that the remedies are to be found. 'Britain', said David Steel to the 1978 Liberal Assembly at Southport, 'is badly governed. It is badly governed because its political institutions are antiquated and undemocratic. This *crucial* weakness is at the *very root* of Britain's continuing economic and social decline.' (My italics.) Steel's introduction to the Liberal Party's manifesto for the 1979 general election declared that:

Political reform is the starting-point. Until we break the two-party strangle-hold, until we get away from the adversary class politics which are embedded in our parliamentary structure, we cannot success-fully tackle the problems of economic weakness and industrial mistrust, of misspent resources in housing, of uncertain management of the public sector and of mishandled relations with our neighbours abroad.[1]

---

[1] David Steel: *A New Beginning for a New Parliament* (Southport, 1978), p. 1. *The Real Fight is for Britain: The Liberal Manifesto 1979*: Introduction, p. 2.

That constitutional reform should be the central item on the agenda of politics flows from the very principles of liberalism. For liberalism has always been a creed which has stressed political values rather than the economic organization of society. 'Liberalism', according to Alan Bullock in *The Dictionary of Modern Thought*, 'in its most characteristic contemporary expression emphasizes the importance of conscience and justice in politics, advocates the rights of racial and religious minorities and supports civil liberties and the right of the ordinary individual to be more effecively consulted in decisions which affect him.'[2] Liberalism's concern for human rights derives from its belief in the centrality of individual choice. 'The free development of individuality,' declared Mill 'is one of the leading essentials of well-being; it is not only a co-ordinate element with all that is designated by the terms civilization, instruction, education, culture, but is itself a necessary part and condition of all these things.'[3]

In the nineteenth century, liberals welcomed the coming both of industrialism and democracy as forces liberating the individual spirit, and making possible the growth of the 'disinterested intelligence, to release it from the entanglements of party and sect — one might almost add, of sex — and to set it operating over the whole range of human life and circumstance'.[4] For the undermining of traditional sources of religious and political authority allowed the individual to choose for himself his own way of life. Indeed, the notion of the individual as essentially a *chooser* is absolutely central to liberal thought. The liberal therefore 'finds the source of political authority in individual wills, the grounds of political authority in individual purposes and the limits of such authority in the minimum required to achieve these purposes'.[5]

A liberal society, therefore, is not characterized by a specific social or economic structure, but is one in which certain

---

[2] Alan Bullock and Oliver Stallybrass: *The Fontana Dictionary of Modern Thought* (1977), p. 347.

[3] J. S. Mill: *On Liberty*, Ch. 3 (Penguin edition, 1974), p. 120.

[4] G. M. Young: *Victorian England: Portrait of an Age* (Oxford paperback edition, 1961), p. 186.

[5] Steven Lukes: *Individualisms*: Paper read at the Political Studies Association Conference, 1967, p. 9.

essentially political values are respected. To insist, as writers such as Friedman and Hayek have done, that such values can only be enjoyed in a market society is to assert what needs to be proved. The founding fathers of modern British liberalism were certainly not committed to such a view. For Mill, Green, and Hobhouse, the free market was of value only in so far as it succeeded in securing individual choice. Nineteenth-century liberal political philosophers asked themselves — what liberties and rights are essential to the aim of moral autonomy, and therefore need protection by government. J. S. Mill's 'self-regarding' sphere of action, the field within which freedom ought to be absolute, comprised personal and civil liberties, such as freedom of thought, speech, and religion, and said nothing about economic liberties such as freedom of enterprise or the ownership of industry. Free trade, even, was justified by Mill not on the grounds of abstract principle, but upon pragmatic grounds as the best means of securing economic benefits.

In the work of later Liberals such as Green and Hobhouse, it was clearly recognized that some of the goods required if individual choice was to become a reality were not such as would be provided by private initiative at all; they were public goods which could only be provided by the community as a whole. These views have nothing in common with those held today by such economic liberals as Hayek and Nozick. Indeed, Mill himself has been taken to task by the *laissez-faire* ideologue Ludwig von Mises for betraying the spirit of liberalism through his admission that the question of the extent of state intervention was an empirical one for political judgement, rather than a matter of *a priori* reasoning. According to Mises:

John Stuart Mill is an epigone of classical liberalism and, especially in his later years, under the influence of his wife, full of feeble compromises. He slips slowly into socialism and is the originator of the thoughtless confounding of liberal and socialist ideas that led to the decline of English liberalism and to the undermining of the living standards of the English people.

Mill is the great advocate of socialism. All the arguments that could be elaborated in favour of socialism are elaborated by him with loving care. In comparison with Mill all other socialist writers — even Marx, Engels and Lassalle — are scarcely of any importance.[6]

Yet, if Mill is a heretic, he is not an isolated one. J. M. Keynes began his essay, *The End of Laissez-Faire* (1926), with the following clarion-cry:

Let us clear from the ground the metaphysical or general principles upon which, from time to time, *laissez-faire* has been founded. It is *not* true that individuals possess a prescriptive 'natural liberty' in their economic activities. There is *no* 'compact' conferring perpetual rights on those who Have or on those who Acquire. The world is *not* so governed from above that private and social interest always coincide. It is *not* so managed here below that in practice they coincide. It is *not* a correct deduction from the Principles of Economics that enlightened self-interest always operates in the public interest. Nor is it true that self-interest generally *is* enlightened; more often individuals acting separately to promote their own ends are too ignorant or too weak to attain even these. Experience does *not* show that individuals, when they make up a social unit, are always less clear-sighted than when they act separately.

We cannot, therefore, settle on abstract grounds, but must handle on its merits in detail, what Burke termed 'one of the finest problems in legislation, namely, to determine what the State ought to take upon itself to direct by the public wisdom, and what it ought to leave, with as little interference as possible, to individual exertion'.[7]

William Beveridge believed that 'Liberalism in the economic sphere ought to stand for *empirical* study of social questions';[8] (My italics.) In 1944, after publication of the Beveridge Report, he became a Liberal MP; and one result of the reforms promoted by the Report was to show that the Welfare State was a pre-condition rather than an obstacle to the enjoyment of practical freedom; that liberty and welfare were complementary rather than competitive. Liberalism, then, is an essentially political philosophy, not a view about the structure of social and economic life; for the Liberal, questions of social and economic organization are questions of *means*, and not of *ends*. The organization of society and the economy is but a means to the enjoyment of liberal values; and so a liberal

[6] Ludwig von Mises: *The Free and Prosperous Commonwealth* (Princeton, 1962), p. 195.
[7] J. M. Keynes: *Essays in Persuasion* (1952 edition), pp. 312–3.
[8] José Harris: *William Beveridge: A Biography* (Oxford, 1977), p. 312.

society is compatible, in principle, with a range of different economic and social systems. Indeed, 'It would not be practicable to outline the precise structure of a liberal society, since of its very nature it would be open, dynamic, subject to constant change and evolution.'[9]

Liberalism thus differs from its ideological competitors whose essential concern is with forms of social organization rather than with political or constitutional issues which are assumed to have been finally settled long ago. For the socialist, it is economic relationships which dominate society. Political authority derives from social groups which possess corporate unity; while the Labour Party exists not to secure individual representation, but to give 'collective expression of democratic sentiment based on the working-class movement and on the constituency organizations of the workers by hand and brain'.[10]

Liberalism is to be contrasted also with the philosophy of social democracy in its pristine version, as embalmed, for example, in Anthony Crosland's, *The Future of Socialism* (1956). For social democracy was essentially a philosophy of economic management whose central aim was to redistribute income and equalize economic power. Social democrats assumed, perhaps too readily, that the state was both an efficient and essentially benign agency for economic change. 'Crosland', David Marquand has argued, 'took the traditional structure of the British state for granted, and failed to see that the centralist, élitist logic underlying it was incompatible with his own libertarian and egalitarian values.' He 'appeared to have abandoned the upholding of liberal values and radicalism in social affairs which the right believe to be the central role of the Labour Party'. For this reason, Marquand believes, 'Crosland's revisionism' itself 'now needs revising',[11] and this is the task which the new Social Democrat Party has set itself. Indeed in its rejection of mechanistic or economic analyses of

[9] *Liberals Look Ahead: The Report of the Liberal Commission* (Liberal Publications Department, 1969), p. i.

[10] A. H. Birch: *Representative and Responsible Government* (1964), p. 123.

[11] David Marquand: 'What the Social Democrats Should Try to Achieve': *London Review of Books*, 7–20 May 1981, p. 9: Nicholas Wapshott: Profile of David Marquand: *The Times*, 26 June 1978.

society, its concern with constitutional issues and with the mobilizing of consent, the Social Democratic Party tacitly dissociates itself from traditional social-democratic philosophies as understood either by the Croslandite revisionists in Britain or the Social Democratic parties in West Germany and Scandinavia. Its position becomes rather that of a *pivot* party of the centre on the model of the German Free Democrats, the Swedish Liberals, the Danish Centre Democrats, or the Dutch Democrats 66.[12]

At first sight, the ideology of modern Conservatism with its emphasis on individual freedom seems rather closer to that held by Liberals. In fact, however, the Liberal conception of freedom contrasts in an interesting and important way with that held by most Conservatives. For the Conservative, freedom is understood as the ability to compete in the market place. Economic freedom is almost a guarantor of political freedom, and indeed it is sometimes implied by Conservatives that the one cannot exist without the other. Political freedom is nothing but the withdrawal of the state from all but its essential tasks — defence, the preservation of law, and the protection of the currency. Liberals, on the other hand, broadly accept the existing role of the state as created by the social-democratic consensus, itself the intellectual product of those 'academic scribblers',[13] Beveridge and Keynes, themselves both Liberals. The Liberal seeks neither to extend nor to reduce the role of the state, but to humanize it through policies of devolution and decentralization and to limit its excesses through a Bill of Rights and a written constitution. What is unacceptable about the role of the state is not its extent, but its remoteness, its failure to attract the allegiance of those whom it governs, So it is that the Liberal favours electoral reform not only to alter the configuration of power at Westminster, but also to mobilize the consent of the electorate for the policies of governments.

---

[12] See Vernon Bogdanor: 'The Social Democrats and the Constitution' in *Political Quarterly*, 1981; and *Multi-Party Politics and the Constitution* (Cambridge 1983) Ch. 2.

[13] John Maynard Keynes in *The General Theory of Employment, Interest and Money* (1936) refers on p. 383 to 'Madmen in authority . . . distilling their frenzy from some academic scribbler of a few years back'.

II

In the nineteenth century, Liberals saw it as their task to remove the barriers to universal suffrage, freedom of conscience and religious worship, competition between individuals, and trade between nations. But from the end of Gladstone's first ministry in 1874 Liberalism faced an intellectual crisis, because it seemed that so many of the Liberal aims had already been achieved. Admittedly, universal suffrage had not yet been attained; but few could doubt that, since the essential principle of parliamentary reform had been accepted, there was no logical stopping-place short of 'one person, one vote'. How could Liberals reorientate themselves towards the new political world to which they were moving? 'Political democracy achieved,' argued Beatrice Potter in 1890, 'what more is there to do, unless you are prepared for Social or Industrial Democracy?'[14] 'The old Liberalism', wrote Hobhouse in 1904, 'had done its work. It had been all very well in its time, but political democracy and the rest were now well-established facts. What was needed was to build a social democracy on the basis so prepared, and for that we needed new formulas, new inspirations.'[15]

So it was, that from 1906 onwards, Liberals in alliance with the nascent Labour Party, found economic and social issues to be at the forefront of the political agenda. Indeed, 'the electoral prospects of the Liberal Party depended upon keeping social and economic issues to the fore — "more than ever before", Lord Crewe had written in 1905, "the Liberal Party is on its trial as an engine for securing social reforms — taxation, land, housing, etc. It has to resist the ILP claim to be the only friend of the workers."[16] It is a paradox that the pre-war Liberal governments which achieved considerable success in economic and social reform, found themselves blocked by those very constitutional issues which had previously formed the life-blood of Liberal Politics, — the House

[14] Beatrice Webb's diary, 31 December 1890, quoted in Peter Clarke: *Liberals and Social Democrats* (Cambridge, 1978), p. 42.
[15] L. T. Hobhouse: *Democracy and Reaction* (1904), pp. 209–10, cited in Peter Clarke: *Lancashire and the New Liberalism* (Cambridge, 1971), p. 173.
[16] Clarke: *Lancashire and the New Liberalism*, p. 393.

of Lords, Irish Home Rule, and the Disestablishment of the Welsh Church.

In 1918 and 1928, the last instalments of nineteenth century constitutional reform were enacted, giving the vote to every adult over twenty-one. It was symbolic that the 1920s saw the beginning of the Liberal Party's long decline, hastened, paradoxically, by the Liberals' failure to reform the electoral system in 1917–18.[17] With the Liberals becoming the third party in the state, constitutional issues were extruded from the political agenda. They were bound to appear an irrelevance in a political system whose actors were defined as Left or Right in terms of their position on a specifically socio-economic cleavage.

The two-party system was buttressed by class feeling and party identification. But with the loosening of traditional loyalties, a political space was created within which there was room for issues of constitutional reform to return to the political agenda. Both of the major political parties have, perforce, been compelled to consider constitutional issues over the last decade and a half — reform of the House of Lords, entry into the EEC, devolution, direct elections to the European Assembly. But they have seen these issues as, at best, an unwelcome distraction from the serious business of politics, which is economic management. For the Liberal, on the other hand, 'Although political debate normally highlights bread-and-butter issues, there is an increasing realization that what are presented as this country's economic or social problems are really those of the structure of government.'

III

Proportional representation is pre-eminent amongst the constitutional reforms demanded by Liberals. Its most immediate effect would be to counter the centrifugal tendencies of the adversarial system and to give greater weight to the political centre. It would, in Roy Jenkins's words, lead to

---

[17] Vernon Bogdanor: *The People and the Party System* (Cambridge, 1981), pp. 129–40.

'the strengthening of the political centre'.[18] Because it would be unlikely that Labour would ever again be able to form a single-party government on its own, proportional representation would also profoundly alter the role of the trade unions. For the unions would no longer be affiliated to an alternative government, but rather to a party which, if it refused all offers of coalition, would become a ghetto party after the manner of the Italian Communists. This would profoundly alter the possibilities open to British governments. It might indeed lead to the trade unions reconsidering their political links with the Labour Party. Certainly they would no longer be able to rely upon a friendly government coming into power and reversing legislation which they deemed inimical to their interest.

With proportional representation, coalition government would become the norm. This would give an advantage to a formation of the centre such as the Liberal/SDP Alliance which could join a coalition with either the Labour or Conservative Parties. Parties at the extremes of the political spectrum would, correspondingly, operate at a disadvantage.

In place of the two-party adversarial system of government, politics would come to be dominated by the progressive centre — the Liberals and Social Democrats, possibly strengthened by the addition of Left-wing Conservatives and Right-wing Labour defectors. For, it could be argued, the two main parties have become increasingly incompatible coalitions held together only by the pursuit of power. Deprived of their life-support mechanism, an electoral system which ruthlessly discriminates against third parties (except for nationalists), the major parties might easily suffer from further defections. The process of realignment could result in public opinion being better reflected in the political parties than it is by an electoral system which locks 'incompatible people, and still more important incompatible philosophies, into a loveless, constantly bickering and debilitating marriage, even if consecrated in a common tabernacle'.[19]

---

[18] *A New Constitutional Settlement* (Liberal Publication Department, 1890), p. 7: Roy Jenkins: *Home Thoughts From Abroad* (BBC: Dimbleby Lecture 1979), p. 10.
   [19] Roy Jenkins: *Home Thoughts from Abroad*, p. 12. See also Philip Williams:

In the 1920s, the failure to change the electoral system was a prime factor in allowing a political cleavage between a socialist party and two non-socialist parties to supersede the pre-war cleavage based upon a Progressive Alliance against a Conservative Party, with a small socialist minority unwilling to co-operate with the Liberals on the Left of the political spectrum.[20] So also in the 1980s, the introduction of proportional representation is crucial to the success of a new 'progressive alliance', and a realignment of politics such that a trade-union-dominated Labour Party adhering to Clause 4 socialism no longer remains a contender for absolute political power. The consequences for British society, as well as for the political system, could prove far-reaching and profound.

What are likely to be the main policies of a government of the progressive centre? Proportional representation would make possible the reintroduction of consensus policies in the economic field. These policies — the construction of an incomes policy, the development of tripartite co-operation between government, employers, and employees, and, more broadly, establishing an institutional framework within which economic objectives can be pursued in an atmosphere of consensus — were all tried in the 1960s and 1970s by the Macmillan, Wilson, Heath, and Callaghan governments. Each attempt, it can be argued, resulted in failure and this has discredited consensus for the party leaders if not for the electorate. Yet, the Liberal claim must be that consensus policies failed because of deep-seated weaknesses in the political system. Conservative governments were unable to secure the consent of the organized working class to policies of economic modernization; while Labour's hostility to the private sector rendered the Party futile as an agent of industrial growth. Above all, the adversary system of politics meant that the two major parties were unable to offer the stability and confidence so necessary for industrial success.

Where predictability is lacking, industrialists, so it is argued, will prove cautious in their investment responses. 'Pure

The Rise — and Possibilities — of Britain's Social Democrats: Dissent, Winter 1982, pp. 70-1.
[20] Vernon Bogdanor: *The People and the Party System,* pp. 129–40.

uncertainty is liable to lead to general lowering of investment in industrial capacity. Expectations about the impermanence of tax changes are liable to lead to very sluggish investment responses with consequent official concern about why policies have not worked, and still further changes in the tax structure thereby fulfilling the original expectations.'[21] According to the Hansard Society's Committee — *Politics and Industry: The Great Mismatch:*

There is some evidence that as soon as the Labour Party began discussing the nationalization of the aircraft and shipbuilding industries (even before the proposal had been put into the form of a Bill) a number of orders were taken elsewhere as customers dislike such uncertainty over the future of the industry. Uncertainty can, therefore, have two effects on investment: it can postpone or lengthen investment projects or it can simply lead to less investment being made.[22]

Continual changes in government policies such as investment incentives, regional policy, indirect taxation, and pay policy are bound to have debilitating consequences upon industrial attitudes. The result is likely to be that the incentives offered by governments to industry come to be discounted, and cease to exert any effect. Proportional representation would, so its advocates believe, transform this situation by providing industrialists with an assurance of predictability in matters such as pay policy and the structure of incentives. Changes of government would more often take the form of changes of coalition partners rather than the ejection of one party from office and its replacement by another dedicated to diametrically opposed policies. Thus, the failure of a centrist government might not lead, as Andrew Gamble, a Socialist advocate of proportional representation hopes, to 'quite novel openings to the Left through the emergence of a clear socialist opposition',[23] but rather to a shift in the political character of the governmental coalition.

There are, of course, obvious dangers associated with this type of constitutional engineering. In a political system in

---

[21] S. J. Nickell: 'The Influence of Uncertainty on Investment: *Economic Journal*, March 1977, p. 65.

[22] Hansard Society: *Politics and Industry — The Great Mismatch* (1979), p. 21.

[23] Andrew Gamble: *Britain in Decline* (1981), p. 226.

which only those whose political views are close to the centre are likely to secure representation in government, those outside the consensus, frustrated by their impotence in Parliament, may be tempted to turn to extra-constitutional methods of influencing public opinion. Nevertheless, the new political alignments which proportional representation could produce, would be defended by Liberals as yielding a more accurate representation of the state of public opinion than could be given by the 'first past the post' system. For the Liberal case for proportional representation is not based wholly — nor even mainly — upon its likely effects on government and Parliament. There is also a wish to reflect public opinion more effectively and to widen the choice available to the individual voter. The Liberal, therefore, feels a special commitment to the single transferable vote method of proportional representation as opposed to party list systems. This system, in the Liberal view, has an educative effect upon the voter, as well as securing fairly close party proportionality. For this reason, the Liberal/SDP Alliance's Constitutional Commission advocated in its report published in July 1982, 'community proportional representation' through the single transferable vote as its preferred system.

The introduction of proportional representation would consititute recognition that the rise of a third force in British politics could no longer be contained, and that British politics would remain multi-party politics for the foreseeable future. Far from sharing the conventional British distaste for Continental-style multi-party politics, the Liberal positively welcomes it. The Liberal Party should not attempt to take its place in a realigned two-party system, but should instead seek a new party structure more capable of reflecting the diversity of opinion in society.

In our view, the party system should reflect the realities of public opinion. The present one clearly works badly, forcing some issues into an artificial mould, obscuring others and generally making government less representative. It should be replaced, and necessarily at this stage, by a multi-party one. The institutions, and particularly the method of election, should be natural channels allowing the system to develop in tune with popular feeling.[24]

[24] *Power to the People: The Machinery of Government* (Liberal Publications Department. 1974). p. 7.

In a modern industrial society, multi-party politics is more 'natural' than a two-party system because there is a far wider diversity of interests seeking representation than can be accommodated by two major parties, whose *raison d'être* is a socio-economic cleavage based upon class. If, moreover, society comprises a large number of different interests, it would be unrealistic to expect that social stability could be secured by the victory of one group of interests over another. Social interests should themselves be represented both in government and in industry in proportion to their support amongst the electorate; and so, the Liberal Party's adherence to proportional representation, which is at bottom a plea for the sharing of power, parallels its advocacy of industrial participation, profit-sharing, and co-partnership in the industrial sphere.

Liberalism, therefore, is a philosophy of social harmony. It makes the optimistic assumption that the forces of rationality and goodwill alone will be sufficient to secure allegiance to the common good of the community as a whole. Unlike the conservative or the socialist, the Liberal does not perceive social life as shot through with conflict, and perhaps he underrates the importance of those factors of power and sentiment which actually hold a political community together. 'The energy that actually shapes the world', Orwell believed, 'springs from emotions . . . which liberal intellectuals mechanically write off as anachronistic.'[25] Liberalism, its critics would argue, is a philosophy appropriate to a small and homogeneous society such as Denmark or Sweden — it is of more dubious application to a country such as Britain, riven as it is by social conflicts both extensive and profound.

IV

But proportional representation is not valued by Liberals only because it will end the adversary political system and make possible a more accurate reflection of popular opinion

[25] George Orwell, *Wells, Hitler and the World State*, in *The Collected Essays, Journalism and Letters of George Orwell*: Volume II: *My Country Right or Left: 1940–1943*: (1968), p. 141.

in the Commons. It is seen also as a pre-condition of further
constitutional reform, as, in David Steel's words, 'the key to
the lock'. For constitutional reform will not be achieved
through the agency of the Conservative or Labour Parties,
parties which, in the Liberal view, retain a vested interest
in the concentration of power legitimized by the notion of
the absolute supremacy of Parliament. The two-party system
is itself inimical to constitutional reform, not only because
each party regards issues of economic management as the
essential substance of politics, but also because the major
parties believe that they alone possess an Aladdin's lamp
in the form of economic policies which, if only they could
be implemented, would save the nation without there being
any need to alter the structure of government. Constitutional
issues, therefore, will only take their place at the centre of
the political agenda when the two-party dominance of
British politics has been broken.

V

For the Liberal, the *leitmotiv*, the golden thread which links
together his various proposals for constitutional reform is the
idea of the sharing of power. Proportional representation
would lead to the sharing of power between the parties in
government, and between government itself and Parliament.
A federal system would make for the sharing of power between
central government and a new provincial layer; while the strengthening and reform of local government would ensure that
community interests are more strongly represented than they
have been hitherto. The Liberal, then, favours not merely constitutional reform, but rather a new constitutional settlement,
which would take the form of a written entrenched constitution:

. . . the Liberal party . . . advocates a thorough-going constitutional
settlement, a 'package approach'. Such a settlement would deal with all
constitutional problems, with all their implications and inter-con-
nections. We will *settle* the Constitution as nearly all other countries
in the world have done and we will do it knowing we are making a
settlement to last. We alone of the United Kingdom political parties
have a clear vision of this.[26] (My italics.)

[26] *A New Constitutional Settlement*, p. 10.

Liberals take pride in their thorough-going advocacy of constitutional reform. The Liberal journal *New Outlook* contrasted the Social Democratic approach to the Liberal one. '. . . faced with an obsolete machine that has irrevocably broken down, the Social Democrat's instinctive reaction is to reach for his screwdriver. Liberal reaction is to look for a drawing board.'[27] Liberals are accustomed to contrast themselves to their Conservative and Labour counterparts by stressing their freedom from ideological constraints. On economic and social policy, the Liberals have certainly followed a path of relativism. They have vigorously opposed absolutist conceptions of economic life such as those based on socialism or the free market, and steadfastly adhered to the philosophy of the middle way developed by Keynes and Beveridge. On constitutional matters, however, it is the Labour and Conservative Parties whose policies are marked by a cautious and sceptical pragmatism, while the Liberal Party has adopted a holistic and utopian approach entirely at variance with the politics of gradualism. Indeed, it is in its attitude towards reform of the constitution that the Liberal Party displays most clearly the nature of its ideology.

The notion of an overall constitutional settlement is appropriate perhaps to a new country which has just gained its independence, or to a country emerging from the experience of dictatorship. It is difficult to see how it can be applied to a mature and developed democracy, many of whose political institutions have remained in existence for hundreds of years. 'The very fact', argued Mill in 1833, 'that a certain set of political institutions already exist, have long existed, and have become associated with all the historical recollections of a people is in itself, as far as it goes, a property which adapts them to that people, and gives them a great advantage over any new institutions in obtaining that ready and willing resignation to what has once been decided by lawful authority . . . .'[28] To secure a new constitutional settlement

[27] *New Outlook*: Vol. 20, No. 8: Editorial: *The Meaning of Social Democracy.* p. 11.

[28] John Stuart Mill: *Remarks on Bentham's Philosophy* (1833) in John Stuart Mill: *Essays on Ethics, Religion and Society: Collected Works,* Vol. x (Toronto, 1969), p. 17.

a government would have to destroy a large number of traditional landmarks which already enjoy a certain kind of legitimacy, in the hope of creating a new and more acceptable focus of authority. It is difficult to believe that hallowed symbols of legitimacy can be attached overnight to new and unfamiliar institutions.

Would it, furthermore, be in accordance with attitudes to democracy which Liberals themselves have argued for, to allow a Liberal, or Liberal/SDP government to legislate for an overall constitutional settlement, with a written constitution, which would be entrenched and therefore difficult to reverse. Liberals themselves have strongly condemned the misuse of the mandate theory by which a party which wins a majority in a general election then uses the supremacy of Parliament to enforce its will on the electorate. It would be difficult for any government to claim a mandate for so momentous and irreversible a change. The offence is compounded surely, if what is enforced, is then also entrenched. Constitutional reform cannot be secured through the synoptic approach of a grand design. It is a sphere in which precision and detail are of the utmost importance. 'I must', said Burke, 'see with my own eyes, I must, in a manner touch with my own hands, not only the fixed but the momentary circumstances, before I could venture to suggest any political project whatsoever. I must know the power and disposition to accept, to execute, to preserve. I must see the means of correcting the plan, where correctives would be wanted. I must see the things; I must see the men.'[29] This is preeminently true of the politics of constitutional reform.

The defects of the Liberal approach were starkly exposed during the one occasion in the post-war period when the Liberal Party actually enjoyed the opportunity of putting its ideas on constitutional reform into practice. The failure of the first devolution bill — the Scotland and Wales Bill — in February 1977 had deprived the Labour government of its parliamentary support, and it was forced to accept a pact with the Liberals to ensure its survival. One of the terms of

[29] Edmund Burke: *Letter to a Member of the National Assembly* (1791), in Edmund Burke: *Works* (Bohn, 1883), p. 549.

the pact was that a new and improved version of devolution would be produced by the Labour government; and the Liberals were accordingly asked for their suggestions. Devolution, or rather federalism, had been Liberal Party policy at least since the publication of its policy document, *Power to the Provinces*, in 1968. Yet the Liberal Party was unable to exert any significant influence upon the thinking of the Labour government. Its thinking had been entirely in terms of general conceptions of government, and not in the precise terms necessary for the resolution of complex constitutional issues. On the central topic discussed in the talks between the government and the Liberals on devolution — whether the proposed Scottish Assembly should be provided with revenue-raising powers — the Liberals proved utterly unable to match the technical sophistication of the Treasury and the Inland Revenue, and they were unable to extract concessions from the government. Yet the principle that the power to raise money should be vested in the same hands as the power to spend it had long been a major part of the Liberal critique of the approaches of the Conservative and Labour Parties to local-government reform and devolution.

For the Liberal Party saw the enunciation of general principles as the central task of the politician. Its leaders did not appreciate that the laying-down of principles marks the beginning and not the end of the political process. It is in the filling-in of detail that the practical politician distinguishes himself from the ideologue.

In truth, the Liberal approach to constitutional reform is marked by a profound rationalism which is hostile not only to the adaptive nature of the British Constitution, but also to the openness and resilience of the philosophical tradition of liberalism itself. The liberal case for freedom is founded ultimately upon a view of the diversity of human nature which makes it impossible for any authority to draw up definitive rules for the regulation of human conduct. So also to impose upon society a definitive course of constitutional development ought to be regarded as artificially limiting the flow of change and in this way pre-empting possibilities of choice for the future. To argue otherwise is to betray a misunderstanding both of the nature of the British

Constitution, largely a product of the practical reforms of previous generations of Whigs and Liberals; and of liberalism itself.

9. Liberals and the Economy*

Andrew Gamble

The danger of planning is that it forgets that all planning is for people. In their enthusiasm the planners are apt to think people exist for the plan. The great protection against this attitude is to have planning by Liberals. For whatever Liberals may be, they are first and foremost concerned with individual men and women.

Jo Grimond.[1]

1. INTRODUCTION

There is an obvious difficulty in writing about Liberal economic policy. The party has been so long out of office that Liberals have had no opportunity to test their ideas. The formulation of policy proceeds in a void; it is all theory and no practice except when Liberal ideas are picked up and implemented by another party. The interaction between policy-making in Opposition and experience of implementing policies in Government is lacking. The Liberals have been a party of permanent Opposition since 1945. Only in 1964-6, 1974, and 1977-8 has the balance of the two major parties in Parliament allowed the Liberals some leverage over Government (in each case a Labour Government), and a limited opportunity to try to put some of their ideas into practice. In the first two cases this was largely negative. The Liberals claimed that the Government's need to keep Liberal support prevented the enactment of socialist measures, particularly the planned nationalization of certain sectors of the economy.[2]

*I would like to thank Peter Knowlson for allowing me to see material on Liberal party economic policy held at Liberal party Headquarters, and Michael Steed for some very useful suggestions and criticisms.

[1] Jo Grimond in P. Furnell and F. Ware, *Planning with a Purpose* (New Orbits 9), 1962, p. 10.

[2] The 1966 Manifesto for example listed the following policy decisions where it was claimed the Government had bowed to Liberal pressure: steel and land nationalization; pensions and rates; regional policy and the Highland Development Board.

In the third case, however, the signing of the Lib–Lab pact guaranteed Liberal support for the Labour Government in return for concessions on policy.[3] This was the nearest the Liberals have approached to re-entering Government since 1945.

There is a further difficulty in writing about Liberal economic policy. The party has sometimes seemed to attach a very low priority to economic issues. One observer in 1975 thought the Liberal assembly at Scarborough very badly managed; there seemed to be no awareness of priorities or any determination to make an impact on the issues that really mattered. As an example he cited economic policy: 'Although their economic spokesman, Mr John Pardoe, was proclaiming that Britain is facing the worst economic crisis in her history, the conference could not find time to debate the question until Saturday morning – and then only the narrower topic of unemployment rather than the broad issue of the economy as a whole.'[4]

This kind of criticism has often been made. It stems from the Liberals' status as a party of permanent opposition, the small number of its MPs, and the apparent irrelevance of formulating detailed policies which will never be implemented. David Steel has quoted James Fenton's observations on the reaction of delegates to his speech at the 1977 Brighton Conference: The delegates . . . 'were not thinking about the content, largely because in all the years they have been Liberals, they have never expected to hear a speech with any content. Content is not really what they're interested in. If they were, they wouldn't be Liberals.'[5]

Yet such parodies of Liberal attitudes underplay the importance of Liberal ideas about economic policy. The party is heir to the tradition of liberal political economy, initially developed by the classical political economists, codified in the Victorian age in the principles of Free Trade, Economy, and *Laissez-faire* which dominated public policy

---

[3] For contrasting views of the Lib–Lab Pact, see David Steel, *A House Divided*, 1980, and Joel Barnett, *Inside the Treasury*, 1982.

[4] Geoffrey Smith in *The Times*, 22.9.75.

[5] James Fenton in the *New Statesman*, quoted by David Steel, *A House Divided*, p. 82.

up to 1914. But the party is also heir to the tradition of social liberalism, developed by Hobhouse, and later Keynes and Beveridge, and associated with the policies of Lloyd George and the 1905 Liberal Government, which justified a greatly enlarged role for government in providing welfare and managing the national economy.

The way in which modern Liberals have reacted to economic problems has been greatly influenced by these two different and at times contradictory legacies from the period of classical liberalism and Liberal Governments. The attitudes of Liberals to the post-war consensus on economic management, to the strategy of modernization pursued in the 1960s, and to the impact of Britain's relative economic decline and the world recession in the 1970s were powerfully influenced by the interplay of these contrasting Liberal ideas about how a Liberal society should be organized. This may be one reason why the Liberal party has always proved so fertile in generating new ideas about economic policy. From the Liberals' Yellow Book *Britain's Industrial Future* in 1928, to the New Liberalism launched by Jo Grimond after 1956, to the attempt in the 1970s to think through the problems appropriate for a 'post-industrial society', the Liberals have never been devoid of ideas or interest in economic questions.

It would be surprising were it otherwise. For allied to the richness of the party's intellectual tradition is the central importance which the performance of the economy has assumed in British domestic politics since 1956. Only very occasionally did it lose this pre-eminence. The problem of relative economic decline has become an obsession for all sections of the political community. Every attempt to remedy the deep-seated weaknesses of the British economy and reverse the decline proved unsuccessful. The economic problems grew worse and a cycle of economic decline, political failure, and electoral rejection was established which resulted in the government changing hands four times after 1959. As the pendulum has swung to and fro, so the attachment of electors to their parties weakened and a climate of ungovernability and political instability was created. The Liberals at times strongly benefited from this. If there is a central theme in Liberal thinking about economic policy it is the constant relating of economic issues to the Party's political and electoral strategy and to its programme for constitutional change, analysed elsewhere in this volume. The Liberals' strongest belief, developed in the last twenty-five years, is that Britain's economic problems cannot be solved and Liberal policies cannot work until there has been a major change in constitutional arrangements.

2. CLASSICAL LIBERALISM

The dominance of liberal political economy in discussions of economic principles derived from the importance Liberals placed on individual liberty. The three central ones were Free Trade, Economy, and *Laissez-faire*, corresponding to the three major areas of economic policy — foreign economic policy, stabilization policy (including public finance), and industrial policy. Free trade meant free movement of goods, capital, and labour, the creation of the widest possible markets. This in turn implied cosmopolitanism and internationalism because it involved greater interdependence between nations and economies, and therefore strengthened the possibility of peace. Peace in turn was regarded as indispensable for world prosperity, and the First World War and its troubled aftermath were considered by Liberals as one of the chief causes of unemployment and depression in the 1930s. Another important consequence of free trade, of buying in the cheapest market and selling in the dearest, was to encourage an ever-widening and more complex division of labour. Britain sold manufactures and services and imported raw materials and cheap food. The maintenance of such international markets in a world of sovereign nation-states required an active policy to ensure that an open world trading order and a viable international monetary system were maintained. These functions were discharged by Britain in the nineteenth century and that they were discharged became permanent concerns of British economic policy.

The second injunction was Economy. Liberals believed that sound money was essential for the smooth working of a market economy and that one of the prime requirements for a stable currency was careful control of public spending so that taxes might be kept to a minimum and easily raised and the government would not be forced either to borrow or to print money. Sound money was considered the best contribution a government could make to stabilizing the economy and providing opportunities for employment and prosperity.

The third principle, *Laissez-faire*, meant that the government would do more than establish and enforce a framework of laws to regulate the economic activities of its citizens. It would create a 'market order' but it would leave individuals free to make whatever choices, whatever exchanges, and whatever contracts they liked, provided they did not offend against the general rules, for example on contracts and property and the freedom of labour, which defined the market order. *Laissez-faire* has often acquired the image of a non-interventionist, inert, and absent state. But the principles of liberal political economy actually implied a strong and interventionist state, constantly intervening to protect the fragile market order — enforcing free competition and removing all obstacles to the unfettered play of market forces. In many respects this involved an expansion rather than a contraction of state activities.[6] Actions which facilitated the broadening of the market were desirable. Liberals supported the free market because it appeared the best means of breaking up concentrations of power, achieving a decentralized economy and so maximizing individual liberty.

The extraordinary progress of the British economy in the nineteenth century was taken as vindicating these principles. But with the gradual establishment of a fully industrialized economy and the rise of mass democracy the adequacy of these principles for guiding public policy began to be questioned. Schools of national political economy began to flourish and the policies and institutional arrangements which liberal political economy sanctioned came under fundamental attack from Social Imperialists and from socialists. Problems of national efficiency and national competition, problems of poverty and unemployment, problems of class division and

---

[6] See Lionel Robbins, *Political Economy Past and Present,* 1976.

the distribution of property and wealth became central to political debate.[7]

The Liberal response to these developments and these challenges were the new doctrines of Social Liberalism. These doctrines entailed giving greater weight than before to considerations of welfare rather than liberty. Elliott Dodds has written that Liberalism 'regards Liberty and Welfare as complementary and both as means to the same end — the creation of opportunity for men and women to become self-directing, responsible persons'.[8] By defining the ultimate aims of Liberalism in this way and refusing to place an absolute value upon liberty, Liberals were able to justify a steady enlargement of state activities. As Desmond Banks put it in his pamphlet, 'Liberals and Economic Planning', in 1963, Liberals sought state activity to 'create those economic conditions without which the individual is not truly free'.[9]

The landmarks of Social Liberalism were the various welfare and redistributive measures enacted by the Liberal Government between 1906 and 1914; the Yellow Book of 1928 which proposed schemes of industrial partnership and national development;[10] the Liberal Manifesto of 1929, 'We Can Conquer Unemployment', which advocated major public works programmes,[11] Beveridge's reports on social security and full employment;[12] and Keynes's new thinking on how to manage a modern capitalist economy.[13] What they all had in common was the belief that only by enlarging the

---

[7] See Bernard Semmel, *Imperialism and Social Reform*, 1962.

[8] Elliott Dodds, 'Liberty and Welfare', in G. Watson, ed., *The Unservile State*, 1957, p. 15.

[9] Desmond Banks, *Liberals and Economic Planning* (Unservile State Papers 8), 1963, p. 15.

[10] *Britain's Industrial Future*, 1928. For a discussion of its importance, see Robert Skidelsky, *Politicians and the Slump*, 1967.

[11] F. W. S. Craig, *British General Election Manifestos*, 1975. Lloyd George's later plans in the 1930s for a 'prosperity loan' are discussed by R. J. McLeod, 'The Development of Full Employment Policy, 1939–45' (D.Phil. Thesis), Oxford, 1978. A useful statement of Liberal thinking in the 1930s is *The Liberal Way* (National Liberal Federation), 1934.

[12] Sir William Beveridge, *Social Insurance and Allied Services*, (Cmd. 6404), 1942, and *Full Employment in a Free Society*, 1944.

[13] J. M. Keynes, *The General Theory of Employment, Interest, and Money*, 1936. For a general survey of Keynes's work and influence, see D. Moggridge, *Keynes*, 1976.

scope of government involvement could the legitimacy of the market order be maintained and the benefits of a liberal society preserved.

3. LIBERALS AND THE POST-WAR CONSENSUS

There are those who regard the reconstruction plans of the war-time National Government and their subsequent implementation by the first majority Labour Government as the greatest triumph of all of Social Liberalism. The Liberals were certainly enthusiastic supporters of the new policies, while Keynes and Beveridge (the latter finally joined the party in 1944 and was briefly an MP) were active in shaping the new balance between the private and the public sectors. Beveridge in public speeches declared that no Liberal Leader since before Gladstone had stood for *laissez-faire*. The necessities of civilized life could not be secured by individuals but had to be won by collective planning and social demand: 'Liberalism with a Radical programme means not interfering with rights but giving additional rights: I suggest that every housewife in this country shall have a right to a tap.'[14]

Under the impact of the war the party was prepared to support far-reaching encroachments on individual liberty to increase social welfare. As Jo Grimond has remembered, 'we were all to some extent socialists'.[15] The Yellow Book had been an important pioneer in exploring the possibilities of better state management and Liberals welcomed the opportunity which the war economy gave for extending public responsibilities and activities. The party adopted a 'pragmatic' attitude towards Labour's measures of nationalization despite its traditional dislike of monopoly and centralized economic power. Where ownership was considered more economic, or where an industry had become a private monopoly, the Liberals supported nationalization, although they continued to oppose arguments in favour of general nationalization or a single form of nationalization, preferring a more diversified pattern. The argument for and against nationalization, the

[14] Sir William Beveridge, *Why I am a Liberal*, quoted by Alan Watkins, *The Liberal Dilemma*, 1966, p. 40.
[15] Jo Grimond, *Memoirs*, 1979, p. 132.

1945 Manifesto declared, was out of date.[16] Each proposal should be decided pragmatically.

Liberals gave greatest backing to the reform of social security and to the assumption by Government of responsibility for full employment. This meant endorsing much higher levels of taxation and accepting that governments had a responsibility not merely to maintain sound money but to engineer high levels of employment, and faster rates of economic growth. Keynesianism, whether Keynes himself would have approved of it or not, emerged after 1947 as a set of techniques for managing the total level of demand to encourage satisfactory levels of employment of resources, including labour, and of investment. One Liberal economist, Alan Peacock, writing in the 1950s summed up the change in economic thinking which Keynes had brought about: 'Keynesians hold that it is the level of the community's expenditure on all kinds of goods and services, and thus the prospective profits of business, which determine the amount of investment undertaken by industry and not the terms on which industry can borrow.'[17] If saving was to be regarded as a check to consumption rather than as a stimulus to investment, then the nineteenth-century Liberal arguments against any redistributive measures through the tax system which would harm the ability of rich individuals to save and invest were no longer valid. The new approach was congenial to many Liberals because Keynesian proposals for manipulating the total level of demand by indirect fiscal and monetary means to stimulate (or restrain) investment and economic activity avoided detailed intervention by governments in the choices individual consumers and individual firms could make. A large part of the increase in public expenditure took the form of transfer incomes. This meant that a mixed economy was still compatible in Liberal eyes with a decentralized economy in which the greater part of economic activity was still governed by the free play of market forces.

In the 1950s, the Liberal party's parliamentary representation fell to its lowest level ever and little new thinking

---

[16] Liberal Party Manifesto 1945, in Craig, 1975.
[17] Alan Peacock in Watson, ed., *The Unservile State*, p. 115.

emerged in the party. Liberals were affected by the general climate of opinion which was critical of the centralization and bureaucracy associated with Labour rule. The party retreated from some of its enthusiasm for planning and intervention. In the 1950 election the Liberal manifesto called for the return of the iron and steel industry to private ownership. In 1951 the Liberals demanded that industry must be set free.[18]

The return of the Conservatives to office in 1951 was not followed by a significant dismantling of the welfare state. The trend towards removing controls from the economy was continued, however, and this was welcomed by Liberals. In the early 1950s the identity and future role of the party was uncertain. The party leadership had resisted calls by Churchill and Woolton in 1950 and 1951 for a realignment on the right of all the forces opposed to socialism. But with the Conservatives committed to moderate pragmatic policies within the general framework that the war and the 1945 Labour Government had established, there seemed no clear role for the Liberals. The consensus on how to manage the economy was at its height in the 1950s and with the great expansion of the world economy under way, there was little that appeared distinctive about Liberal policy, apart from an insistence on the need for free trade and the advocacy of co-ownership schemes.

Nevertheless there were some controversies in these years inside the party. There remained a sizeable element of Liberal opinion which was untouched by Social Liberalism and which continued to advocate free-market policies and attack not merely the 'excesses' of centralization and bureaucracy that had grown up under Labour, but the necessity and desirability of an enlarged public sector and a managed economy at all. Some of these groups did not stay within the Liberal party, but became separate organizations like Edward Martell and his People's League for the Defence of Freedom.[19] Others like Arthur Seldon devoted their energies

---

[18] Liberal Party Manifestos 1950, 1951, in Craig, 1975.
[19] The League is discussed by Alan Watkins in *The Liberal Dilemma*, and by George Thayer, *The British Political Fringe*, 1965.

to setting up the Institute of Economic Affairs (1957) which became the chief propaganda unit for free-market ideas and was to grow greatly in influence in the 1970s.

Radical individualists in the 1950s put forward arguments derived from liberal political economy about the overriding importance of free trade, competition, and sound finance. Such views found echoes in the Conservative party but were for the most part ignored by the Conservative leadership. If the Liberals had followed the ideas of Major Oliver Smedley, for example, they would certainly have acquired a distinctive position and would later have been recognized as forerunners of the New Right of the 1970s. In a speech delivered in 1955, reported by the *Glasgow Herald*, Major Smedley declared:

> I say, and shall continue to say, that the worst thing you can do with your money is to hand it over to be spent by the State . . . Far better keep it in your money-box and sleep with it under your pillow at night . . . Anywhere is better than letting it pass through the slippery fingers of the State. There is no need yet for a campaign for the non-payment of taxes, lawfully levied and assessed. But the handing over of our savings to the State is not yet compulsory, and there we have an opportunity of making our protest against Government extravagance. Money is losing value because the Government will not exercise control over their own expenditure and the constantly expanding issue of paper money with which they finance it.[20]

These attitudes were shared by a much wider spectrum of Liberal opinion. What tends to be overlooked is how, until recently, economists with an orthodox training who became interested in the problems of political economy naturally gravitated to the Liberal party. The Liberal party historically was the only consistent defender of the importance of free markets, the institution around whose study the discipline of economics was constructed. The national political economy of Keynes and Beveridge which placed welfare above liberty and therefore tended to give greater weight to the co-ordination of the economy through state management and administration rather than through markets was never universally accepted. Many Liberal economists held out against it. They may not have expressed themselves in the language of Major Smedley

---

[20] Major Oliver Smedley, quoted by Alan Watkins, pp. 72–3.

but their underlying approach was the same. They set in train criticisms of the enlarged state sector which were to become the basis for the formidable revival of Liberal political economy in the 1970s. In the 1950s debates raged around the question of whether welfare benefits should be provided universally or selectively, and whether they should be provided through the State.[21] Some Liberals, despite everything that Keynes and Beveridge had written, remained deeply suspicious of the state and questioned the desirability of entrusting tasks to public agencies when there were other means of accomplishing them.

One major feature of recent British politics is that when the revival of liberal political economy did come it was the Conservative party with which it was associated, and not the Liberal party. So economic liberalism and Liberal economics diverged to add to the confusion of political terminology. The Liberals on the whole chose to remain with Keynesianism and the perspectives of Social Liberalism. That they did so was partly because the radical individualists of the 1950s, who would have purged the party of its Social Liberalism, never made much headway. They were resisted by the party Establishment who did not want to see the Liberals staking out political ground too distant from the consensus policies which the two main parties were pursuing. They were resisted also by the Radical Reform Group, which believed the task of the Liberals was not to retreat from Social Liberalism but to propose ways in which the institutions and policies of the welfare state and the managed economy could be improved and strengthened. This meant state action to redistribute wealth and decentralize power. In 1956 the party acquired a leader who inclined to the views of the Radical Reform Group, Jo Grimond.

4. THE PURSUIT OF MODERNIZATION

Grimond brought two major changes to the party. The first was a new strategy in the attempt to achieve a realignment of

---

[21] See Alan Peacock, 'Welfare in the Liberal State', in G. Watson, *The Unservile State*, pp. 113-30.

the left, the creation of a new radical force in British politics which would replace the Labour party. The second was an emphasis on the formulation of policy. The party had little prospect of any share in Government but the activity of making and communicating policy was an important part of re-establishing the credibility of the party as a serious electoral competitor.

Considerable effort was put into policy-making. Groups such as the Unservile State Group, the New Orbits Group, and the Oxford Liberal Group emerged. Series of pamphlets including New Orbit, New Directions, Liberal Focus, and the Unservile State Papers were published. Most important of all a series of policy panels were established which produced major reviews of Liberal policy. In the economic field these included taxation and industrial affairs.

The sum of all this activity became known as the New Liberalism. Its character was fixed by the electoral strategy Grimond was pursuing, his desire to make the Liberals the core of a non-socialist radical party. This ruled out a programme designed to roll back the frontiers of the state and remove the obstacles to the free workings of markets, notably trade-union power. A much more attractive option beckoned, one more in keeping with the climate of the times. This was to throw the Liberal party fully behind the plans that were emerging for modernizing the British economy and British society without disturbing the essential features of the postwar consensus.

Grimond believed that Conservativism could be challenged by a radical programme built around the need to take self-government to a new stage. But it was significant that the means to do this were predominantly statist and collectivist. The central themes of the new Liberalism included the encouragement of economic growth through governmental planning, a concern with economic, political, and social modernization at home, and the transfer of Britain's interests abroad from the attempt at world power to full acceptance of a European role.

The case for a strategy to modernize the British economy stemmed from an assessment of Britain's post-war performance that was rapidly gaining acceptance amongst a section of

Britain's opinion leaders.[22] This held that despite the un-
paralleled prosperity of the 1950s, the achievement of full
employment and economic growth, the British economy was
beginning to lag seriously behind its main competitors. The
main cause was identified as the foreign economic policy
which successive British Governments had pursued since the
war. They had endeavoured to protect sterling as an international currency and to achieve a surplus on the balance of
payments large enough to pay for both the overseas military
expenditure necessary to maintain a world role for Britain
and a high level of overseas foreign investment. Despite
the improvement in Britain's export performance this
was producing periodic balance of payments deficits and
consequent runs on sterling. To protect sterling from
devaluation successive Chancellors deflated the economy,
inaugurating a stop-go cycle which was proving fatal to
business confidence and long-run investment plans. The
economy was expanding at a much lower rate than it was
capable of doing. It was also believed that removing the
external constraint on growth would permit the adoption
of a programme to remedy many of the other persistent
weaknesses of the British economy.

The Liberals pioneered this analysis in party political
debate. They developed a new foreign economic policy which
played down the traditional priority attached to free trade
and instead declared emphatically in favour of Britain joining
the EEC, finding a way of dispensing with the international
role of sterling, and curbing overseas military spending. The
Liberals' position was summed up in the title of a pamphlet
by Jo Grimond, *Growth not Grandeur*. In it he declared:
'The Government has pursued a policy which has given
priority to grandeur rather than growth.'[23] Britain's relative
decline was due to the misguided attempt to maintain what
remained of Britain's world power. The Liberals argued that
Britain's world power had been eclipsed, and that it was
fruitless in the contemporary interdependent world economy

---

[22] Particularly influential was Andrew Shonfield's book *British Economic
Policy since the War*, Harmondsworth, 1958.

[23] Jo Grimond, *Growth not Grandeur* (New Directions), 1961, p. 8.

trying to preserve economic sovereignty. Membership of the EEC would unshackle British economic policy.

With the balance of payments constraint on British growth removed a steady rate of expansion of the economy could be planned. Stabilization policy would be altered so as to make economic growth the major priority. Liberals advocated a 4 per cent per annum target and a five-year plan and greatly increased public spending, especially on capital projects. As *Partners in a New Britain* put it: 'If Britain is to become once more a dynamic progressive nation instead of the stagnant one of the past ten years we must plan for rapid growth.'[24]

The third plank of the modernization strategy concerned industrial policy. Here the Liberals brought forward again proposals for co-ownership and profit-sharing, intended to heal the rift between the two sides of industry and establish consensus within firms to complement national consensus on the targets of the plan. Co-ownership to promote industrial partnership and industrial democracy had long been a central Liberal policy aimed at removing the sources of class conflict and furthering the Liberal aim of decentralizing power. The ideal Liberal community and economy would be one composed of independent producers, so ensuring the greatest possible degree of equality and independence. This would be an economy without any division between a class owning the means of production and a class of propertyless workers. The actual capitalist economy that had emerged was obviously far different from this, with its concentration of power and wealth, its giant production units, and its armies of wage workers. Co-ownership in its various forms became the Liberal answer to this problem of a modern industrial society. The advantage of large-scale enterprise would be maintained, but the disadvantages would be countered by giving all workers a stake in the enterprise and ensuring that firms continued to operate efficiently by making the competition fierce.

Liberal pamphlets and policy statements in the early 1960s resound with confidence in the prospects for successful modernization. The handbook for Liberal candidates and speakers summed up Liberal policy as a five-point programme:

[24] *Partners in a New Britain* (LPD), 1963.

1. Launch a five-year plan to ensure that industry was at full capacity. 2. Make Britain more efficient through bringing industries up to date by stimulating competition and encouraging research and development. 3. Make better use of Britain's resources, especially our skilled manpower. 4. Share the wealth which increased productivity brings more equitably. 5. Take a leading role in international schemes to expand world trade and pool currency reserves.[25] Britain it was said suffered from a disease. What was needed was a national team effort. The overriding priority was to raise economic growth.

The commitment to a higher rate of economic growth had already been endorsed by the Liberal Assembly in 1961. A resolution was passed which declared that faster growth was necessary in order to achieve Liberal's social objectives — on education, pension, transport, housing, and aid to under-developed countries. Economic planning, wrote the authors of a pamphlet entitled *Planning with a Purpose*, should be systematically geared to making the British economy 'more modern, efficient, and cost-conscious'.[26] This was a common theme. A Liberal society should welcome change and expansion and Liberals advocated the full use of every new technological innovation. Grimond argued that Liberals must question all established methods and institutions, submitting them to the test of whether they contributed to a more dynamic society and expanding economy.[27] The most forth-right declaration of these ideas came in the 1964 manifesto:

Britain has lagged behind since the war because the 'Establishment' in politics, in Whitehall, in industry, and the trade unions have too often been unresponsive to the possibilities of the new age. To put this right the way Britain is run must be drastically reformed; the new men and women who understand modern technology must be given wider opportunities to use their talents; economic growth must become a major aim through more skilful management of the nation.[28]

---

[25] *Partners for Progress* (LPD), 1964.
[26] P. Furnell and F. Ware, *Planning with a Purpose*, p. 4.
[27] William Wallace, 'The Liberal Revival — the Liberal party in Britain 1955-1966' (Ph.D. thesis), Cornell, 1968, p. 68.
[28] Liberal Party Manifesto 1964, in Craig, 1975, p. 273.

5. THE CHALLENGE TO THE CONSENSUS

After the 1966 General Election with the return of a substantial Labour majority, the Liberal political strategy of seeking a realignment of the Left was temporarily exhausted. Liberals once again had had to stand on the sidelines watching the other parties take up their ideas — entry into the EEC, a National Plan, a modernization programme. The high hopes that had been placed in modernization quickly collapsed, however, as first the Conservative and then the Labour Government found management of the economy ever more difficult and hazardous and as the incidence and severity of crises and policy failures grew alarmingly.

The two opposition parties reacted differently to the débâcle. The Conservatives abandoned their faith in modernization through planning and government intervention in the economy and, under pressure from a vociferous section of the party which was becoming imbued with ideas of economic liberalism, the leadership began to declare the need for the market to be reasserted, the whole apparatus of tripartite consultation on growth dismantled and new government agencies in the expanded public sector wound up.

The Liberals' diagnosis of the problem was very different. They clung to the modernization strategy and attacked the Labour Government for abandoning it. They were particularly critical of the Government's refusal to devalue sterling, until compelled to do so in November 1967, because this meant the Chancellor was forced to scrap the growth targets of the National Plan and to impose a major deflationary package on the economy in 1966. At the 1966 Conference, against the advice of the executive, a motion was passed calling for devaluation if other measures failed.[29] There was a strong attack on the wage freeze in a resolution moved by Peter Bessell. He attacked it on four grounds; because it meant government interference with free collective bargaining; because it encouraged piecework and overtime instead of higher productivity; because it had halted productivity

---

[29] An amendment from Devizes which was backed by the executive called for devaluation only after Liberal policies had been tried. It was defeated by 431 votes to 340.

bargaining; and because it would either be ineffective or would create shortages. He also attacked unemployment with the ringing declaration: 'The message from this assembly is that one capable man unemployed is intolerable.'[30] At the 1967 Conference a resolution moved by Christopher Layton, one of the party's leading economic advisers, stated: 'this Assembly deplores the Government's abandonment of full employment and of a high rate of economic growth. It believes that an annual increase in national income of at least 4 per cent stemming from a sharp rise in investment and exports must be the top priority of economic policy.'

Although they were disillusioned with the results of modernization the Liberals did not abandon the strategy as the basis of their thinking. They did not seek to differentiate themselves from Labour's stance as the Conservatives had done. This may have weakened their electoral prospects in 1970 but the gain for the Liberals was a consolidation of their thinking on several aspects of the modernization strategy. They became committed for example to the idea of a permanent and statutory incomes policy as an indispensable means for combating inflation, which had begun to accelerate in the late 1960s. The principle was first affirmed at the Conference in 1967 and has been reaffirmed on several occasions since, except in 1976, when a clause affirming the party's intention 'to sustain a firm prices and incomes policy for the remainder of this decade, using statutory powers if necessary' was deleted from a resolution on unemployment.[31] This was opposed by the party leadership and a commitment to a statutory incomes policy reappeared the following year at the prompting of John Pardoe. Jeremy Thorpe as Leader had made this a central feature of the election campaigns in 1974. Liberals in the past had always been wary of compulsory national wage-bargaining. They had been critical of the early steps towards an incomes policy and were critical of Labour's *In Place of Strife* proposals, because they reinforced national wage-bargaining. If there had to be an incomes policy Liberals at this time wanted it to be voluntary.

[30] Peter Bessell, quoted in *The Times*, 22.9.66, p. 11.
[31] See the report in *The Times*, 18.9.76. Earlier Liberal attitudes to incomes policy can be found in Nancy Seear, *Policies for Incomes* (Unservile State papers 13), 1966.

Their preference for solutions that encouraged decentralization of decision-making led them to advocate plant and
productivity bargaining. But Liberals were never prepared to
propose anti-union legislation, and this meant they needed
a policy to cope with the immediate and pressing problem
of inflation while Liberal reforms of pay bargaining and
industrial relations were taking effect. Liberals hoped that a
statutory incomes policy would eventually be unnecessary,
but in the short run they came to think it an indispensable
tool for managing the economy without resorting to the
social-market tactic of creating mass unemployment. They
have produced a number of novel ideas as to how to run a
permanent incomes policy, including a major measure of
redistribution, a national minimum wage, and an inflation
tax — to be levied on companies and employees if prices or
wages exceeded a certain percentage increase. This featured
prominently in the February election manifesto in 1974.
By 1979 it had been toned down. The manifesto in that
year states; 'we would introduce a sustained prices and
incomes policy based on wide consultation and enforceable
at law. Our incomes policy would be supported by tax
measures and a national minimum income. It would reward
increases in value-added.'[32]

The commitment to a 'sustained' incomes policy was
linked to two other major themes, the damaging effects
of adversary politics and the need for a major redistribution
of power and wealth in society. But the precise interpretation
of this latter aim has caused considerable controversy in
the party. The Young Liberals who caused such uproar at
Liberal Conferences in the 1960s, particularly in 1966 and
1977, and the groups pursuing community politics, uni-
lateralism, and ecological politics in the 1970s tended to
interpret the Liberal commitments on tax reform, industrial
structure, and industrial democracy in more radical ways
than the Liberal leadership. Young Liberal proposals in the
1960s for a wealth tax and for workers control were both
heavily defeated.[33] The influence of 'radical individualists',

---

[32] Liberal Party Manifesto, *The Real Fight is for Britain*, 1979, p. 10.

[33] See the reports in *The Times*, 23.9.66 and 22.9.67. An amended motion
advocating industrial participation was passed.

however, was slight in the party in the 1960s and 1970s. Steady progress was made in developing the party's proposals on tax reform, which came to revolve around plans for a credit income tax, and indexation of taxes and benefits, and in the adoption of the co-ownership proposals originally advanced by the Industrial Affairs policy panel in 1962. These proposals were finally embodied in a resolution accepted by the Conference in 1968. The Liberals became committed to amending the Companies Act so as to give greater representation to employees, allowing them to participate in the selection of boards of companies over a certain size on the basis of parity with shareholders. Works committees were to be established in all plants with more than fifty workers. In the resolution passed at the Brighton Conference in 1977 the main strands of a Liberal industrial democracy were defined as (1) workplace councils with state-defined rights of consultation and information; (2) election of boards on common voting rolls for employees and shareholders; and (3) increased financial participation by employees.

The tax reforms Liberals wanted to see have also gone through several formulations. In the 1970s John Pardoe was particularly important in persuading the party to advocate a radical shift in the burden of direct and indirect taxes. Liberal policy was crystallized in a resolution passed at the 1978 Assembly, and tax reform featured prominently in the Liberal election campaign in 1979 and in the bargaining with Labour during the Lib–Lab pact.[34] The 1979 Manifesto called for the introduction of a credit income tax, aimed at abolishing the means test and substituting cash credits for personal allowances, social security payments, and national insurance benefits. It also proposed a major switch from taxes on incomes to taxes on wealth and expenditure. This would have involved income tax starting at 20 per cent with a top rate of 50 per cent (it was at the time 83 per cent), a substantial increase in the tax threshold, and new gifts and wealth taxes. These reforms would be accompanied by other

[34] Liberal policies were set out in detail in the resolution passed at the 1978 Assembly. The Liberal party publishes the full text of all resolutions passed at its conferences, although there is no complete record of the debates themselves.

changes including the introduction of self-assessment of tax liability, the indexation of some tax rates, the replacement of the National Insurance employers' contribution by a regionally varied payroll tax, and a major reform of local-government finance to allow rates to be abolished and to give local authorities the powers to levy their own taxes to fund the local services they wanted to provide. These ideas (particularly the shift to indirect taxes) are more in line with traditional Liberal ideas about taxation and individual liberty, although they would not necessarily reduce the overall level of taxation or make the tax system more inegalitarian in its effects. Some of the reforms (particularly on local-government finance) would decentralize the way in which taxes were collected and distributed, but others (particularly the credit income tax and the wealth tax) would equip governments with powerful new fiscal instruments for pursuing egalitarian social policies. Few Liberals seem to have been attracted by proposals to erect a fiscal constitution − placing legal and constitutional limits on the extent to which governments can raise taxes and defining closely the purposes for which taxes can be spent.

The Liberals pinned their faith on effecting through their tax and industrial reforms a major change of attitude and a new spirit of enterprise and co-operation. This was the key to solving Britain's economic problems. As John Pardoe wrote in his pamphlet, *We Must Conquer Inflation*: Liberal industrial democracy is in the forefront of our plans to conquer inflation. It is the only way in which we can change the wage-demand process in a democratic society.'[35] But if such reforms were ever to be implemented then the system of adversary politics had first to be ended, because it destroyed continuity in policy, preventing either a sustained programme of planning or a sustained incomes policy. Liberals had long attacked the two-party system on the grounds that it entrenched class politics − the party of owners confronting the party of workers. They had always stressed that they

[35] John Pardoe, *We Must Conquer Inflation*, 1974, p. 23. John Pardoe and Richard Wainwright emerged in the 1970s as the Liberal Party's two leading economic spokesmen in Parliament.

were a classless party in the sense that they were not tied to any major interest and were able to consider dispassionately the right economic policy for the nation. The 1966 Manifesto blamed the slow progress of the modernization strategy on the two-party system: 'Both parties have their roots firmly in one section of the community or another. The Conservatives both ideologically and financially are still tied to the interests of capital. Equally Labour are tied to the interests of the Unions, often to the detriment of both.'[36]

The diagnosis grew much more critical in subsequent years with the dramatic escalation of Britain's economic problems and an equally dramatic growth in the inability of governments to cope with them. The acceleration of inflation with all its attendant dislocation of the economy and expectations, the return of mass unemployment and the onset in the mid-1970s of the first generalized world recession since the war, and the emergence of a major fiscal crisis, were accompanied by serious industrial unrest and fears for political stability. No Government proved capable of riding the storms. The Wilson Government fell in 1970, the Heath Government in 1974, the Callaghan Government in 1979. All were judged to have failed in their central objective — managing the economy successfully and remedying its persistent weaknesses. Policy in certain areas was subject to violent fluctuations. For Liberals the only possible solution was constitutional changes which would ensure the formation of stable coalition governments, ending the zig-zag of policy caused by the alternation in office of the two class-based parties. In his foreword to the October 1974 Manifesto Jeremy Thorpe declared: 'Liberals are unashamedly committed to breaking the two-party system in which the Party of Management alternates with the Party of Trade Unionism, each committed to the reversal of their predecessors' policies. Both interest groups represent vital elements in our society. Neither should ever be allowed to dominate the

---

[36] Liberal Party Manifesto, 1966. In the early 1960s Michael Young had argued that there was an opportunity for a radical consumers party to redress the influence of the producer groups.

thinking of the government of the day.'[37] In 1979 David Steel was even more forthright:

We have tried confrontation politics for long enough. In 1964, in 1970, in 1974, incoming governments promised that they held the key to Britain's industrial and social problems, if only they could undo the achievements of their predecessors and push their own prescriptions through Parliament. The hopes they raised have all been cruelly disappointed. It is high time to try a different pattern of government, which is based upon the support and the consent of the broad majority of the electorate. That alone can now provide the basis for the long-term programme of reform which Britain so desperately needs . . . until we break the two-party stranglehold, until we get away from the adversary class politics which are embedded in our Parliamentary structure, we cannot successfully tackle the problems of economic weakness and industrial mistrust.[38]

In the 1970s the opportunity to pursue sustained economic policies was thus seen by Liberals to depend upon constitutional reform. The response of the Liberal leadership to the wreck of policies and the disappointing of hopes in the years after 1959 was not a challenge to the basis of the post-war consensus, but a search for ways in which that consensus might be restored and strengthened. The party leaders refused to launch a traditional Liberal assault upon public spending or to challenge what many former Liberals now regarded as the main threat to a marked economy — the power of the trade unions. Instead they advocated continuing attempts to reach agreement with all interests involved in industrial society on policies that could secure prosperity, participation, and economic and social progress.

The Liberal leadership held fast to this line since it was so closely tied to their conception of the role of the Liberal party in British politics and the possibilities of entering government. The emergence of the SDP and the possibility that the realignment of political forces which had eluded the Liberals for so long might at last be at hand further reinforced the Leadership's commitments to its policies.

---

[37] Liberal Party Manifesto, *Why Britain Needs Liberal Government*, 1974, p. 1.

[38] Liberal Party Manifesto 1979, pp. 1–2. The validity of an adversary politics analysis of British economic policy is the subject of a forthcoming study by Professor S. A. Walkland and myself. See also Richard Rose, *Do Parties Make a Difference?*, 1980.

There were other currents of opinion in the party which drew different lessons from the failure of the modernization strategy and the challenge to Keynesianism and the welfare state which the end of the long post-war boom had brought. There were some like Jo Grimond who now recanted their former faith in the possibilities of benign state management and rediscovered the virtues of a Liberal anti-state position. Grimond, the architect in the 1950s of the new Liberalism, could be found in the 1970s regretting that it was the Conservatives who had seized on the new liberal ideas stemming from Hayek, Chicago, and the Institute of Economic Affairs and had developed a strategy for a social market economy. He came to see the failures of economic management as resulting from the size of the public sector and the abuse of their monopoly power by the trade unions. 'It is the size and nature of the public sector', he wrote, 'which makes the economy so difficult politically to manage.'[39] He praised the clarity and coherence of Keith Joseph's speeches and urged the party to reject state socialism and corporatism and instead 'reassert more fertile traditions, the free market plus co-operation plus community development. On these three pillars a self-respecting modern community could be built.'[40]

Grimond looked forward to a realignment on the Right. The main divide in politics, he argued, had come to be between those who would fight for a free society and those who still supported the Labour party.[41] This was the position he and the party had rejected in the 1950s with the result that many of the radical individualists had drifted away. In the 1970s there were many Liberal activists who while they agreed with Grimond's emphasis on anti-State perspectives, and on the importance of co-operatives and community development, disagreed strongly about the sanctity of the free market. This was not because they doubted the value of markets but because they observed how existing markets in an industrial society often did not function to create a liberal society. Where Grimond, like social market Conservatives,

---

[39] Jo Grimond, *The Common Welfare,* 1978, p. 52. He goes on to argue in this book that the case for charging for social services now convinces him.

[40] Grimond, *Memoirs,* p. 261.   [41] Ibid., p. 262.

saw trade union power as the worst form of centralized power, the radical Liberals tended to sympathize with trade-union power as primarily defensive in character and were much more prone to condemn concentrations of corporate power, for instance multinational companies. The response of these Liberals to the breakdown of consensus on economic management and the new world economic problems of the 1970s was to question the necessity and the desirability of economic growth, the power and the priorities of the corporate sector, and the affluence of the industrialized West, and to begin discussing the problems of organizing a post-industrial society, restructuring work and leisure, planning technological change, and conserving resources. There were calls for a new Liberal Yellow Book and arguments for an economic policy that aimed at low or zero growth.[42] Since the party was still so strongly committed to a modernization strategy the idea of *aiming* for no growth at all was highly subversive of existing Liberal thinking. But it could draw on ideas put forward by John Stuart Mill and Keynes and it was fueled by increasing concerns about the effects of industrial societies upon their environment. An amendment supporting zero growth was rejected at the 1972 Conference, but the Liberals led the way in pioneering ecological perspectives in British politics, and the world recession, the return of mass unemployment, and the appearance of new technologies, particularly microprocessors, brought new support. To those who thought that economic growth was undesirable were added those who thought it was no longer feasible and that the problem facing industrial societies was how to adjust to a long period of economic stagnation. As John Pardoe put it in 1981: 'Liberals hold many different views of growth, ranging from the view that it is all bad through the view that some is good and some is bad, to the outright view that you can't have enough of it. But the facts are that whether we want growth or not we are almost certainly not going to get it.'[43] By this time the party

---

[42] See, for example, Harry Cowie, *A Chance to Work*, 1981 and *Full Employment Without Inflation*, 1982. Cowie was the Liberals' Director of Research in the 1960s and has remained one of the party's leading policy-thinkers.

[43] John Pardoe at the Liberal Party Assembly 1981, quoted in *Liberal Economic Strategy*, Policy Division, December 1981.

had already abandoned its earlier stance in favour of growth. In a key resolution passed in 1979 it was asserted that 'sustained economic growth as conventionally measured is neither achievable nor desirable'. The reasons included the increasing scarcity of natural resources and the international imbalance of economic power.

Such views, if acted upon, indicated a rather different future economic policy and political strategy for the Liberals. In place of a realignment of the centre to sustain a programme of state management, expansion, and modernization, it suggested a realignment of those forces on the political Left which wanted economic policies that would challenge existing concentrations of power, existing priorities of production, and the existing organization of industrial and domestic labour. These debates about the shape of a post-industrial society had only just begun by the end of the 1970s but looked certain to grow in importance in the 1980s.

6. CONCLUSION

The Liberal party at the beginning of the 1980s was equipped with a distinct and reasonably coherent set of economic policies. Liberal goals were quite clear but, as the period of the Lib–Lab pact showed, the translation of these into practical policies may prove more difficult than Liberals have sometimes imagined. Liberal 'victories' such as the partial rescinding of the 5½p. petrol-duty increase in the 1977 Budget, the cut in income tax by 1p in the 1978 Finance Bill, help for small businesses, enabling legislation to assist the spread of profit-sharing schemes, were rather meagre compared to the Liberal vision of a transformed industrial society.

The party had clear and in many cases distinctive policies in all three major branches of economic policy. In foreign economic policy it was committed to the EEC and an eventual European Federation; in stabilization policy it advocated an incomes policy to control inflation, and tax reforms and a limited reflation[44] to reduce unemployment; while in in-

[44] See the details of the reflationary package of £9 billion spread over three years, designed to create one million jobs, as laid out in *A Chance to Work*.

dustrial policy it was committed to introducing co-ownership and stimulating competition.

The Liberals faced a dilemma in the 1970s because the unravelling of the post-war consensus was as painful for Liberals as for social democrats and many socialists, since the Liberals had invested so much ideologically in its success. Despite some new radical thinking there were not many signs that the party was about to forsake the positions it had long held. Monetarism was fiercely attacked in pamphlets and policy statements,[45] but the obvious gap in the party's armour was that it was forced to concede the limits of traditional Keynesianism, so had few immediate policies for dealing with unemployment and the critical state of British industry. The party had become more critical of public expenditure but many of its Conference resolutions still proposed new spending programmes. The party was also determined to avoid any appearance of hostility to the trade unions, but its thinking on relations between the unions and any future Liberal Government was not greatly advanced. There remained a general presumption in favour of intervention. The market economy was certainly not praised in Liberal publications as Sir Keith Joseph and the Centre for Policy Studies praised it. The Liberal economic ideal remained in the words of a 1970 Young Liberal policy statement: 'an economic system which enables each individual to achieve fulfilment through his work, which distributes the proceeds of industry to all, and which, denying excessive power to the bureaucracy and to those who own capital, guarantees to each worker the right to share in the direction and rewards of his labour'.[46]

These were fine sentiments. But if Liberals should find themselves in government could they cope with the immediate and severe pressures of economic management in ways that opened up rather than frustrated opportunities to implement their radical reorganization of the institutions of the economy?

[45] See e.g. Cowie, 1981 and 1982, Pardoe, 1974, R. Finnie, *The Alternative Economic Strategy* (1981) and *The Economy and Industry* (1980); and John Williamson, *British Economic Recovery* (mimeo), Policy unit, 1981.

[46] Quoted in M. Meadowcroft, *Liberal Values for a new decade* (LPD), 1980.

10. The Liberals and Europe

Alan Butt Philip

The Liberal Party has been conspicuous in its consistent support since 1945 for European unification. The party has at various times backed proposals to set up a European Coal and Steel Community, a European Defence Community, the Western European Union, the European Free Trade Area, and the European Economic Community. The Liberal Party in the 1980s supports the idea of economic and monetary union and seeks to rebalance and strengthen the institutions of European Community, especially the European Parliament. Yet this commitment to European unification appears on closer inspection not to be quite as firm and consistent; nor has it necessarily sat easily alongside the long-standing internationalist tradition of Liberalism.

LIBERAL INTERNATIONALISM

The Liberal tradition of internationalism owes much to the history of liberalism in the eighteenth and nineteenth centuries. By stressing the rights of the individual and of self-determination the Liberals were hardly friends of the then international order, as determined by the Congress of Vienna. The liberal concern with liberty, human decency, and progress did not recognize political boundaries: it was and is universal. Mr Gladstone's famous campaigns over the Bulgarian horrors (1876) and the Armenian atrocities (1896) were early evidence of the concern which contemporary Liberals show for the victims of tyranny and racialism. Liberals have generally sought to assist popular democratic movements to overthrow feudal monarchies and to substitute

---

[1] The author wishes to acknowledge the assistance given to this research by Miss Muriel Burton, who has made her own unpublished study of the Liberals' attitudes to European integration. The judgements made in this paper are however the sole responsibility of the author.

constitutional government. Liberalism and nationalism, early allies in the struggles to establish democracies in Europe, were gradually to part company in the late nineteenth century, as men such as Lord Acton came to recognize the political and moral dangers inherent in exaggerated conceptions of the ideas of the nation-state and self-determination.

In Britain the Liberal Party in the late nineteenth century was decidedly anti-Unionist: it favoured decentralization and constitutional reforms which might have loosened the links between the constituent parts of the United Kingdom. This standpoint in support of the grievances of the Irish, the Scots, and the Welsh (the first two points in the Newcastle Programme of 1891 were Irish Home Rule and Welsh disestablishment) corresponded with the Liberals' growing awareness of the drawbacks and the perils of large nation-states mobilized by popular nationalism. Many Liberals found themselves at the rough end of anti-Boer and jingoistic agitations in the early years of the twentieth century. Their abhorrence of wars, especially where mass destruction of civilian as well as military personnel was involved, led them to pay more heed to the need for international order and collective security. In this, Lloyd George's international peacekeeping efforts between 1918 and 1922 were typical of the Liberal commitment to a managed peace on terms that the defeated could respect. Liberals in the inter-war years played a central role in the organization of the League of Nations Union in Britain and many were well-known advocates of world government. In the 1930s the Liberal Party became increasingly alarmed at the breakdown of the Versailles Treaty settlement and at German and Italian expansionism. Many Liberals allied themselves with Churchill in calling for rearmament at home and sanctions abroad against those countries which did not respect their international obligations. Europe's experience of Nazi domination in the 1930s and 1940s left Liberals more than ever committed to collective security and to supranationalism, especially in Europe, as the means by which future wars could be prevented.

LIBERAL REACTIONS TO EUROPE AND THE
EUROPEAN COMMUNITIES 1945–75

The way in which Liberals were to choose to apply these general principles in the post-war years was far from clear in 1945. Liberal opinion was sharply divided, at least at leadership level, between those like Professor Gilbert Murray and Dingle Foot who stressed the Liberal interest in strengthening international ties world-wide and those such as Frances Josephy and Lord Layton who argued for a more European focus to Britain's foreign relations, and even perhaps a federation of European states. In the House of Commons this was matched by a difference of approach between Clement Davies MP who saw European unity as a step along the road to world government and Wilfred Roberts MP who argued that joint economic planning of the European economies should be undertaken with the benefit of Marshall Aid. A resolution endorsing 'a functional approach' to the unity of Europe was carried by the 1947 Liberal Assembly and the following year an even stronger resolution was passed by the Assembly, a month before the famous Hague Congress.

Yet the debate on this occasion revealed a clear division over the issue of European federalism. The resolution of 1948 strongly supported the formation in Western Europe of a political and economic 'association' in the context of the Marshall Plan and the Treaty of Brussels. It went on to state: 'This association of European states must also deal with the long-term problems of common economic development, including in particular the scaling of barriers to international trade; of common defence and the definition and enforcement amongst its members of a Charter of Human Rights.' The resolution advocated the creation in Western Europe of a 'political union strong enough to save European democracy and the values of Western civilization, and a trading area large enough, with the Colonial Territories, to enable its component parts to achieve economic recovery and stability'. It also called for an 'emergency policy' for a Council of Western Europe, comprising the sixteen ERP countries and West Germany, with international staff to co-ordinate social,

economic, and defence policies, to be followed later by a
'democratic federation of Europe' with wide powers brought
into being by 'a constituent assembly composed of representatives chosen by the parliaments of the participating
states' which would frame a federal constitution for Europe.[2]
Not for the first time Liberal leaders – such as Lady Violet
Bonham Carter, Lord Samuel, and Philip Fothergill – advised
caution and they were able to add to the resolution amendments which stressed that the suggested European association
should not conflict with United Nations, Commonwealth, or
American interests.

But on the key issue of a federal Europe it was the younger
delegates in 1948 who insisted on this commitment and
supported the strong line taken by Lord Layton, Wilfred
Roberts, and Frances Josephy. Roberts followed this up with
an all-party motion on similar lines which attracted the
signatures of ninety MPs.[3] A clear and practical test of
Liberal opinion emerged in the summer of 1950 with the
Schuman Plan, which led to the signing of the Treaty of
Paris in 1951 and the setting-up of a European Coal and
Steel Community in 1952. While Labour viewed M. Robert
Schuman's ideas with scepticism and the Conservatives
refused to commit themselves to joining the ECSC, Liberal
spokesmen such as Lord Layton and Sir Andrew McFadyean
not only endorsed in principle the plan to put the coal and
steel industries of Europe under a common authority, but
also fully accepted the supranational character of the
proposals. This was the theme repeated by Clement Davies,
the Liberal leader, in the House of Commons on 27 June
1950 when he seconded a Conservative motion supporting
the Schuman Plan. But two notable Liberal dissentients,
who were later to join the Labour Party, were Lady Megan
Lloyd George and Dingle Foot: they could not accept such
a pooling of sovereignty involving basic industries in Britain
or Davies's view expressed some years later that the ECSC
was 'the finest step towards peace in the world which has
ever been made'.[4]

---

[2] *Liberal News,* 16 April 1948.   [3] HC Debates, 5 May 1948, Col. 1305.
[4] HC Debates, 21 February 1955, Col. 899.

The abortive plan to set up a European Defence Community was also supported by the Liberals until the French rejected it in 1954. After this the period between 1956 and 1959 saw evidence of some vacillation by British Liberals in regard to European policy. The Liberal Party was still committed in principle to European integration along federal lines, but had some difficulty in giving a coherent response once the British government embarked upon negotiations to set up a European Free Trade Area as an alternative to UK membership of the European Economic Community. Shortly before Jo Grimond succeeded Clement Davies as Liberal leader at the end of 1956 the Liberal Assembly meeting in Folkestone had passed a resolution calling for Britain's active participation in the setting-up of a Common Market. But the Treaty of Rome was signed in March 1957 without Britain, and the Liberal leadership appears then to have opted to support the European Free Trade Area idea as second best. Thus one year after the Folkestone resolution, the Liberal Assembly at Southport supported a motion calling for Britain to take a 'positive lead' in the European Free Trade Area negotiations.

A major factor in the apparent backpedalling in 1957 on previous Liberal commitments to Europe seems to have been the change in the party leadership. Whereas Clement Davies had been prepared to leave European policy to other Liberal MPs such as Donald Wade and Arthur Holt, Jo Grimond clearly signalled that a free trade area arrangement, if it could be obtained was preferable to the customs union which was to be the basis of the new EEC.[5] But with the breakdown of the negotiations at the end of 1958 which led to the division of Western Europe into EFTA and EEC camps, a clearer Liberal line emerged. The new EFTA (European Free Trade Association) was to be devoid of political content, lacking institutions or any supranational commitment. Liberals when faced with such a choice opted decisively for the EEC road towards European unity and promptly found themselves politically out on a limb. The election of Mark

[5] *Liberal News*, 1 February 1957 and J. S. Rasmussen, *The Liberal Party* (London, 1965), pp. 133–42. Other commentaries on the Liberal approach to the European Communities can be found in H. Cowie, *Why Liberal?* (1964), pp. 114–22 and R. Douglas, *History of the Liberal Party 1895–1970* (1971), pp. 273–5.

Bonham Carter as MP for Torrington in March 1958 resulted in a more incisive approach to European issues, and throughout 1959 Bonham Carter and Holt made speech after speech in the House of Commons arguing both that it was in Britain's and in the Commonwealth's interests to join the EEC and that the consequences of staying apart from the Community would be more serious for Britain than the difficulties which membership might create.

Although the Liberals did not give pride of place to the question of EEC membership at the 1959 general election, half the Liberal candidates mentioned Britain's relationhsip with the European Community in their election addresses.[6] In December 1959 a Liberal amendment in the House of Commons regretting 'the failure of H. M. Government to associate Great Britain with the countries comprising the EEC' was brushed aside and British membership of EFTA was then endorsed in the Conservative-dominated Commons by 182 votes to three.[7] From 1959 onwards there was no wavering in the official Liberal line on the EEC and a rapid change of view about the EEC among business, political, and civil service élites in 1960-1 merely confirmed Liberals in their belief that they had been right about Europe all along. The leadership of political opinion in Britain on the subject of the EEC clearly passed out of Liberal hands when the Prime Minister announced in July 1961 that Britain would be opening negotiations for EEC membership. The European Community thereby moved to the centre of the political stage, and has remained a bone of contention between Tory and Labour ever since.

But the strains which both these parties experienced when, eventually parliament came to consider the terms on which Britain could join the EEC meant that the small group of Liberal MPs in the 1970-4 House of Commons were able to play a decisive part in securing British accession. Although in October 1971 MPs voted by a majority of 112 in favour of the principle of EEC membership (with 89 dissident Labour MPs more than compensating for the government's loss of

---

[6] D. Butler and R. Rose, *The British General Election of 1959* (1960), p. 132.
[7] HC Debates, 14 December 1959.

support from 41 Conservative MPs), when the necessary legislation came to be voted on by the House of Commons the pro-European Labour MPs stayed loyal to the official Labour stance.[8] The government did not recover the support of all its own anti-EEC MPs, thus leaving the political balance in the Commons on a knife-edge. Night after night five of the six Liberal MPs voted in divisions on the government side:[9] night after night the government won its case by majorities of between 4 and 54. The crucial vote on the second reading of the European Communities Bill was won by a mere eight votes on 17 February 1972.

The next landmark in the development of Britain's relations with the European Communities was the holding of the referendum in June 1975 to approve or reject the terms of accession which had been renegotiated by the new Labour government under Harold Wilson. The Liberal Party was profoundly sceptical about the whole renegotiation exercise but was happy to play a full part in the ensuing referendum. Jeremy Thorpe, the Liberal leader, had always opposed the referendum device as an affront to the supremacy of parliament, a view endorsed by the party as a whole although some Liberal MPs, including Jo Grimond and David Steel disagreed. The entire Liberal leadership co-operated with the 'Britain in Europe' campaign nationally and this was echoed at constituency level in joint campaigns with pro-European Conservatives and some Labour enthusiasts. The Liberal Party also mounted its own parallel campaign in favour of British membership of the European Communities. This stressed the more far-reaching political commitments of Liberals to a directly elected European Parliament, to a strong Community regional policy, and to economic and monetary union, while the economic advantages claimed for British membership by the 'Britain in Europe' campaign

[8] *Keesing's Contemporary Archives* (1971), p. 24930, names those MPs who did not follow their party's line. Sixty-nine Labour MPs voted with the government and twenty Labour MPs abstained. Thirty-nine Conservative MPs voted against the government and two abstained.

[9] The sixth Liberal MP, Emlyn Hooson (Montgomery), took the view that Britain should have joined the European Communities at the outset and that it was now too late to join on satisfactory terms. But by the time of the 1975 referendum he did not advocate British withdrawal from the EEC.

were given much less emphasis.[10] This separate Liberal
campaign however was largely swamped by the official
pro-EEC campaign, and was not helped by lack of finance
following two general elections. The Liberal Party spent only
£500 on its own campaign and donated anoter £500 to the
'Britain in Europe' campaign, which later declared it had
spent over £1 million on the referendum.[11] The two-to-one
margin of victory for the pro-EEC campaigners naturally
pleased the Liberals, who were unused to being on the
winning side at the polls. There were sources of embarrassment
to the party: for one of the only two local-authority areas in
the country which voted against British membership was
Shetland, whose MP was Jo Grimond; further a disproportionate number of those voting against British membership
appeared from electoral and opinion-survey evidence to be
drawn from Liberal ranks, suggesting that Liberal leaders
and activists were out of line with over 50 per cent of the
party's voters.[12]

THE DISSENTING LIBERALS

Despite the often monolithic support within the Liberal
Party for committing Britain to membership of the European
Communities, there has always been a distinct minority
taking an opposite view. For a period between 1957 and
1958 even the Liberal leader, Jo Grimond, could be counted
as unenthusiastic about the EEC preferring a European free-
trade area to a customs union.[13] In the decade after the end
of the Second World War there were many Liberals who did
not believe that Britain's future lay almost wholly with her
European neighbours and allies: they still placed great weight
upon Britain's trade and political ties with North America
and the Commonwealth, and did not want Britain to sac-
rifice these or to treat Europe as a most-favoured region.
Most of these Liberals became reconciled to Britain's reduced

---

[10] D. Banks, *The Liberal Programme for Europe* (1975).

[11] D. Butler and U. Kitzinger, *The 1975 Referendum* (1976), p. 86.

[12] Ibid. pp. 271-2. A Gallup Poll taken shortly before the Referendum found
48 per cent of Liberals in the 'Yes' camp, 21 per cent in the 'No' camp, and 31
per cent abstaining.   [13] See above.

role in the world by the mid-fifties: some, like Dingle Foot, Megan Lloyd George, and Manuela Sykes, left the party, but for other reasons. Another group of dissentients were those who resisted the concept of a federal Europe growing out of the European Communities. Lord Samuel urged caution in the 1940s, and so did Lord Ogmore in the 1960s. Other Liberals resisted the technocratic image of the EEC, its lack of democratic control, the apparent impossibility of reform from within, and complained of its adverse impact on peripheral regions and developing countries: Emlyn Hooson, Peter Bessell, and Paul Tyler belonged to this category. Yet the most strident criticisms of the European Communities came from the traditional free-trade wing of the party who saw the Communities as capitalist cartels forcing dear food on the unsuspecting British. Roy Douglas, Oliver Smedley, S. W. Alexander, and Air Vice-Marshal 'Pathfinder' Bennett were the leaders of this group, but they found they carried less and less influence in the party on a variety of economic issues as the years passed. They formed a small Liberal anti-EEC caucus at the time of the EEC referendum in 1975 but made no distinct impact on the campaign. Their argument had been lost within the party as far back as the 1961 Assembly in Edinburgh when only six delegates voted against a resolution welcoming Britain's application to join the EEC. What is perhaps surprising is that despite having a few MPs and candidates in winnable seats as supporters as late as the early 1970s, the anti-Common Market Liberals were unable to drum up more interest in their case inside the party. Many of those with doubts about the party's European policy seem simply to have become reconciled to the inevitable and, perhaps in the interests of party unity, to have given up the fight and stayed within the fold, or, like Oliver Smedley and Air Vice-Marshal Bennett, to have left the party and carried on their anti-Market stance by other means. The Liberal dissenters on the EEC issue were to prove too politically divided amongst themselves to form an effective group within the party.

LIBERALS AND THE EUROPEAN PARLIAMENT

A central factor in Liberal support for the European Communities was their creation of supranational political institutions in Western Europe. Liberals who sought world government as well as those who yearned for political stability considered the institutions of the Community as an achievement in themselves, but ripe for further development. Yet there was always a desire by Liberals to bring in a truly international and democratic element into the functioning of these European institutions by means of an elected assembly or parliament which could exercise democratic control over them. So much was clear even in the 1948 resolution carried at the Liberal Assembly in Blackpool, although it called only for an indirectly elected assembly. The Liberal commitment to parliamentary methods of government made the demand for a democratic European assembly inescapable as soon as any major supranational powers were ceded by the national parliament. Thus when the referendum campaign was under way in 1975 Liberals, almost alone, stressed the importance of holding direct elections to the European Parliament while other pro-Europeans, like Edward Heath, sought to play down this commitment. An element of party interest can also be attributed to the Liberals' highlighting the commitment to a directly elected European parliament. Article 138 of the Rome Treaty calls for such elections to be held using 'a uniform procedure' and, aware that no other European democracy uses the British 'first-past-the-post' electoral system, Liberal spokesmen, including Jeremy Thorpe, saw in direct elections a lever for securing the introduction of proportional representation in Britain.

In the early years of British membership of the European Communities the Liberal Party sent two representatives to the nominated European Parliament — Russell Johnston MP and Lord Gladwyn, a former British Ambassador to Paris and the United Nations. According to some parliamentary conventions, the British Liberals could only expect one European seat, but a second seat was offered by the Heath government mainly because the Labour Party refused to take up its allocation of seats in the European Parliament. Following the 1975 referendum Labour decided to nominate a full delegation to the Parliament and, after a parliamentary row, Lord Gladwyn ceased to be a member.[14]

The surprise commitment at the end of 1974 of the European Council to direct elections led to the signature in September 1976 of an Act of the Community providing for an elected European Parliament but with each member state choosing its own electoral system and procedures. In the spring of 1976 the Callaghan government also lost its overall majority in the House of Commons, as a result of by-election defeats, and this was suddenly to provide the Liberals with some possible leverage in the House of Commons. At the same time some Liberals were publicly asking the question whether they should boycott the European elections if the method of election did not include some element of proportional representation.[15] The conclusion of the 'Lib–Lab pact' in March 1977 between the Labour government and the Parliamentary Liberal Party therefore not surprisingly included some undertakings about these forthcoming European elections. The first was a firm commitment to introduce the legislation necessary for the elections to the European Parliament to be held. Although the Labour government had agreed in Brussels the previous September to the holding of these direct elections, the Labour Party was officially opposed to them and there had been many suggestions that Labour should not even participate in the elections. The agreement between Mr Callaghan and Mr Steel committed the government for the first time to provide the parliamentary time and support to ensure that

---

[14] The row concerned both the decision to reduce Liberal representation in the delegation to the European Parliament and the way in which the choice between Russell Johnston and Lord Gladwyn had been made, initially without consulting the Liberal Party. Lord Gladwyn, a former UK Ambassador to France and the United Nations, was one of the early supporters of British entry into the EEC, setting out his case in *The European Idea* (1966).

[15] This issue was raised in *New Outlook* in 1976 and prompted the Liberal Party's national council to urge the party to look at the boycott proposal in the event of a first-past-the-post system being adopted. See the *Directory of Liberal Party Resolutions 1967–78* (1973), pp. 70–1.

the European Parliament elections took place.[16] Secondly the Labour government became committed as a result of the Callaghan–Steel agreement to recommending that the voting system used for these elections should be one of proportional representation. Although the Cabinet agreed to this — with some dissent — the Parliamentary Labour Party was not called upon to do so, and when a vote was taken on 13 December 1977 only 147 Labour MPs supported the regional-list form of proportional representation endorsed by the Labour and Liberal leadership: 115 Labour MPs voted against the regional-list system, nearly fifty Labour MPs abstained, and the vote was lost by 319 to 222.[17] The defeat by so many Labour MPs of a cherished Liberal policy affecting the development of the European Parliament provoked the Liberal Party to call a special national Assembly in January 1978 calling into question the whole Lib–Lab pact: but David Steel and his parliamentary colleagues survived this challenge without difficulty.[18] By this time the Liberals had become resigned to fighting the direct elections under an electoral system which would probably deprive them of their one remaining member of the European Parliament, Russell Johnston MP. In the event this pessimism was fully justified: the Liberal Party polled 13 per cent of the vote in Great Britain but failed to win a single seat. The irony and injustice of the largest Liberal Party in Europe and the most pro-European political force in Britain being excluded from the new European Parliament was not lost on many British observers and was scathingly attacked abroad.[19] A delegation of ten Liberal Euro-candidates travelled to Strasbourg for the opening of the new Parliament on 17 July 1979 to protest at the exclusion of Liberal representatives, claiming that the Liberal share of the vote entitled them all to sit as MEPs: their case was put by the leader of the Liberal group in the Parliament, Herr Martin Bangemann, at the opening session. In the autumn of 1979 the Liberal Party,

[16] D. Steel, *A House Divided* (1980), pp. 36–42.
[17] HC Debates, 13 December 1977.
[18] The Lib–Lab pact was endorsed by a majority of 1727 votes to 520 by the special Assembly held on 21 January 1978.
[19] See *Le Monde*, 12 June 1979.

with encouragement from the National Committee for Electoral Reform, sought a ruling from the European Court of Human Rights but this was subsequently refused. Thus British Liberal influence in the European Parliament could only be exerted by proxy: Russell Johnston was made an honorary member of the Liberal and Democrat group while Richard Moore, a former adviser to Jeremy Thorpe, joined the group's secretariat in a senior position. Meanwhile through its international contacts the Liberal Party has tried to lobby hard for the European Parliament to adopt a measure requiring the use by Britain of a proportional-representation voting system at the next European elections to be held in 1984. As a start a Belgian Liberal was chosen to chair the Parliament's subcommittee drawing up the measure, but even though the Parliament has agreed to proportional representation, the real political obstacles will of course be encountered in the Council of Ministers, in Downing Street, and in the House of Commons.

BRITISH LIBERALS AND EUROPEAN LIBERALS

After the Second World War a number of Liberals in several countries decided to formalize the existing international contact between Liberals by founding the Liberal International. Together they made a common declaration of principles — at a conference in Oxford in 1948 — and were able to secure the support of many Liberal parties throughout the world, and also of individuals who had no Liberal party in their own country or who were exiles from countries where democracy had been extinguished.[20] Although there was representation from America (especially Canada) and Asia, the bulk of Liberal International's support came from Western Europe. The Liberal tradition is one of the three historic political families in West European politics, alongside Christian Democracy and Social Democracy. There are many Liberal parties in Europe but individual countries' political history, culture, and ecology has over time heavily contributed to these parties developing often sharply differing

[20] *Liberal International: World Liberal Union* (1977).

attitudes.[21] Some writers have distinguished the Anglo-Scandinavian Liberal tradition with its radical and tolerant Christian orientation from its Continental counterpart — a liberalism that is rooted in nineteenth-century economic liberalism and the anticlerical struggles of that epoch.[22] Such a distinction, although useful, does not tell us much about what separates individual liberal parties from each other. The issue of European integration has not brought Liberals in Europe as a whole together: instead it has created a two-tier internationalism for Liberals in which only EEC Liberals enjoy specially close relations with each other. Liberals in Scandinavia (except Denmark), Switzerland, Austria, and the Iberian peninsular have become outsiders as a separate organization for EEC Liberals has been spawned — the Federation of European Liberals and Democrats — to organize and campaign for liberalism in the European Community, and especially in the European Parliament. The closeness of ties developing between many European Liberal parties within the Community is still something of an élite experience, and has been achieved at a price. True, the formation of ELD has brought new blood into the Liberal camp — notably the Giscardian Parti Républicain and the Italian Republican Party; but the Danish Radikale Venstre and the French left-wing radicals who work within the Liberal International framework have been forced on ideological grounds not to join ELD. Norwegian Liberalism has been dealt a very heavy blow by the EEC issue: the Liberal Party split on this issue and only the anti-integrationist Liberals are now represented in the Storting, and in much reduced numbers. Nor should it be forgotton how divided were the French Radicals under Mendès-France when, in the mid-1950s, they had to decide whether France should join

[21] For fuller discussion of the variety of Liberal political attitudes in Europe see R. Moore and C. Morgan, *The Liberals in Europe* (1975); M. Steed, *Who's a Liberal in Europe?* (1976); S. Henig (ed.), *Political Parties in the European Communities* (1979); and G. and P. Pridham, *Towards Transnational Parties in the European Community* (1979).

[22] See, for example, M. Salvadori, *The Liberal Heresy* (1977) and M. Steed, op. cit.

the EEC.[23] The British Liberal Party was clearly spared the agonizing doubts and splits that some other Liberals experienced on the European integration issue, and it was regarded as a matter of course that once Britain joined the European Community British Liberals should begin to work very closely with other Liberals in the EEC, especially as direct elections to the European Parliament were foreshadowed, and hence a common Liberal campaign across Western Europe was to be expected. The experience of rubbing shoulders with so many Liberal government ministers on the Continent of Europe in the course of preparing for direct elections can only have strengthened British Liberals' enthusiasm for power-sharing and coalition government.

The first move was made in 1973 at the annual congress of the Liberal International when a resolution was passed requiring the setting-up of a European Liberal party organization for which only EEC member parties would be eligible. This resulted eventually in the founding of the Federation of European Liberals and Democrats in Stuttgart in March 1976 accompanied by the issue of a common Declaration to which the founding parties subscribed. At the Liberal Assembly in Scarborough the previous autumn a resolution had been carried endorsing the ELD Federation plans but stipulating that the new Federation should not include the French Republican Independents, supporters of President Giscard.[24] When the first ELD delegate congress met in The Hague in November 1976 the French Republicans slipped in their membership application the day before it opened and it was automatically accepted. This threw the British Liberal and French left-wing Radical delegations into confusion: the latter walked out of the congress but the British decided reluctantly to stay. The Hague congress was followed by congresses in Brussels (1977) and London (1978) leading up to an international rally in Luxembourg in April 1979 to

---

[23] See P. Williams, *Crisis and Compromise: Politics in the Fourth Republic* (1964) and F. O'Neill, *The French Radical Party and European Integration* (1981).

[24] The exposition of Liberal objections to the French Républicains Indépendants and their successor party, the Parti Républicain, is given clearest expression in M. Steed, *The French Threat* (1976), also published in *New Outlook*, vol. 16, No. 1, January 1976.

launch the European Liberals' direct-elections campaign. The congresses were able to agree joint policies on most subjects relevant to the Community with comparatively few major disagreements — mainly expressed by the French on the development of European integration and regionalism. These policies were then incorporated in a joint ELD manifesto for the 1979 European elections and it was upon this manifesto that the British Liberals based their campaign, adding a few paragraphs of their own.[25] The British Liberals were however mandated by the Liberal Assembly in Blackpool in September 1980 to move the expulsion of French Republicans from the ELD, as a result of delegates' anger at the Republicans' political line in the European elections and their links with the British Conservative Party: but this move found no support from other ELD parties and embarrassed the British representatives on the ELD executive. The British Liberals found themselves in the uncomfortable position of not liking some of their political associates but having no alternative home. The reasons why the Liberal leadership in Britain did not share some of their radical activists' misgivings about ELD membership can be briefly stated. The ELD Federation was a Liberal International and European Liberal leaders' initiative in which the British Liberals, especially Jeremy Thorpe, had played a full part from the outset. It was therefore most unlikely that they would ever seek to undermine their own invention, especially as the Liberal leaders across Western Europe had established a good rapport amongst each other. Instead leading British Liberals appealed for tolerance from their radical supporters. Secondly, the British Liberals found they had little tangible support elsewhere in the ELD for taking a strong line with the French Republicans: even members of other Liberal parties who disliked the Republicans' politics recognized that the Giscardian members of any Liberal group in the European Parliament were too numerically important to lose. In fact as a result of the first direct elections seventeen of the forty Liberal MPs were French Giscardians, of whom four were Radicals — and thus

[25] *Programme for Europe* (1979). See also the *Times Guide to the European Parliament* (1979).

linked to Liberal International. The lack of coherence of the resulting Liberal group was quickly shown up when the European Parliament voted at the end of 1979 to reject the Communities' 1980 budget: the Liberal group was split down the middle with all but two of the Giscardians voting in favour of the budget and thus against almost all their Liberal allies.[26] Thirdly, some British Liberal ideas of forming a smaller but more radical Liberal grouping in the European Parliament and outside foundered on several obstacles: for most of the ELD parties showed no interest in such an idea; and all the suggested allies, such as the Dutch D'66 and the French left-wing Radicals, were numerically weak; the British Liberals had no MEPs at all after elections, and the combined forces of radical liberalism in the European Parliament would not even be large enough to count as a parliamentary group, with all the facilities and procedural powers that such status entails.

The fourth element in the British Liberals' acceptance of ELD membership alongside the French Republicans was financial. Although there have been years when the Liberal Party has had some difficulty in paying its annual subscription to the ELD, the financial rewards at the time of the 1979 European elections were considerable — in cash and in kind. Liberal headquarters in London received approximately £175,000 in the years 1978 and 1979 from ELD for fighting the European elections and ELD received this money from the Liberal and Democrat group of members of the European Parliament.[27] This finance effectively paid for the lion's share of the campaign costs and would certainly not have been forthcoming from any other source. The presence of the French Republicans in the ELD group in the Parliament effectively increased the amount of money the ELD made available to British Liberals.

[26] Debates of the European Parliament, 13 December 1979, OJ No. 249, Annex, pp. 200-1.
[27] Annual Reports and Accounts of the Liberal Party Organization 1979 and 1980. The financing of the European elections is also discussed in D. Butler and D. Marquand, *European Elections and British Politics* (1981).

LIBERAL POLICIES IN AN EEC CONTEXT

The Liberal opponents of British membership of the European Communities undoubtedly had a point in highlighting the consequences of membership for the traditional Liberal rallying cries of free trade and cheap food. Pro-Community Liberal spokesmen frequently had to project their ideal view of the world on to the Community level in order to fend off such opposition: the Community would thus be presented as the best means of achieving many established Liberal policies.

The European Communities have certainly operated a trading policy that was different from the relatively open trading system, with Commonwealth preference, which was the typical British arrangement. The common external tariff of the EEC which effectively puts a ring-fence of protection around member states is far from palatable to the free traders. But while the EEC may result in protection against third countries, it is also designed to bring about complete free trade within the Community: so a loss is balanced by a gain. In addition it became clear early on that Commonwealth preference, affecting the least developed countries, could be reproduced on an EEC scale if former British possessions were given the same privileged access to European markets as their French counterparts. Thus membership of the EEC was presented by Liberals as a way of widening the markets open to most of the Commonwealth, although some of the larger states, especially the former dominions, would not be included. This was one of the themes pressed by Mark Bonham Carter at the Llandudno Liberal Assembly as early as September 1962.[28]

The other sensitive area of policy was inevitably agriculture. The UK government's decision to seek membership of the EEC came at a time when the deficiency-payments system of subsidizing farm incomes was proving expensive and unpredictable. Liberals were therefore prepared to look sympathetically at alternatives. The common agricultural policy, based on intervention in the market to maintain

---

[28] S. Holt stresses the break with the free-trade tradition this implied in G. Ionescu (ed.), *The New Politics of European Integration* (1972), p. 69.

common prices, was not yet fully operational nor apparently as costly as the British deficiency payments system. It did however offer the prospect of expansion to the agriculture industry and this was emphasized by Jeremy Thorpe at the Liberal Assembly in Edinburgh in 1961. Agriculture is a subject of major significance in the Liberal Party because so many of its MPs and its most promising constituencies are to be found in highly rural areas.[29] So, despite the consumer bias of traditional free-trade principles, the Liberal leadership was well disposed to commit itself to a policy which promised rural advantages. Subsequently criticism of the common agricultural policy strengthened in the party throughout the 1970s, although the special anxieties of the hill-farming areas about the future of their subsidies were overcome by the passing of the less-favoured areas directive in 1975.[30] Nevertheless by 1980 the party's agriculture spokesman, Geraint Howells, MP for Cardigan, was calling for British withdrawal from the CAP and the Liberal Assembly in Blackpool that same year perhaps unwittingly gave the impression that Liberals were no longer prepared to accept the objective of agricultural self-sufficiency within the Community.[31] The strong Liberal criticism of the CAP, although featured in the party's 1979 general- and European-election manifestos, was not however pressed very far with other Liberal parties in the EEC: for British Liberal allies in the Netherlands, Denmark, and West Germany take a rather favourable view of the CAP as it affects their farmers. Fisheries have also been a contentious issue for pro-EEC Liberals because Liberal MPs have had local constituency interests to protect, especially inshore fishing: this has prompted

[29] The three most agricultural constituencies in the United Kingdom are all traditional Liberal bastions — Montgomery, Cardigan, and Orkney & Zetland. A list of the 100 most agricultural seats is given in D. Butler and D. Kavanagh, *The British General Election of October 1974* (1975).

[30] The less-favoured areas directive (Council Directive 75/268/EEC) legitimized the existing British hill-cow and hill-sheep subsidies by permitting the payment of 'compensatory allowances' in specified 'less-favoured areas' throughout the European Community.

[31] The 1980 resolution accused the CAP of being 'a major barrier to both the economic and the political development of the EEC' by virtue of its 'inflexibility, injustice and inefficiency'.

tough and critical stands by Cornish Liberal MPs, by Jo Grimond as MP for Orkney and Shetland and by Alan Beith, the MP for Berwick-upon-Tweed. But Liberals in general, with the exception of the Scottish Liberal Party, have preferred to leave this issue to be handled by those directly affected except in the case of the 'cod war' with Iceland in 1976 where the Liberals' national council repudiated the strong-arm tactics of the British government.[32]

On economic and industrial policies there have been far fewer policy difficulties for Liberals in a Community context. Having long called for greater policy co-operation and co-ordination among European and other developing countries the onset of common European economic policies posed no problems for Liberals, provided political control at the supranational level was assured. Thus at the 1962 Assembly John Pardoe persuaded the party to accept monetary integration, the pooling of UK currency reserves, and a five-year plan for industry integrated with the European target rate of growth once British was part of the Community. Later on Liberals were happy to support the EEC commitment to economic and monetary union in 1969 and the development of the 'snake' and, later still, the European Monetary System which Liberals consider Britain should have joined early in 1979.

Nor have the industrial policies of the European Communities created difficulties for British Liberals. Rather there has been dismay that so little has been achieved by the Community in the restructuring of key industrial sectors (other than coal and steel) and in the pooling of research and development expenditures and of technology. The competition policy, with its emphasis on restraining price-fixing, monopolies, and mergers and removing trade distortions, is fully supported by Liberals, as are the Community's moves to harmonize company law and make industrial democracy mandatory for larger firms. But Liberals deplore the lack of an effective common energy policy, while for the most part being unaware of the Community's commitment to and financing of the expansion of nuclear power — a policy to

---

[32] See *The Directory of Liberal Resolutions*, p. 7.

which British Liberals are opposed within the United Kingdom.
Environmental issues in general have been of keen concern to
Liberals since the late 1960s and they would welcome a
more effective Community impact in this sphere, especially
as regards pollution.

From the time Britain became a member of the Communities, Liberals have argued for common measures to
improve employment prospects and opportunities, and for
the expansion of the European Social Fund, whose emphasis
on training for future employment corresponds well with
Liberal thinking about Britain's needs. The priorities given
by this Fund for disadvantaged groups in the labour market,
including women, migrant workers, and the handicapped,
have also been welcomed. In contrast, the development of
a European regional policy, with the European Regional
Development Fund as its principal instrument, has not given
so much satisfaction. The Liberals have long recognized the
importance of a successful and effective regional policy as a
prerequisite for eventual economic and monetary union in
the Communities. They have not been convinced that the
Regional Development Fund has yet been applied towards
policies or projects which could not otherwise have been
financed from national sources. In this area too they are
therefore seeking less national interference and more Community control over policy and fund administration, with a
far greater proportion of the Community's resources devoted
to the structural funds rather than agricultural price-support.

Liberal demands in the UK for strengthened Community
institutions with supranational authority and a more balanced
relationship between Commission, Council, and Parliament
have echoed the views of their ELD partners in much of
Europe.[33] Political co-operation in the foreign-affairs sphere
has also met with firm support. British Liberals have pressed
for a stronger Community posture in defence of human rights
both world-wide and within Member States, by incorporating
the European Convention on Human Rights into Community
law, thus granting all Community citizens enforceable rights

---

[33] D. Banks, *Liberals and a Federal Europe* (1974).

of redress ultimately by the European Court of Justice.[34]

In many ways Liberals have felt very much at home with the theory of how the Community should work and develop: they have not found it difficult to be 'communautaire'. The frustration of Liberals, such as Ralf Dahrendorf, with the Community as it functions at present and at its lack of development has yet to call in question the whole Community idea.[35] But David Steel at least has gone on the record in asserting that the economic principles pursued by the Community may need to be modified if world trade becomes increasingly more 'managed' than 'free'.[36]

CONCLUSIONS

Liberal support for the European Communities stems logically from the development over the last seventy years of Liberal attitudes towards nationalism and the need to secure new international economic, military, and political arrangements designed, to preserve peace and democracy in Europe. This predisposition towards supranationality was confirmed for Liberals by the experience of the Second World War and supported by a strong international Liberal tradition which places individual liberty and security above the demands of nation states and their claims of national sovereignty. The Liberal leadership generally provided a strong lead to Liberal supporters on the issue of British membership of the Communities; what would have happened to the Liberal Party if Jo Grimond had pressed his early preference for a European free-trade area rather than a customs union remains a tantalizing question. The exclusion of Liberals from the British establishment and from political power in the 1950s and 1960s probably helped the Liberals to appreciate Britain's reduced position in the world more accurately than their Labour or Conservative counterparts. In addition the Liberals

---

[34] M. Holmstedt, S. Hughes, and D. Ive, *Where Next? Human Rights — the Next Thirty Years in Western Europe* (1980).

[35] For example, R. Dahrendorf, 'A New Goal for Europe' (1971), reprinted in M. Hodges (ed.), *European Integration* (1972), pp. 74–87.

[36] David Steel's 1981 Federalist Lecture reported in *The Times*, 27 October 1981.

had no vested interest in preserving the supremacy of
Westminster and Whitehall: indeed all their political instincts
favoured a redistribution of power to supranational and to
devolved political institutions. Thus it was not opportunism as
at least one writer has claimed,[37] but a combination of
political principle and location within the political system
which led the Liberals in Britain to take a strong and un-
equivocal line in favour of membership of the Communities.
In addition the Liberals can claim some share of the credit
for the passage of the European Communities Act by the
House of Commons in 1972 and for the result of the 1975
referendum. For such constancy of purpose, the largest
Liberal Party in Europe was rewarded with no representation
at all in the first directly elected European Parliament.

Yet there are some important aspects of this Europeanism
in the Liberal ranks which do not sit well with other themes
emphasized by the British Liberals. The trend towards local
'community politics' and grass-roots democracy, which
advanced within the party throughout the 1970s, is the very
antithesis of Liberal demands to increase the powers of
supranational bodies in the European Communities. Even if
the usual justification of transferring powers to the appropriate
level of government is accepted, a more poignant paradox
can be discerned. The Liberals have for decades endorsed a
vision of a democratic, open-trading, supranational Europe
which unfortunately does not accord with the reality of
the European Communities in the 1970s and 1980s. The
Community and its decision-making processes are plagued by
nationalism and the claims of vital national interests. Fundamentally the Communities are not supranational bodies but
intergovernmental institutions which manage European issues
behind closed doors and which largely escape political control.[38] The popular hallmark of the Communities' institutions
is not their open and democratic nature but their deadlocked,
technocratic, and sometimes insensitive behaviour. It could

[37] A. Watkins, *The Liberal Dilemma* (1966) and by implication also in R. J.
Lieber, *British Politics and European Unity* (1970), p. 146.
[38] For further elaboration of this view, see R. Dahrendorf, op. cit., and H.
Wallace, W. Wallace, and C. Webb, *Policy-Making in the European Communities*
(1977).

be argued that the Liberals have become trapped, by virtue of their support for a Europe that might have been but is not, into propping up a profoundly illiberal set of international institutions which Liberals throughout Europe will find almost impossible to reform or to replace.

11. The Liberal Party, Local Government, and Community Politics

(a) THE LIBERALS AND LOCAL GOVERNMENT

Bryan Keith-Lucas

The Nineteenth-Century Legacy

The need for decentralization of government was, to a Victorian Liberal, an essential article of faith. It was the Whig lawyers, led by Brougham and Francis Place, who pushed the Municipal Corporations Act through Parliament in 1835. It was Liberal MPs, and particularly Joseph Hume, who pressed persistently for reform of the county administration, and the substitution of elected councillors for the benches of nominated magistrates who had ruled the counties for centuries. The act creating the elected county councils was however finally passed (after many abortive Liberal bills) by a reluctant Conservative government under Lord Salisbury, as a concession to the Liberal Unionists. It was the Liberals, in Gladstone's last administration, who established the parish councils and the urban and rural districts.

So too in the literature of local government, the principal champions of local autonomy and municipal enterprise were the Liberals — John Stuart Mill in his *Considerations on Representative Government*, George Brodrick in the Cobden Club *Essays on Local Government and Taxation* (1875), and C.T.D. Acland in the Cobden Club symposium *Local Government and Taxation in the United Kingdom* (1882). The most passionate opponent of centralization, and unwavering champion of the parish as a local-government unit, was Joshua Toulmin Smith, a Liberal, in his polemical publications *Local Self Government and Centralisation* (1851) and *The Parish: its Obligations and Powers* (1985). The standard account of the evolution of local government in the Victorian age was written by an Austrian Liberal, Josef

Redlich,[1] assisted by Francis Hirst, who was later to be chairman of the Cobden Club, and one of the last of the true Gladstonian Liberals.

By the later part of Victoria's reign it had become an essential part of the creed of every Liberal that centralization was an evil to be opposed whenever possible, and that there was an innate virtue in the local democracies of towns and villages — and particularly of villages. Alexis de Tocqueville's aphorism was often quoted; 'Local assemblies of citizens constitute the strength of free nations. Town meetings are to liberty what primary schools are to science — they teach men how to use and enjoy it. A nation may establish a system of free government, but without the spirit of municipal institutions it cannot have the spirit of liberty.[2] The Liberal commitment to the doctrine of the innate virtues of free local authorities was supplemented by a traditional and romantic belief in the historic merits of parish government. The demand was not for innovation, but for turning back to our ancient constitution, to the institutions of our Anglo-Saxon forebears, and reviving the folk moot and the court leet. This romantic picture of the Golden Age of local liberty was historical nonsense, and was as much part of the Gothic Revival as Strawberry Hill, Sir Walter Scott, or the Eglinton Tournament. By the later years of the century few serious politicians accepted it uncritically, but yet it had played a great part in influencing thinking about parish government.

Perhaps the greatest achievement of the Liberals in this field in the nineteenth century was the passing of the Local Government Act, 1894, commonly known as the Parish Councils Act. This was greeted with unrestrained enthusiasm, and unqualified optimism, by the party members. Dr Spence Watson, President of the National Liberal Federation, in the preface to the *Parish Councillor's Handbook*, wrote of that act:

In every parish, however small, there will grow up, with the sense of free citizenship, a recognition of responsibilities as well as the knowledge

---

[1] *Englische Lokalverwaltung* (1901) translated into English as *Local Government in England* (London, 1903), reissued (Book 1 only) in 1958 and 1970 as *The History of Local Government in England* (Macmillan).

[2] *Democracy in America* (Vintage Edition, New York), p. 63.

of rights. Each man and woman, as the spirit of self-government grows by use, will realize that in the wise administration of the humblest parish affairs there resides the best guarantee for the common good.

Great as the powers given by this Act are, and great as the material benefits may be, there are indirectly greater blessings still in store. It will abolish patronage and banish privilege. For the rule of the few it will substitute the responsibility and co-operation of the many.

It is the Charter of the peasant's liberty — a Charter framed and passed by a Liberal Government, which recognizes that the true well-being of the state depends rather on the welfare of the many than the wealth of the few, and that our country's future is safest and the common weal best insured when entrusted to the care of all her people.

The Liberal Party has always contended for the building up of rural local government on the unit of the parish by bringing the principle of self-government to every cottage door.[3]

The act was seen as completing the structure of democratic local government started by the Municipal Corporations Act of 1835. This task, it seemed, had now been substantially achieved. Dr Redlich, in his *Local Government in England*, proclaimed that:

From the standpoint of reorganization the tasks and problems of the future are of secondary importance. The grand principle of representative democracy has been fully applied to local government, and securely established by the series of measures which culminated in the Act of 1894. In England, at least, De Tocqueville's prophecy of the triumph of democratic ideas was substantially fulfilled before the close of the nineteenth century.[4]

This view naturally involved a dilemma for the Liberals. If they had truly achieved their goal, what remained for them to do? For nearly a century they had made the development of democratic local government an essential part of their programme; now there was little more to be said or done about the subject. The job was done.

Civic Enterprise

As ever happens in politics, the final settlement soon proved to be incomplete, and to call for further change and

---

[3] Corrie Grant: *The Parish Councillor's Handbook*, with a preface by Dr R. Spence Watson (Liberal Publications Department, 1894), pp. 4,5.

[4] Op. cit., p. 215.

modification. The social pattern of the last years of the nineteenth century may have seemed as if it were established for all time, and the local-government system as if it too would last for ever. But the whole fabric of society was about to be shaken by the impact of war; the petrol engine was about to change the relationship of town and country, and to break down the isolation of the villages and market towns; the women's suffrage movement was beginning to alter the accepted assumption of the male right to govern; the Labour Party was about to emerge as a separate and growing force.

In the period between the wars the interest in local government centred mainly on the struggle over the Poor Law, with Neville Chamberlain dramatically opposed to the socialists of Poplar, and on the conflict between the expanding county boroughs and the counties, who fought to protect their threatened boundaries and rateable values. On neither of these questions did the Liberal Party adopt a clear and distinctive policy.

The most constructive thinking in the party in this period was probably that of Ernest Simon, Lord Mayor of Manchester, and for a time a junior minister in the Department of Health; later Lord Simon of Wythenshawe, a Labour peer. In his book *A City Council from Within*[5] he pleaded for wider powers for local authorities, by the relaxing of the *ultra vires* doctrine, which restricted the councils so narrowly in what they could do for the benefit of their people. He wanted to extend the scope of municipal trading into such fields as milk supply and coal; he wanted to get away from the restrictive traditions of ceremonial mayors and lawyer town clerks; above all he wanted to raise the status and dignity of municipal affairs from the slough of Victorian mismanagement to the heights of Athens in the fifth century BC. He dreamed of a great and regenerated Manchester of which men could be proud, as Pericles was of Athens.

Attitudes however have changed since the 1930s when Simon argued so trenchantly for municipal enterprise. The nationalization policy carrried out by the post-war Labour government, and experience of some of the disadvantages of

[5] London, 1926, Ch. VIII.

public control, have somewhat blunted the demand for municipal trading and enterprise. No longer is this a major item of Liberal policy for local government. Even in the Labour party, interest in municipal ownership has practically disappeared. It was Labour Governments which removed gas and electricity, hospitals and water from local-government control.

Regionalism

Other Liberals had other visions; Gladstone had fought for Home Rule in Ireland, unfortunately in vain; others dreamed of a revived patriotism for Wales, a renaissance of Welsh culture and the Welsh language. This was partly a romantic movement, linked with Druids, Gorsedd Circles, the Eisteddfod, and the memory of Owen Glendower. But it was also a political movement, born of a distrust of centralization and government from Whitehall. Stuart Rendel and David Lloyd George stressed the separateness of Wales, which they refused to see just as a province of England. With this there grew a more general demand for devolution — for separate regional government not only for Wales, but also for the regions of England. In 1905 the Fabian Society published its plea for regional assemblies — *The New Heptarchy*; in 1919 Professor Fawcett published his book, *The Provinces of England*.

After the second war the question of regionalism became again a major political issue. On the one hand an increasing number of services were being entrusted to a variety of regional bodies, nominated, but not elected, and so not responsible to the electors — regional hospital boards, gas boards, electricity boards, and, a bit later, regional sports councils, tourist boards, passenger transport authorities, water boards, economic planning councils, and a number of others. On the other hand, the demand for self-government was growing in Wales and Scotland, and to a lesser degree in Cornwall. The Liberal Party was sympathetic to these movements, and as a party committed to decentralization, was naturally in favour of devolution, though not of independent nationalism. The leadership of these movements, which might

have been grasped by the Liberals, was taken by the Plaid
Cymru and the Scottish Nationalists, parties prepared to go
further than the Liberals, and demand not merely devolution,
but self-government, or even total independence, and to back
that demand in more aggressive ways.

It was the upsurge of this nationalist feeling, translated
into votes in parliamentary elections, that led to the Labour
Government setting up in 1969 the Royal Commission on
the Constitution, to consider the relations between the several
countries, nations, and regions of the United Kingdom.

The Liberal Party had already stated its views in a pamphlet
Power to the Provinces.[6] In this the case was argued for the
creation of a federal structure for Great Britain, with Northern
Irish, Scottish and Welsh Parliaments, and elected assemblies
with less far-reaching powers for the provinces of England.
There would be a Federal Parliament at Westminster to deal
with such matters as foreign affairs, economic planning, and
defence.

This pattern formed the basis of the party's evidence to
the Royal Commission on Local Government (Redcliffe-Maud)
and to the Royal Commission on the Constitution (Crowther),
in which the case was also argued for a Bill of Rights, a
reformed Upper House, and a written constitution. The
proposal to introduce another level of government — the
Parliaments of Ulster, Scotland, and Wales and the assemblies
of the English provinces — raised at once a further difficulty.
There were already four levels of government — Parliament,
county councils, district or borough councils, and parish
councils. Britain was negotiating for entry into the Common
Market, which would involve a fifth tier. If there were to
be also yet another, would not the country be grossly overgoverned? Indeed, was it not already overgoverned with only
four tiers? The Liberals had traditionally been the party most
opposed to government interference.

Thus the commitment to a federal structure, and to the
European ideal, inevitably had repercussions on the Liberal
Party's thinking about local government. It became apparent

---

[6] A Liberal Party Report, published in 1968 by the Liberal Publications
Department.

that at least one level of administration should be abolished, and this should not be the parishes, to which the party had a traditional attachment. The counties would have to go.

Areas and Boundaries of Local Authorities

At the same time the pattern of local-government boundaries, based on the ancient areas of the counties, the boroughs, and the parishes, was becoming irrelevant, as the towns expanded into new suburbs under the jurisdiction of neighbouring county councils, and the isolation of villages and towns was broken down by the revolution in methods of transport. The area of the rural districts had been dictated by the distance that farmers would travel in their pony traps when they went to market. The motor car had changed all that.

It was however not until after the second war that it was generally accepted that drastic change was needed in the pattern of local government, and not until 1972 that any substantial change was achieved, albeit very imperfectly. But the Liberals had been talking and discussing the need for change for some years, even though their political influence was then at its lowest ebb, and so their chance of achieving any reform was slight.

In 1961 a party committee was appointed 'to consider the structure, finance and organization of local government in England and Wales, and what Liberal policy should be in relation to this'. The committee reviewed all aspects of the subject, and paid particular attention to the problem of the size and boundaries of local authorities.[7] They proposed the merger of the smaller counties, the abolition of the distinction between urban and rural districts, the creation of urban parish councils, and the establishment of a directly elected Greater London Council. This however would have had considerably narrower functions than those ultimately given to the GLC by the London Government Act, while the second-tier authorities — the London Boroughs — would have been more important.

[7] *Local Government*: A Report to the Liberal Party (Liberal Publications Department, 1962).

This committee would not have retained the extraordinary anomaly of the Corporation of the City of London. It was 120 years since Lord Brougham had declared that 'it was utterly impossible that many months should elapse before municipal reform should be extended to the City of London'.[8] It was just 100 years since John Stuart Mill had described it as 'that union of modern jobbing and antiquated foppery, the corporation of the City of London'.[9] But still it remained, unreformed except in minor ways, as an absurdity which could be defended by the Royal Commission on the Government of Greater London only on the grounds that it was beyond the limits of logic.[10] The City still retained the boundaries established in the reign of King Richard II; all its pomp and wealth was unrelated to the government of the Metropolis as a whole, and the committee suggested that this should serve a wider purpose for the benefit of the whole of London.

The London Government Bill however followed the policy of the Royal Commission, and proposed to leave things as they were. The Liberal spokesman in the Commons, Eric Lubbock (Lord Avebury), moved an amendment to merge the City into a large central borough, to be built up from the City, Westminster, Holborn, and Finsbury, and some parts of other areas. The amendment, however, was not accepted. Apart from this, the Liberals in the Commons played but little part in the debate on the bill. There were however only seven of them at this time, to cover all subjects in Parliament.

Outside London the committee made a number of recommendations which were incorporated in the Local Government Act of 1972, including the abolition of aldermen, which the Liberals had long been advocating, on the grounds of their undemocratic nature.The Act did, however, include a number of provisions to which the Liberals could not subscribe; particularly the merging of boroughs, urban districts, and rural districts into very much larger, and allegedly 'more viable' units. This involved in many cases the amalgamation

[8] Parliamentary Debates, 3rd Series, 2 March 1843, col. 238.
[9] *Representative Government* (Everyman edition), p. 350.
[10] 1960. Cmd. 1164. p. 237.

of communities of very diverse natures. For example, the City of Canterbury, with its great historic traditions, was merged with the small port of Whitstable, with its failing trade in oysters, with the minor seaside resort of Herne Bay, and with the agricultural villages of Bridge-Blean Rural District. All community of interest was thereby lost.

This policy was in direct conflict with the traditional Liberal respect for the small community as a local-government entity. There was, however, little protest from the Liberal bench in the Commons (once more reduced to six hard-pressed members), and Lord Foot, in the Lords, accepted the proposed structure defined by the bill. The one substantial objection came from the Welsh Liberals — Emlyn Hooson protesting against the size of the proposed new counties of the Principality, but in vain.

The upheaval and confusion involved in the implementation of the 1972 Act made it apparent that no further major reorganization would be tolerated for a number of years to come. The Liberals did not agree with all the provisions of the Act, but yet there appeared to be little point in pressing for further substantial change in the general pattern of local government. There was still scope for internal improvements, for changes in the relationship with Central Government, and extension of the powers of local authorities, but the structural framework had to be accepted for a number of years at least.

One aspect of the structure, however, did have a special interest for the Liberals. They had long argued for all services being provided at as low a level as might be practical. It was a Liberal Government that had established the parish councils, with exaggerated hopes. The concept of small local assemblies of the people of the villages was one which commended itself particularly to the party members. In the report of 1962, and in the evidence given by the party to the Redcliffe-Maud Commission in 1968, special emphasis had been put on the importance of parish councils, and in particular on the need for such bodies in the urban areas, perhaps where a rural village had been swallowed up in the suburbs of an expanding town, or in those parts of a city or town where there was a clear sense of community, as in Notting Hill, Cheetham Hill, or Hillhead.

A later party committee, which reported in 1980,[11] took up this theme again, arguing for wider powers for parish councils, on the lines suggested by the Redcliffe-Maud Commission. The committee saw the parish councils not as a minor appendix to the main structure of local government, but as an essential element in the democratic system, which should be extended to all parts of the country.

The Independence of Local Authorities

In all the discussion about local government there is an essential conflict between two opposing views of democracy. Some would argue that true democracy involves, inevitably and essentially, the right of small communities to run their own affairs in their own way, through their elected councils; to be mean or generous, careful or extravagant, as they will; to provide their services in such ways as they may choose, including the right to have schools of whatever nature they prefer — comprehensive or segregated, grammar schools or bilateral, sixth-form colleges or multilateral schools. They would argue that only thus can experimentation be carried out, and the people have the power to control their own affairs.

Others would argue that the democratic government of a nation is incompatible with the right of some parts of that nation to refuse to comply with the decisions of the nation's, democratically elected Parliament. It is maintained that if the nation as a whole has chosen to follow a policy — perhaps of comprehensive schools, or of the sale of council houses, or of rigid retrenchment in public expenditure — it is unacceptable that some local councils should reject these decisions and refuse to implement the national policy.

The Liberal Party has in the past firmly endorsed the first of these arguments; it has traditionally supported a policy of decentralization, and of the right of local authorities to make

---

[11] *Power and Responsibility to Local Government*, 1980. The same principle was expressed in Conference resolutions in 1971 and 1972.

their own decisions without control from the centre — from Westminister or Whitehall. Gladstone, referring to Dodson's Local Government Bill of 1881, wrote:

Your measure should not only be a great Local Government Bill, but a great decentralization Bill; that to the utmost possible extent administration by the local authority, subject to fixed rules and conditions . . . should be the principle of our local expenditure, and should replace the principle of administration from the centre which has of late been forcing itself into our system.[12]

But the dilemma remains; should the liberty of local authorities go so far as to allow them to do things which are abhorrent to the Liberal conscience? Should there be no control over them when they propose to do what is manifestly stupid, illiberal, or ill-considered?

This problem came to the fore at the Party Assembly in 1979. A resolution was proposed in the words that:

This Assembly reasserts its belief in the maximum freedom of action for local authorities and the consequent necessity for central government to limit its role to imposing broad statutory duties, whilst recognizing the inevitability that some local authorities may at times pursue policies contrary to those of the Liberal Party.

This Assembly accordingly:

(a) logically must welcome the action of H. M. Government in removing compulsion as regards the introduction of comprehensive education and

(b) condemns the action of H. M. Government in forcing all local authorities, regardless of their individual circumstances, to sell council houses upon centrally prescribed terms and conditions.

During the debate there was argument for and against this proposition, some defending the doctrine of freedom of choice for elected local authorities, others maintaining that, in view of the party's support for the principle of comprehensive education, it should press for this to be made universal, and applied in all local-government areas.

The motion was referred back, and a committee was appointed under the chairmanship of Lord Evans of Claughton, the party spokesman on local government in the House of Lords. Even within this committee the argument continued, but ultimately the view prevailed that freedom for local

---

[12] Gladstone to Dodson, 10 Jan. 1882, British Library, Add. Mss. 44235, f. 142.

authorities to act as they see fit is an essential part of Liberal philosophy, and must override any desire to guard against those authorities adopting policies which Liberals oppose or dislike, or to make them follow policies, however desirable, which they themselves reject.

Thus in its report *'Power and Responsibility to Local Government'* the committee declared that local authorities should be free to take important decisions themselves; in-novation, experiment and initiative should be encouraged, rather than uniformity and standardization; local authorities should be allowed to provide services in a variety of ways, and determine the level of these services.

This declaration of principle was in line with the evidence given by the party to the Redcliffe-Maud Commission on Local Government, and the statement of Sir Henry Fowler in introducing the Parish Councils Bill in 1893 — 'I do not suppose that these parish councils will not make mistakes . . . Parish councils will make mistakes, parish councils will be extravagant, parish councils will possibly do foolish things; all that is inevitable in any system of popular government. But I am ready to run the risk of my rural friends making mistakes.'[13]

The Working of Local Government

The central theme of both the party report and the evidence to the Redcliffe-Maud Commission[14] was the need to set local councils free from the control of Ministers and civil servants, but there were also many other recommendations about the way local authorities are organized, and how they carry out their functions. First among these were proposals to alter the constitution of the councils to make them more responsive to public opinion. The party urged the case for proportional representation in local elections, but failed, as usual, to convince the other parties. They argued for the abolition of the aldermen — a proposal which was implemented

---

[13] Parliamentary Debates, 4th series, 21 March 1893, cols. 695-6.
[14] Written Evidence to the Royal Commission on Local Government in England (HMSO).

in the Local Government Act of 1972, as was also their recommendation for a four-year term for local councillors on a regular rotation between the different types of local authority. They pressed the case for allowing candidates to show their party allegiance on the nomination and ballot papers, which was introduced by the Representation of the People Act, 1969, and for the district auditors no longer to be able themselves to surcharge a councillor, without reference to an independent court or tribunal. This was implemented in the Local Government Act of 1972.

On the other hand, there were some proposals which have not been accepted, mostly in the field of local-government finance. The party reports have urged the need for a wider base for local taxation than the rates, and suggested that a number of central-government taxes should be transferred to local authorities, on the same principle as the 'Assigned Revenues' of 1888. It was suggested that the motor-vehicle licence duties, driving-licence fees, and taxes on entertainments should be given to the local authorities, in addition to the rates, so as to make them less dependent on the grants from central government, which inevitably involve some degree of central control.

Unlike the Conservative Party, the Liberals have not proposed the abolition of the rating system, but have for a long time favoured site-value rating instead of the present arrangements. They also advocated in 1962 that a rate of 50 per cent should be levied on all unoccupied properties — a proposal which was implemented in the Local Government Act, 1966.

Though many of the proposals put forward by the Liberal Party in their reports on local government have later been incorporated into legislation, they cannot and would not claim the sole credit for reforms. Some were advocated also by the Labour Party, and others owe much to their being included in the recommendations of Royal Commissions and Departmental Committees.

Liberal Councillors

The practical impact of Liberals in English local government in this century is very hard to assess. It is only in recent years that the majority of local councillors have been elected on a party ticket; until the 1950s the smaller local authorities were predominantly composed of 'independent' councillors, though a high proportion of these were in fact Conservative in their sympathies. In 1952 in nearly half the boroughs of the country the independents were still the largest group, while the rural district councils were nearly all composed almost entirely of independents. In only a handful of the boroughs were the Liberals the largest party — Bacup, Halifax, Huddersfield and Mossley. Of these only Huddersfield had a clear majority of Liberals. After the municipal elections of 1953 only two of these were left with Liberals as the largest group — Huddersfield and Mossley.

Ten years later, after the elections of 1963, there were five boroughs in which the Liberals were leading — Aldershot, Finchley, Glossop, Mossley and Tewkesbury; in Bacup the Labour and Liberal parties each had nine seats, while the Conservatives had five.

In 1981 the Liberals had an absolute majority in the Isle of Wight, the City of Hereford, Adur in Sussex, and Medina in the Isle of Wight. In one other district they were the largest group — Wyre Forest in the county of Hereford and Worcester.

The party has suffered badly from the electoral system, which exaggerates the gains of the larger parties, and diminishes the influence of the smaller. More even than the parliamentary system, it results in the representation of the Liberals being less than proportionate to their votes. None the less, it does not appear that a change in the voting system, by itself, would have given the Liberal party control in any additional councils, though it would increase the number of their seats in a number of councils. For example, in 1979 the electors of Stockport voted 45.3% for the Conservatives, 26.6% for the Labour candidates, and 24.6% for the Liberals, but the result, in terms of councillors elected, was that the Liberals got two seats out of the twenty being contested. In Gloucester the Liberals got 19% of the vote, but only 3% of the seats.

So in no case has any major local authority had for any length of time a council on which the Liberals held an overall majority. This means that one cannot point to important achievements of Liberal councils in this century, as one could, for example, in Birmingham under Joseph Chamberlain in the 1870s. In the earlier part of the century one might include E. D. Simon's work in Manchester, and in particular his persuading the Council to develop Wythenshawe as a satellite town, and no account of the part played by Liberals in local government this century would be complete without some reference to the rate strike in Wales against the Education Act of 1902, led by David Lloyd George. It did not, however, result in any permanent consequences, except as a stepping-stone in Lloyd George's political career.

In more r cent years the influence of Liberal councillors can probably be seen most clearly in the Liverpool City Council, where they have never held a clear majority, but have just been the largest party, and so have accepted the duties of the governing group. It was here that 'community politics' had its most impressive success; the number of Liberal Councillors rose from three (out of 160) in 1965 to 43 (out of 99) ten years later. Their impact was probably strongest in the field of housing, in such matters as the policy of building council houses specifically for sale, and the introduction of a 'tenants' charter'. How much more they might have achieved had they had a clear majority can only be a matter for speculation.

Conclusion

Historically the main significance of the Liberal party in local government has not been in the field of physical achievements. There are few, if any, bridges, motorways, or housing estates which can be claimed as the fruit of Liberal policies. But one significant development can be claimed; the recognition of the importance of community politics; the realization that local-government elections need not be merely a minor reflection of the struggle for power in Parliament, but may be won on purely local issues. In Liverpool particularly, but to a lesser degree in many other local-government areas, the Liberals have based their campaigns on local matters, rather than the central government, its promises and successes or failures. This aspect of Liberal policy is dealt with in the next section of this book, and so will not be pursued here.

Apart from this, the main contribution of the party to the history of local government has been in the realm of ideas; the championship of the independence of local authorities, and their freedom from central control; the absolute importance of the small communities, and their inherent right to manage their own affairs.

It may of course be suggested that the Liberal policies were idealistic rather than practical; that a party which was so long out of office, and so was not responsible for the management of the nation's economy, could afford to deal in dreams rather than realities; that if the Liberals had had to face the administrative problems of government they, like other parties, would have had to compromise with the harsh facts of the real world. Freedom for local councils sounds splendid, but a government committed to national economy and retrenchment is bound to bring the local authorities under control. So also its commitment to proportional representation may be seen as the natural reaction of a party which fails to win elections under the present system. Commitment to the concept of regionalism may be a form of romanticism, which in practice would lead to division and Balkanization. The faith in parish government may be a romantic dream, born of bad history and the Gothic Revival.

These are criticisms of the Liberals' approach to local government which cannot be totally ignored. There is truth in the view that Liberal writers — many of them academics — tend to be idealists, and that their ideals would conflict in some cases with the demands of practical government. Civil servants do not welcome variation and difference among local authorities, nor do they want to deal with numerous small bodies, when they could so much more easily deal with a few, large, ones. In its evidence to the Redcliffe-Maud Commission the Ministry of Housing and Local Government (as distinct from the Minister) argued for a structure of local government with only thirty or forty main units in the country. It claimed that 'there is a clear need to reduce drastically the number of authorities with major financial responsibilities, so as to secure an improvement in their budgeting and control arrangements and in their relationship with central government'. The Ministry complained also that it 'cannot trust a multitude of small local authorities to spend money wisely'.[15]

There is so wide a gulf between the Liberal approach and that of the civil servants that it is perhaps impossible to try to reconcile them. The Liberal attitude is rooted in idealism, but it does not necessarily follow that it is impractical. Many of their proposals have in fact been incorporated into the legislation of recent years; parish councils have amply justified their creation; local variation and initiative are perhaps essential elements in a democratic nation.

This attitude to local independence and freedom from central control may be compared not only with the approach of the central government of Britain, but also with thinking in Western Europe. The draft Charter of Local Self Government[16] was adopted by the Conference of Local and Regional Authorities of Europe in 1981, and submitted to the Committee of Ministers of the Council of Europe. This draft proclaims, among other things, that 'powers given to local government shall normally be full and exclusive. They may not be undermined or limited by administrative action on the part of a central or regional authority', that 'local authorities shall have a general residual right to act on their own initiative with regard to any matter not expressly assigned to any other authority nor specifically excluded from the competence of local government', and also that 'public responsibilities shall be exercised by preference by those authorities which are closest to the citizen'.

Liberal principles would seem therefore to be very much in line with the thinking of continental Europe, as well as forming an important part of the British tradition of thought on local government.

[15] Written Evidence of the Ministry of Housing and Local Government, p. 75. HMSO, 1967.

[16] Council of Europe: Resolution 126 (1981) (1) on the Principles of Local Self-government: Strasburg, 29 Oct. 1981.

(b) COMMUNITY POLITICS
Stuart Mole

Origins

The general election of 1970 was traumatic for the Liberals, reducing their parliamentary representation from thirteen seats to six. It was becoming more and more difficult to believe that the Party could enjoy a continual upward increase in support to the point at which it could break the two-party system. Indeed, the parliamentary party was no larger in 1970 than it had been at the nadir of the Party's fortunes in 1951. It was natural for those candidates and activists who remained to begin an agonized re-examination of the Party's strategy, its organizational competence, and indeed the validity of its separate and distinct political purpose and appeal. Many left the Party despairing of overcoming the inertia of the political system, but for those who stayed on, 'community politics' seemed the main hope for the future.

At the 1970 Eastbourne Assembly, the Party looked afresh at its electoral strategy. The outcome of the debate was a firm commitment, to community politics. 'Our role as political activists', the Assembly declared, 'is to help and organize people in communities to take and use power; to use our political skills to redress grievances; and to represent people at all levels of the political structure.'

The growth of community politics rested on three main social factors. First, with the growth of technology, giant industrial organization, and supranational bodies, the individual felt increasingly unrecognized, atomized, and ignored. Whether in the work-place, in relation to government and its agencies, or in his home environment, the citizen found it less and less possible to express his individuality. The state now seemed to govern every aspect of his life: the decline of communities accompanied the rush for size, and the result was social rootlessness.

Second, the individual seemed to be the victim of insensitive and often inhuman policies. Faced with a complex range of local and statutory services, he looked on with a mixture of suspicion, frustration, and incomprehension. The paradox was that the agencies of a benign welfare state seemed themselves to have become oppressive.

Third, the established political parties, faced with the challenge of bureaucracy, seemed unable to respond. Social change was rapid — but despite the rhetoric of reform and Harold Wilson's vision of a new Britain forged in 'the white heat of technological revolution', political aspirations remained unsatisfied and hopes unfulfilled. Students and many other young people turned aside from conventional politics into extra-parliamentary radical protest; into single-issue pressure-group politics; or into the more individualistic embrace of the 'counter-culture' through drugs, mysticism, or a variety of 'alternative' life-styles.

All this proved fertile territory for the growth of community politics. As a critique, community politics rests on firm Liberal foundations. Joseph Chamberlain articulated the same underlying theme when he established the National Liberal Federation more than one hundred years ago. He spoke of those:

who reject the principle, which should be at the bottom of all Liberalism, that the best security for good government is not to be found in *ex cathedra* legislation by the upper classes for the lower, but in consulting those chiefly concerned and giving shape to their aspirations whenever they are not manifestly unfair to others — these all view with natural apprehension a scheme by which the mob, as they are ready to term the great bulk of their fellow countrymen, are for the first time invited and enabled to make their influence felt . . . [17]

Community politics represents an attempt to regenerate democracy and recast democratic institutions so that power is driven downwards to the most basic level possible. That level will be the community or pattern of communities, whether in the work-place or in local government. The idea is both simple and utterly familiar within the Liberal tradition of devolution and decentralization.

But community politics is more than a critique. It is also a process, offering a basis for social change not directed exclusively through existing structures; and a method by

[17] Joseph Chamberlain: 'A New Political Organization' in *Fortnightly Review*, 1877, p. 126.

which Liberals might seek to acquire influence and power.

The techniques of community politics had been first fashioned in the Newtown area of Birmingham by Wallace Lawler, for a time the lone Liberal on the City Council, then MP for Ladywood between 1969 and 1970. In many ways he offered a model of how the 'New Liberalism' could and should develop. The Party had to abandon the leafy suburbs and cease to be the intermittent receptacle of passing Tory discontent. Instead, it had to head for the inner cities, for the core of Labour support, and for the heartlands of deprivation and discontent. The weapons were simple – advice centres, community newsletters, petitions, action groups, and grumble sheets. The political approach was based on an identification with a tight-knit, traditional, local community threatened by wholesale redevelopment trans-forming and depopulating the area.

Liberals who came to Ladywood wondered at the solid displays of orange posters in working-class streets and at the new fierce loyalty of former Labour stalwarts. It seemed a marvellous oasis of Liberalism in a most unpromising desert. If it could be done here, of all places, they mused, even at a time when the Liberal Party barely registered on the national political barometer, surely it could be done *anywhere*.

Liverpool

And so it was. In Liverpool, the Liberals, building on the work of Cyril Carr and Trevor Jones, became the largest party on the City Council in 1973. This was a major break-through, for there had been no Liberal administration in Liverpool since the turn of the century. But the event was also of national importance to the Liberal Party. It constituted a major electoral success, at least on a par with a parliamentary by-election victory. It provided a valuable test of Liberal competence to govern. Above all, as the only major urban authority under Liberal control it gave an opportunity to test the theory of community politics against the practice of municipal government.

The growth of the Liberal Party from its initial foothold in Church Ward, Wavertree, followed the classic path. Like their compatriots in Birmingham, Liverpool Liberals ranged themselves against a prevailing orthodoxy which dominated the Conservative and Labour Parties. In the twenty years before local government reorganization, control of the City Council had changed six times. But, apart from a continuing conflict over comprehensive education, Labour and the Conservatives maintained a consensus on the major questions of policy affecting the City. This was particularly true of redevelopment. Large areas of the City centre had been cleared and inner-city communities were uprooted and transported to outlying housing 'bantustans'. Those who remained had to live in a desolate wasteland, awaiting the coming of the grand concrete design which would make the transformation complete. Urban motorways carved a brutal path through settled communities, while extravagance at the City Hall appeared unabated. It was not a happy juxtaposition.

The Liberal Party stirred a ready response in individuals and communities caught in such a process. In tune with the prevailing national mood of the Skeffington Report, with its ideas for public participation in planning, Liberals sought to give a voice to those whose wishes had hitherto been overridden. The politics of the bulldozer, they argued, must be replaced by an approach which listened to the wishes and needs of the people and adapted planning policies accordingly.

The 48 Liberals elected in 1973 faced 42 Labour members and 9 Conservatives. Their hold on power was, therefore, always tenuous. Yet they promised a completely new style of government. Consultation, participation, and open government were to be the watchwords. A virtue was made of abandoning blind commitment to preconceived policies. In its place, consultation with local communities was to have an integral part in policy formulation. Greater openness was introduced into the conduct of the Council's business with committees and subcommittees thrown open to press and public alike. Council meetings were televized on a number of occasions, although the rumbustious proceedings were scarcely edifying to those unused to scouse politics. Finally, half an hour was set aside at each Council meeting for the presenting of citizen's petitions.

In line with this approach, the Liberal administration launched an ambitious plan designed to encourage community development and establish grass-roots democracy. A Community Development Committee was formed, backed by a sizeable budget, with the intention of helping the plethora of community councils, neighbourhood and residents' groups. But difficulties soon arose, and, after heated debate, the Liberals' plan for a system of democratically elected community councils ran into the ground, following combined opposition from Conservative and Labour councillors.

The Community Development policy also came under review. An enthusiastic overall commitment to community ventures failed to overcome some of the more human side effects. Local groups, outside democratic control, can quickly become little more than pressure groups peddling a particular sectional or political interest. Equally, generous grant aid to local organizations sometimes meant inefficiency, with ill-defined and uncoordinated appointments of community workers. Later attempts by the Liberals to control the misuse of local-authority grants were characterized by their opponents as attacks on the very voluntary and community groups which they had once promoted. On wider financial matters, the Liberals were able to scrap almost immediately a number of grandiose schemes which would have placed a heavy burden on the ratepayers for dubious benefit.

Operating without an effective majority and under pressure from the Conservatives, no less than Labour, the Liberal administration maintained a tight budgeting grip. Indeed, a more vigorous and effective approach to the estimates and the rate-making allowed Liverpool to reduce its domestic rate by 1p in the pound when setting its 1975/6 budget. This was in marked contrast with practice elsewhere. The claim was thus made that vital services, upon which those in need depend, were universally protected and improved. At the same time, performance review allowed old inefficiencies and waste to be rooted out and economies made.

More recently, the impact of a highly punitive approach by central government to local-authority finance has inevitably meant rate and rent rises and a constant battle to maintain basic services. Minority control, lost in 1976, regained in

1978, and narrowly lost again during 1979–80, again passed to the Liberals in 1982, despite the local election results. The Liberals entered the election as the second party, with four seats fewer than the Labour Party. Despite a net gain of two seats from the Liberals and an increased share of the vote, Labour refused to take control as long as a hostile majority maintained their seats in the council and its committees.

Undoubtedly, Liberals viewed a further period of power with mixed feelings. Added to exceptionally difficult financial circumstances, with the City hard hit by the recession and rising unemployment, Liberals have had to cope with other social problems, from riots to falling school-rolls. School reorganization, with the consequent amalgamation or closure of some schools, has stirred fierce emotions and bitter accusations that the administration had failed to live up to its high standards of community involvement.

For their part, the Liberals replied that reorganization, though painful, is vital if pupil–teacher ratios and school resources are to be maintained. They charged Labour with deliberately orchestrating protest for political purposes. On the positive side, they also pointed to a series of innovations designed to involve parents in their children's education, from daytime shared use of school premises for adult-education classes to parents' support units, encouraging the closest possible parental connection with the school.

Perhaps the most successful area of Liberal activity has been housing provision. The influence of community politics is clear. Since 1978, no bulldozer has been applied to a house unless it was structurally unsound. The Housing Chairman of that year responsible for this policy, now MP for Liverpool Edge Hill, David Alton, also points with pride to the twenty-five Housing Action areas, covering 8,500 properties, declared in 1978/9 alone.

Today 30,000 houses are in Housing Action areas. Of these 85 per cent are now fully modernized and the remainder have been given basic amenities. In David Alton's own parliamentary constituency of Edge Hill, he highlights the benefits of local Liberal representation. Ten years ago, 50 per cent of all the houses in the area were without inside toilet, running hot water, or bathrooms. Demolition was the official answer.

Today those homes have been retained with less than 15 per cent now requiring basic modernization work. Liberals have also pioneered Building for Sale schemes. Some 3,000 low-cost private homes for sale have been built or are in prospect, with the local authority providing derelict inner-city land in partnership with private developers, Finally, the City Council has also established housing co-operatives, with estates collectively managed by the tenants themselves.

But there have been problems and pressures which have undermined the purity of the community politics approach. The most immediate of these was in coping with the sudden influx of new recruits to the Party's ranks at the time of the 1973 breakthrough. Youthful idealists were naturally welcome — two Liberal councillors elected in 1982 were students at Liverpool University — but political rejects and opportunists also found the fledgling Party irresistible. Some came from a Labour Party, already alive with conflict between the Old Guard and an emerging authoritarian 'hard' Left. The absence of any proper candidate-vetting procedure and a desperate scramble to find sufficient candidates for the 1973 election brought other problems, and much unwelcome publicity.

As for the future, minority control of the City Council is increasingly viewed with little relish. 'Another year of rotten decisions and all the blame',[18] was how David Alton put it. A spell in opposition, some argue, would allow Liberals to gather their energies, cement the Alliance with the SDP, and rejuvenate the Party's dedication to community politics.

Other pressures inevitably bear down on the theory of community politics. The Liberals have always fiercely advocated decentralized power and local decision-making, yet in the aftermath of the riots in 1981, the City Council found itself with wholly inadequate powers to tackle the problems. The irony is that the new instrument of centralized authority set up to revive the riot-hit areas is the Merseyside Urban Development Corporation. Prominent among its membership is Sir Trevor Jones, the Liberal Leader of the

[18] David Alton in conversation with the author, 8 July 1982.

Council — forced, despite all his inclinations, to go where the power lies.

The Electoral Impact

The story elsewhere, if less spectacular, showed some similarities with what had happened in Liverpool. 1972 saw the beginning of a local-government revival. In 1973, 1,000 Liberals were elected on to the new County and District Councils, establishing footholds in London, Leeds, Sheffield, Liverpool, and Birmingham. The District and County elections in 1976 and 1977 saw the process seriously checked, at a time when the Party nationally had lost much of its 1974 popularity and had become embroiled in embarrassing scandal. But there were still advances into new areas such as Tower Hamlets in London's East End. By 1979, the forward movement was once more widespread. Despite apprehension about the dangers of fighting a difficult General Election on the same day as local polling, the outcome was highly satisfactory, with 1,013 councillors being returned.

Since then, the process has accelerated, with a steady crop of by-election victories; full or minority control of District Councils like Hereford, Wyre Forest, Adur, and Medina; and 300 gains in the 1981 County elections, including control of the Isle of Wight and a narrow victory at Richmond in the GLC elections. But in 1982 further advances were checked by the war in the Falklands which led to a swing to the Conservatives, although Liberal candidates performed better than those of the SDP.

In parliamentary by-elections, also, the application of community-politics techniques has had dramatic effects. For community politics played an important role in the by-election victories not only of Ladywood in 1969, but also Ripon in 1973 and Liverpool Edge Hill in 1979.

Even more recently, those same techniques were used to the full in William Pitt's huge win in Croydon North-West in 1981. Never before had a Liberal won in a by-election a seat which was marginal between the two main parties, from such a low base, and with a candidate whom most had written off as 'poor'. The true impact on the Alliance of

Croydon has been masked by the equally impressive effect of personality — in the shape of Roy Jenkins and Shirley Williams at Warrington, Crosby, and Glasgow, Hillhead. Yet, as the Beaconsfield by-election and the local elections of 1982 showed, neither the impact of personality, the new credibility of the Alliance, nor community politics can insulate a locality from an adverse tide in national opinion. But elections are far from being the sole purpose of community politics.

Criticisms and Tensions

Given its dramatic impact in local and parliamentary by-elections, it was scarcely surprising that community politics should have quickly attracted fierce criticism.

The first main charge, deployed in the main by Conservative and Labour opponents and by those outside the Liberal Party, was that the approach was politically incoherent, inflammatory, inimical to the idea of parliamentary government, and destructive of the quality of leadership.

Eric Heffer accused 'pavement politicians' of having a 'contempt for parliamentary democracy'. Harold Wilson spoke of a party which had a 'policy for every street corner' but no coherent approach to the great national issues of the day. Others saw community politics as undermining political leadership. On this latter point, Roy Jenkins argued that: 'It is the duty of leaders to seek to synthesize and give reality to people's aspirations, not to separate and exploit their conflicting grudges.' Finally, Christopher Chataway, in 1974 shortly before leaving politics altogether, raged that 'the insidious growth of so-called community politics . . . has finally rendered the life of the politician intolerable'.

A rather more muted version of the same criticism has come from some within the Liberal Party. They acknowedged the popularity of the approach among the activists who attended Party Council and the Assembly and found that they could scarcely dismiss something which was obviously electorally successful. They therefore recognized the value of community politics 'in its proper place' but feared lest national policy-making and presentation should be neglected and the position of Parliament as a forum of national debate be undermined.

A third body of critics was composed of those who accused practitioners of having abandoned the true techniques enshrined in the 1970 Eastbourne Resolution and allowed 'community politics' to degenerate into election gimmickry of the most parochial kind. In particular, the growing influence of the Association of Liberal Councillors, a body apparently obsessed with technique and practice rather than principle and theory, seemed to provide proof of the corrupting influences of municipal power.

However, few of these critics practised what they preached. Characteristic of this group was Peter Hain who, while writing prolifically on the subject, always held aloof from the tedious, mundane, and unremitting effort of community politics, preferring instead the more glamorous, sharp single-issue campaign.

Most Liberals were, not surprisingly, unimpressed by the wounded complaint that community politics was making the life of the MP intolerable. It would after all seem the least they could do in return for an electoral system which effectively stripped them of parliamentary representation. In any case, Liberal MPs, elected for seats which could never be treated as other than highly marginal, were well used to the necessity for a high constituency profile and a heavy casework load, on top of their other Party and parliamentary duties.

None the less, it was recognized that community politics did indeed place a greater strain on the elected representative and make the electorate more demanding and critical. But that, after all, was its purpose. The answer was not to remove the pressure but to improve the effectiveness of the representative by providing greater aid and facilities at a local level. Furthermore, Liberals argued, the community politician was seeking to establish an ultimately more responsible and honest relationship with the electorate. By moving closer to the people, the MP or councillor was better able to inform and talk to the electorate on national and international issues, having re-established the relationship of trust that continuing cynicism had eroded. Indeed, it appeared generally more honest to emphasize the representative role of the MP, and provide a proper back-up service, than to present the MP merely as part of a team that blames all the nation's problems on its predecessors and promises unlimited benefits as soon as it comes to power.

But what of political leadership? Was it diminished by 'separating and exploiting conflicting grudges'? Indeed so, came the reply, but this was scarcely something about which a political two-party system, based on the divisive appeal of class, had reason to be pious. Poor political leadership and the unscrupulous manipulation of grievances was scarcely a necessary consequence of community politics.

Indeed, perhaps a politician who was closer to his electorate and who provided more points of contact would be better able to understand and represent their fears and aspirations and, in turn, more able to explain the limitations and realities of national and international circumstances. This would surely improve the quality of representation, for leadership cannot exist in a vacuum. Furthermore, it is arguable that recent electoral trends have shown a growing public distaste for what has since the mid-nineteenth century been the traditional gladiatorial function of parliament. Parliament, as a forum of debate, far from educating and mobilizing electoral support, seems to have added to public cynicism and disillusionment about politics.

Community politics at the very least puts a higher premium on the effective and conscientious MP; and it could be that in all parliaments greater emphasis should be put on the role of the MP as a social worker and mediator between the citizen and the administration. As merely a supporter of the government or the opposition, a Member appears at worst an ineffective cog in an impersonal machine and at best a manipulative research agent for an aspiring or present government. But as a representative traditionally concerned with the redress of grievances, an apparent free man in battle with government and bureaucracy alike, he possesses some obvious freedom of action and is observably the political arm of the people.

The influence of community politics may therefore percolate through as an added pressure for parliamentary reform; in an improvement in the conditions and status of the Member; a reform of cumbersome procedure that at present keeps the MP locked up in Westminster; a decline in party control and an increase in relevance and expertise through a network of specialist comittees. Whether on a parliamentary or a local level, community politics is about the feeling of powerlessness an individual has in his relationship with the institutions that govern his life; and the need to alter that relationship, by his own efforts as much as those of the politician, so that the channels of accountability and responsibility no longer remain closed and the individual is able to play an active part in determining his social environment.

Within the Liberal Party community politics has come to be generally accepted, and its electoral importance no longer seriously questioned. Yet some Liberals still feared the corrupting effects of local power. Would the party slip into strident Poujadism, devoid of policy and unconstrained by historic Liberal principles? The perils of populism were shown by the experience of the SNP which, in 1968, captured control of a number of Scottish burghs. The saltire was raised above the town halls, yet the resulting indecision, incoherence, and confusion quickly brought about the inevitable electoral penalty.

For over a decade Liberals have resisted this temptation. It could easily have happened in Liverpool, after the capture of the City Council in 1973. Yet ten years afterwards, Liberals continue to exercise some kind of tenuous control. Community politics has given hundreds of Liberal activists direct experience of some kind of power through local government, while in an increasing number of authorities Liberals are exercising control. The result has been more informed policy-making at national level and a far higher level of debate of local-government issues than before.

Yet the general acceptance of community politics within the Liberal Party has only gone to reinforce the views of another category of critics who believe it to be a form of cheap electioneering.

Frank recognition of the electoral motivation of community politics is important. But the last decade has seen community-politics activists come to moderate their original ideas in three particular respects.

First, local election campaigns have to be more than a straightforward attempt to reap just rewards for virtue and hard work. The point was forcibly impressed on many Liberals who had originally been elected councillors in the early 1970s. Many made the elementary mistake of assuming that they would be virtually unassailable providing no potential rival worked as hard, or as long, or to as much effect in their locality. Politics was kept out of politics — and some election campaigns became little more than a modest if comprehensive catalogue of advice centres held, community newsletters delivered, and successful local campaigns conducted over the previous three years.

The result was disastrous. Some had so anaesthetized the political process that the electorate believed the community work would continue regardless of the election result. The lesson was duly learned. If elections are the measure of community politics, they must be fought as political campaigns by party candidates against political opponents.

Second, it has come to be recognized that a voter supports a party because of his favourable perception of the candidate's campaigning image. Few voters conduct a detailed appraisal of comparative party policies; only a minority find a single policy issue so compelling as to determine their vote absolutely; and gratitude and respect, while counting for something, provide a candidate with no guarantees about voting behaviour.

It is the task of the candidate to blend those ingredients together to construct an image of himself and the Party which is favourable to the voters and which conveys sufficient urgency and excitement to motivate the elector to cast his vote. The difference between the Liberal Party and its Conservative and Labour rivals lies in the fact that the image of the latter is expressed in class terms. In the case of the Liberal Party, whose voting support is not centred on a predominant class base, the Party's image is far less defined. This is both a disadvantage (leading many to believe the Party lacks policies) and an advantage in so far as it allows Liberals to construct an appeal across the class divide.

Third, Liberals have reluctantly now come to acknowledge the connection between local and national events, images and campaigns. Some have believed that a vigorous enough local campaign, rooted in solid community involvement, can effectively insulate that effort from damaging factors at national level.

The community-politics strategy undoubtedly lifted the party in 1972-4 through the local and Parliamentary by-election successes of those years. But at the same time, it encouraged activists to overestimate the power of the strategy by discounting such national factors. Community politics created an extraordinary dynamic. But the credit for harvesting the six million votes of February 1974 lay as much in the fine national electoral campaign which Jeremy Thorpe was able to fight.

Conclusions and Future Challenges

The emergence of the SDP and the formation of the Alliance provides community politics with an interesting test. Clearly, the overwhelming majority of Liberals found the concept of realignment highly appealing. It offered the realization of the long-held strategic change spoken of by Jo Grimond twenty years earlier with the prospect of a new alliance of like-minded groups. Very few had believed that the Liberal Party could achieve a rapid breakthrough on its own and they therefore welcomed a new force which might assist the process. Yet there were some who counselled caution on philosophical grounds. Were Liberalism and Social Democracy actually the same thing?

For those who had expressed their Liberalism through community politics, the answer appeared to be 'No'. After all, the growth of community politics had largely been the result of disenchantment with the social-democratic approach. Peter Hain had expressed this, in its most strident form, six years earlier. Writing in *Community Politics* he said:

Wherever we look, social democracy has failed abjectly to deliver the goods. Comprehensive schooling, while a step forward from the old élitist system, has had not more than a marginal effect in eradicating educational inequality. Housing policies have contributed to social alienation and disintegration. That cardinal principle of social democracy, economic growth, has accelerated the destruction of the environment and rallied opinion to the workship of 'bigger is better'. Frantically searching around for a lifebelt, social democracy has turned to technocratic solutions, and the planners and experts have been invited in to save the day.

He continued:

All of these attempts have failed. And they have failed, not for lack of good intentions, but because they have skirted around the central issue: to create and nurture a consciousness for self-help and a spirit of community solidarity that can only become a reality in self-governing, egalitarian communities. Such an aim cannot be left to psychologists or any other social technician: it is a political issue.[19]

Despite Peter Hain's well-publicized departure from the Liberals into the Labour Party, his words would still awaken a nagging fear among many of his erstwhile colleagues.

Michael Meadowcroft, a highly respected figure in the Party and a successful practitioner of community politics in Leeds, struggled publicly with this dilemma. In debate at the Liberal Assembly with the former Labour MP David Marquand and in subsequent writings, he sought to define the differences and similarities between Liberals and Social Democrats and to ask whether the Alliance would involve a cost to Liberalism which would outweigh any conceivable gain.

In 'Social Democracy: Barrier or Bridge' he suggested that:

An alliance would gain for Liberals the support of a number of parliamentarians with considerable experience of government, extra media coverage and the help of SDP members and activists in Liberal-fought seats. It could lose for us, particularly in the urban areas, those radical activists who have been attracted to the Liberal movement precisely because of our community politics emphasis and our opposition to the centrist politics — often identified locally with social democrats — that have had such a long-term detrimental effect on our cities.

Michael Meadowcroft's conclusion was hesitant, and qualified by many reservations. None the less, he was willing to assist in the task of constructing the Alliance on the ground.

After all, sceptics were told, Wilsonian Social Democracy

[19] Peter Hain (ed.): *Community Politics* (London, 1976), p. 29.

was scarcely the same thing as the new Social Democratic Party. Some of the faces might be familiar, but the policies were different — with electoral reform, decentralization, and industrial democracy high on the list of new-found causes. Indeed, Liberals were quick to point out that in such joint policy statements as 'A Fresh Start for Britain' (1981) not one major Liberal policy item has been omitted or amended through the necessity for agreement with the SDP. Finally, it is pointed out with some glee that if Liberals and Social Democrats disagree on 10 per cent of policy, that represents a far higher degree of unanimity than could normally be expected from within the Liberal Party, among its own members.

Even so, difficult negotiations over parliamentary seats, with Liberal activists conceding more than they ever thought likely, could once more bring doubt to the surface. Indeed, the Liberal Party Chairman, widely regarded as a traditionalist, wrote in the February 1982 edition of the 'Liberal Clarion':

If the Parties have much in common objectives for the future they could scarcely be more different in immediate past experience. On the one hand, the revival of the Liberal Party has been based upon deep commitment to a style of politics which gives pride of place to the value of local communities and local determination. Perhaps the most powerful modern expression of our devotion to liberty has been the resolve to return power to the people.

By contrast, the leaders of Social Democracy look back to years of power, often exercised by central diktat with little regard for the views of the people in receipt of a torrent of legislation. Doubtless this experience of power lends credibility to the Alliance but it is also in danger of creating a Party not only more centralized than our own but also less concerned with genuine local democracy than the Conservative Party and, in some respects, the Labour Party. In a Liberal Society those who lead must be the ultimate servants. There is no room for Wagnerian bosses.

Community politics, as we have seen, has given to many Liberals grass-roots experience and understanding of local politics. These activists believe that political success is won not by dramatic breakthroughs, but by a long and patient process of local organization and advance. The community politicians are a remarkably cohesive group within the Party and their spokesman is the Association of Liberal Councillors which gained considerably in influence in the Party during the 1970s. It is amongst the ALC that the greatest degree of scepticism towards the Alliance is to be found; it is indeed natural for community activists to be suspicious of the SDP, which some regard as a Party organized from the top, reliant upon the charisma of powerful leaders, rather than hard work at local level.

It is from the ALC that rebellion against the Alliance would be most likely. One form which this might take would be for rogue Liberal candidates to stand against Alliance nominees at a general election. If David Steel was forced to respond by issuing an Alliance 'coupon', he could appear as a latter-day Lloyd George in conflict with a significant section of his own Party. The consequences for the survival of Liberalism could be severe.

Even if there is universal, albeit grudging, acceptance of the agreed balance of seats within the Alliance for the next general election, doubts could easily re-emerge. If the Alliance secured less than 30 per cent of the vote, and no more than 40 or 50 seats, many Liberal activists would feel cheated by a deal for which they had sacrificed much, but which, they would argue, gave them little more than the Liberal Party could reasonably have secured on its own.

Much will, of course, depend on whether the Alliance were to hold the balance of power, giving the Liberals a share in government and the chance of securing proportional representation. This would certainly prevent recrimination. But if these hopes were not realized, retribution would surely follow — with community politics becoming the focal point for those opposed to the strategy of the Alliance.

For community politics is not only an electoral technique which has been proved to be highly effective; it is also a key ingredient in the formation and growth of the modern Liberal Party. Whether it becomes a positive force in the Alliance or a destructive and divisive one must depend in part upon the skills of the parliamentary leadership of both parties and the effectiveness of the national campaign which they are able to mount.

Conclusion: The Liberal Party, the Alliance, and the Future

Two central features of the modern Liberal Party emerge with striking clarity from these essays. The first is the remarkable continuity of doctrine and ideas which the Party displays. Parties are, of course, far more than repositories of opinion; they are also vehicles for the advancement of social interests. Yet it remains true that the sort of elector who would find the ideas of the Liberal Party sympathetic during the time of Gladstone or Asquith would also be inclined to support the Liberal Party or the SDP today. The main themes — constitutional and political reform, decentralization of power, economic and social reform, internationalism — have hardly changed, although their priorities at different times have legitimately varied.

But the second theme which emerges is that the Liberal Party exists in a political and electoral environment which is alien to it. Primarily, of course, it is the electoral system which conditions the life of the Liberal Party today. We need only compare the influence of the Liberals with that of the Free Democrats in Germany to appreciate this point. In 1980, the Free Democrats secured 10.6 per cent of the vote in West Germany; while in 1979, the Liberals gained 13.8 per cent of the vote in the British general election. In post-war elections, the FDP has never secured more than 12.8 per cent of the vote; while in the two elections of 1974, the Liberals gained 19.3 per cent and 18.3 per cent of the vote respectively. Yet, whereas the FDP has been able to participate as a coalition partner in West German governments since the founding of the Federal Republic, except for the years 1956–61 and 1966–9, the Liberal Party has not participated in government since the war, and its prospects of political influence depend upon the accident of one of the other parties not gaining an overall majority of seats. In addition, the electoral system has denied the

Liberal Party representation in the European Parliament, although in the European elections of 1979 it gained one-eighth of the vote, more than was secured by some Continental Liberal parties which obtained representation.

Yet this is not the only way in which the Liberal Party is adversely affected by the electoral system. For, while the Liberal vote is distributed fairly evenly across the country, this is not reflected in its representation in Parliament. Its MPs will come from constituencies where there has been a lucky by-election, or a successful breakthrough in a particular locality. They are therefore almost bound to be unrepresentative. Since the Party has no safe seats, moreover, it cannot easily attract able Liberals into standing for Parliament; while the curious geographical pattern of its representation makes it difficult for the Party to mount a national electoral campaign which concentrates upon the same issues throughout the country. It is understandable, then, that proportional representation should lie at the fore-front of Liberal priorities. For electoral reform would entirely transform the position of the Party, making it either a quasi-permanent coalition partner as with the FDP; or, such is the depth of disillusionment with the two major parties, a party of government in conjunction with the Social Democrats.

II

If proportional representation has been part of the programme of the Liberal Party since 1922, and the central priority for Liberals since 1974, it is, nevertheless, only since David Steel became leader of the Liberal Party in 1976 that a viable strategy for securing it has been developed. Jo Grimond's realignment strategy did not of itself involve proportional representation, for it entailed the eventual re-establishment of a two-party system. Grimond sought simply to reverse what had happened in the 1920s. Instead of Labour, with the aid of left-wing Liberals replacing the Liberal Party, the Liberals, with the aid of right-wing Labour, would replace the Labour Party. As Michael Steed has said, the Liberal Party 'retained the sense of being a majoritarian party which had temporarily lost its natural place in the system'.[1] Once realignment had occurred, the new radical Grimondite party would take its place in a new two-party system, and in due course, form a single-party government of its own.

The Labour Party's election victory in 1964 and 1966 undermined this strategy because it showed that Labour remained a governing party; while the Liberal débâcle in the 1970 general election showed that the long slow march to restore the Party to power in its own right could prove never-ending. Nor had the Liberal Party's electoral advances in 1974 been able to secure for it a position of influence in government.

David Steel sought to remedy the Party's parlous position through a strategy of co-operation with other Parties. His experience as a back-bencher, co-operating with Roy Jenkins at the Home Office on abortion law reform, with back-benchers from other parties in the campaign against the 1968 Commonwealth Immigration bill restricting the right of entry of East African Asians with British passports, and his leadership of the anti-apartheid campaign, had all convinced him of the benefits of such a strategy. 'The experience', he said 'has not made me any less of a Liberal, nor compromised the independence of Liberalism.'[2] When he became leader in 1976, therefore, David Steel determined to extend this strategy whatever the opposition from Liberal activists who believed that it diluted the pure milk of the Party's doctrine. For it was, in Steel's view, absurd to support proportional representation which, in Britain, logically entailed support for multi-party politics and coalition government, without being willing to co-operate with other parties. In June 1974 he unavailingly pressed Jeremy Thorpe to come out openly in support of coalition; and in his first speech at the Liberal Assembly as Leader, at Llandudno in 1976, he declared 'We must be bold enough to deploy the coalition case positively. We must go all out to attack the other parties for wanting power exclusively to themselves no matter

[1] Michael Steed: The Liberal Party in Henry Drucker (ed.): *Multi-Party Britain* (1979), p. 78.
[2] Peter Bartram: *David Steel: His Life and Politics* (1981), p. 125.

how small a percentage of public support they possess.'

The Lib–Lab Pact of 1977–8 was a logical consequence of this approach. It was, said Steel in June 1977, a 'new experiment in political co-operation', and its central feature was the joint consultative committee through which Labour ministers and their Liberal 'shadows' jointly discussed future policy. For it was through this committee that 'the Liberal Party could be seen by the whole nation to be sharing in the business of government. Moreover, the existence of the committee . . . would help to scotch the notion in the public mind that only one-party government could work effectively.'[3] It was because he wanted to present the Liberal Party as a party of government, rather than because he sought specific legislative gains, that Steel led the Liberal Party into the pact; and it was for this reason that he continued the pact against the wishes of many Liberal activists after he had failed in December 1977 to secure proportional representation for elections to the European Parliament.

David Steel has also played a major role in encouraging the break-out from the Labour Party, and the establishment of the SDP. He acknowledged this role in an article written for the Liberal journal, *New Outlook*, entitled *The Alliance: Hope and Obligation*, published in 1981.

The question then immediately arises: could not the Liberals achieve the breakthrough on their own? I believe the answer is 'No – not at one general election.' . . . The leap from a handful of MP's to a Party of Government is one which few people consider at all likely and it is a problem of credibility. . . .

I do not deny that my role, as I saw it, in encouraging a social democratic break-out from the Labour Party and the formation of a new Party was, and is, a high risk strategy. But I also believe that it is the approach which provides us with the only chance to break the existing two-party system and present the electorate with a credible alternative government, in one move, at the next General Election.

I know that some will argue that my job a year ago should have been solely to encourage Labour dissidents to join the Liberal Party as the only agency capable of change. Had I pursued that line I do not believe that the Labour Party – and British Politics – would have been shaken to anything like the same degree by the earthquake caused by those willing to quit the Labour Party.

[3] Ibid., p. 149.

The possibility of a new Social Democratic grouping maximized the numbers of those prepared to cross the divide. The presence of an SDP, whose leaders and membership recognize an ally and friend in the Liberal Party, maximizes the potential appeal of the forces of realignment.[4]

Once the SDP was formed, therefore, David Steel pressed for agreement on policy and, against the wishes of many Liberal activists, an electoral pact.

The leadership of David Steel, therefore, has been as important to the formation of the Alliance as the decision by David Owen, Shirley Williams, and William Rodgers to break away from the Labour Party. Indeed, it is not over-estimating his influence to argue that, under different leadership, either the Alliance might not have come into existence at all; or alternatively its shape would have been very different.

In accepting the implications of the Party's commitment to proportional representation, and in maximizing the opportunities for co-operation with other parties in a period of political fluidity greater than anything Britain has seen since the 1930s, David Steel has made a distinctive contribution to Liberal Party politics. He has indeed already influenced the Party at least as much as Jo Grimond and more than any other leader since Lloyd George.

III

Nevertheless, the future role of the Liberal Party is still unclear. If the Alliance fails, it may remain nothing more than a receptacle of temporary protest votes, a civically-minded alternative to abstention. In the past, the Party has often relied less on the merits of its policies than upon the unpopularity of the other two Parties. Lemieux has shown how much of the Liberal vote in February 1974 resulted from 'negative issue protest'.[5] Voters supported the Liberals not because they agreed with their policies, of which they had only a hazy understanding, but because they

---

[4] *New Outlook*, September 1981, p. 7.
[5] P. H. Lemieux: 'Political Issues and Liberal Support in the February 1974 British General Election' in *Political Studies*, 1977.

disapproved of the policies of the party they had previously supported. Often, therefore, their support for the Liberals had little to do with liberalism. Disillusioned Conservative supported the Party because they opposed Edward Heath's decision to take Britain into the Common Market; while erstwhile Labour voters came to support the Liberals because they regarded Labour's policies on immigration and race relations as too permissive!

Because so much of its vote has been a negative one, Liberals have found it difficult to project their identity to the public at large. Nor does such a basis of support seem secure enough to enable the Liberals to become a responsible party of government.

Alternatively, the Liberals could remain simply a pressure group for ideas, a party for members of what Ralf Dahrendorf has called the 'thoughtful minority'.[6] It would be the Party for those unwilling to adhere to any single overriding affiliation whether that affiliation is perceived in either class or ideological terms. Dahrendorf believes that since modern society necessarily involves increasingly complex social affiliations, the size of this minority is bound to increase. However, such a conception of the Party's role would also condemn it to minority status for a considerable period of time.

The Liberal Party could again become what is was between the years 1926 and 1929, an intellectual think-tank, what Keynes called 'an almost perfect tabernacle for independent thought which shall at the same time be not too independent but in touch with realities of politics and of political life'.[7] As a popularizer of ideas and issues, the Liberals would draw attention to problems which the major parties ignored. This would enable the Party to exert an influence upon policy even if it was not in government; as with the Progressives in the United States in the 1920s, who although electorally unsuccessful, prefigured many of the central features of Franklin Roosevelt's New Deal.

Many Liberals, however, would argue that such a role

[6] Ralf Dahrendorf: 'Liberalismus' in Peter von Juling (ed.): *Was heisst heute Liberal?* (Hamburg, 1978), p. 29.

[7] John Maynard Keynes: *Collected Writings*, Vol. xix (Cambridge, 1981), p. 733. Letter to J. L. Garvin, 9 February 1928.

would not be sufficient to secure the spread of Liberal
ideas. For the two major parties would be too dominated by
vested interests and ideological blinkers to perceive their
relevance. That, they would suggest, was the fate of Keynesian
ideas on unemployment in the 1920s. Because the Liberal
Party lacked political leverage, these ideas were not accepted
by the Labour or Conservative Parties. For the same reason,
Britain failed to join the Common Market in the 1950s when
she might have been able to negotiate more favourable
terms, and failed to adopt non-sectarian policies of economic
modernization during the 1960s and 1970s. For Liberal policies to succeed, therefore, the Liberal Party must be stronger.

A third role which the Liberal Party might play would be
that of the FDP in West Germany, a corrective to the absolute
philosophies of the two major parties. It would become the
party of balance and compromise. Whether such a role is
possible does not, of course, depend upon the Liberal Party
alone. Under the plurality electoral system, it depends upon
the chance of whether the other parties need Liberal help
in the Commons, as between February and October 1974,
and in the years 1977–8. But with proportional representation
the position of the Liberals as a corrective force will be
guaranteed, as it is in West Germany.

Yet such a role also holds dangers for Liberals. It could
make it difficult for the Party to preserve its identity. The
Liberal Party is accustomed to see itself as a radical force; and
Roy Jenkins, the leader of the SDP, called in his Dimbleby
Lecture of 1979 for the development of a new 'radical
centre', perhaps a contradiction in terms. For the radicalism
of the Liberal Party is hardly part of the middle ground of
British politics. Liberal MPs, as Philip Norton brings out so
clearly, tend to regard socio-economic issues, the central ones
for most voters, as strictly secondary. The Liberal Party is
a Party of radical individualists. Liberal voters, for the most
part, are not. Liberal radicalism has concentrated upon
policies such as reform of the abortion and homosexuality
laws, and an attack upon what the party regards as restrictive
immigration policies. William Pitt, the victor of the Croydon
North-West by-election has indeed called the existing immigration laws a form of 'institutionalized racialism'. Roy

Jenkins, also, has been associated with many of these issues. He was Home Secretary when David Steel piloted his private member's bill legalizing abortion through the Commons in 1967; and he has been responsible for race-relations legislation designed to prevent discrimination against ethnic minorities. Such concerns are those of a minority, albeit a courageous one. Would they survive the transition of the Liberal Party from a party of ideas to a party of government?

The Liberal Party — and the SDP — have to confront a basic dilemma. Faced with the reality of Mrs Thatcher's radicalism and the possibility of Mr Benn's radicalism is there scope within the British political system for a third form of radicalism, as espoused by the Alliance? Or is the Alliance in reality a conservative force seeking to recreate the Butskellite consensus which the other parties have abandoned? Is the Alliance a radical formation; or a centrist one? It cannot be both.

The Social Democratic Party was formed as a breakaway from the Labour Party. Two of the three leaders who broke away — David Owen and Shirley Williams — sought a realignment on the Left, replacing Labour by a party modelled on the German SPD. The new party would be of the Left, but it would be revisionist, disclaiming Clause 4 and the commitment to wholesale nationalisation, and rejecting trade-union affiliation. This realignment on the Left could come about either in alliance with the Liberal Party, or through the Social Democrats acting on their own. The first alternative, the Grimondite one, involves replacing Labour by a united Social Democrat–Liberal Party. It would signify the coming together of two different but closely related streams of thought — the Liberal and the Social Democrat which, as Peter Clarke shows, were torn apart after the First World War.

Yet, the problem which Grimond never succeeded in resolving remains. How can a realignment on the Left be secured with the votes of the discontented Right, and the aid of a Party which is a receptacle for temporarily discontented Conservatives? It is for this reason that David Owen sees co-operation with the Liberals as purely temporary, until proportional representation is achieved. When that happens, the two parties should go their separate ways. Yet this does not resolve the problem. For the electoral profile of the SDP is far closer to that of the Liberals than to Labour. And the SDP is seen by the electorate as a party of the centre rather than a party of the Left.

It would appear natural, then, to imagine the SDP working together with the Liberals not as a new Left-wing party, but as a central bloc seeking a pivotal role in British politics. The rather decorous leadership contest in 1982 between Roy Jenkins and David Owen was generally held to be one about the direction which the SDP would take; and Jenkins's victory seemed to confirm that the SDP would in fact join the Liberals as a party of the centre — but Owen's vote was higher than had been predicted, and showed, perhaps, that there were more supporters of a Leftward orientation in the SDP than had been imagined.

IV

The Alliance, of course, offers the Liberal Party the possibility of another role, that of a party of government. If that happens, it would have to become a more homogeneous and disciplined party paying proper deference to its leaders who would have to gain ministerial credibility. A transformation of this kind would be more difficult for the Liberals than for the SDP. For the leaders of the SDP are men and women of government, while most of those who have joined the Liberal Party have been aware that they are joining a slightly anarchic party far from the seat of power. The Liberals, therefore, could be faced with strong tensions between its parliamentary leadership and its extra-parliamentary activists. It is understandable perhaps if many of the latter fear electoral success more than failure.

Whether the Alliance succeeds in breaking the two-party system depends upon whether it can convert the dissatisfaction with the Labour and Conservative Parties into stable and permanent electoral support. At first sight, the opportunities for doing so would appear to be very great. The public's increasing disillusionment with the managerial incompetence and extremist rhetoric of the two major parties has created a climate of electoral volatility in which a new political formation can hope to gain support. For the paradox is that, as the rhetoric of party divisions has widened, so ironically the class basis of voting behaviour has eroded, and social attitudes have converged. Such a situation offers considerable possibilities, though not only for the Liberal Party. It also allows Mrs Thatcher to hope for a realignment of attitudes along a radical populist and authoritarian basis; and Mr Benn to hope that the grievances of the unemployed, the aspirations of youth, and the sectional interests of workers in the public sector can be combined in a new socialist coalition.

But the Liberal Party — as an already established political organization, yet in no way responsible for the country's growing political and economic difficulties — might seem ideally placed to take advantage of the crisis. Centrist and catch-all in its appeal, it seems to offer to the electorate a return to conditions of stability together with a programme of economic modernization capable of reversing the long years of economic decline. 'The Alliance', as Andrew Gamble has argued, 'is proclaiming that it alone is the truly classless party, the party that puts nation before class, the party that is moderate and pragmatic in pursuit of the common good, and which has no association with any sectional interest'.[8]

The Alliance, however has plainly not yet succeeded in converting temporary support to a permanent sense of identification. This does not mean that it will prove unable to do so. For political parties can themselves influence social trends creating new political alignments as they do so. They are, to some extent at least, masters of their fate. The 1980s may well prove a decade when the whole structure of British politics undergoes a seismic change. The Liberal Party faces an opportunity such as it has not enjoyed for over sixty years; and one unlikely to recur. The essays in *Liberal Party Politics* describe the Liberal Party as it begins to navigate in uncharted waters. They cannot predict whether the voyage will be successful, or indeed what the destination will be.

[8] Andrew Gamble: 'The Rise and Rise of the SDP' in *Marxism Today*, March 1982, p. 8.

Select Bibliography

Historical

R. B. McCallum: *The Liberal Party from Earl Grey to Asquith.*
John Vincent: *The Formation of the Liberal Party, 1857–1868.*
John Morley: *Life of Gladstone.*
Roy Douglas: *The History of the Liberal Party, 1895–1970.*
Chris Cook: *A Short History of the Liberal Party 1900–1976.*
Roy Jenkins: *Asquith.*
Kenneth O. Morgan: *Lloyd George.*
Trevor Wilson: *The Downfall of the Liberal Party 1914–1935.*
Peter Clarke: *Liberals and Social Democrats.*
Alan Bullock and Maurice Shock (eds.): *The Liberal Tradition.*

Contemporary

J. Rasmussen: *Rentenchment and Revival: A Study of the Contemporary Liberal Party.*
Alan Watkins: *The Liberal Dilemma.*
Arthur Cyr: *Liberal Party Politics in Britain.*
Lewis Chester, Magnus Linklater, and David May: *Jeremy Thorpe: A Secret Life.*
Alistair Michie and Simon Hoggart: *The Pact.*
Peter Bartram: *David Steel: His Life and Politics.*
Michael Steed: 'The Liberal Party', in Henry Drucker (ed.): *Multi-Party Britain.*

Psephological

David Butler and Donald Stokes: *Political Change in Britain.*
Ivor Crewe, James Alt, and Bo Särlvik: 'Partisan Dealignment in Britain 1964–1974' in *British Journal of Political Science*, 1977.
James Alt, Ivor Crewe, and Bo Särlvik: 'Angels in Plastic: Liberal Support in 1974' in *Political Studies*, 1977.
P. H. Lemieux: 'Political Issues and Liberal Support in the February 1974 British General Election' in *Political Studies*, 1977.

G. Gudgin and P. J. Taylor: *Seats, Votes and the Spatial Organisation of Elections.*
H. Himmelweit *et. al.: How Voters Decide.*
I. Crewe: 'Is Britain's Two-Party System Really About to Crumble' in *Electoral Studies*, 1982.

Books by Liberals

J. M. Keynes: 'Am I a Liberal? and Liberalism and Labour' in *Essays in Persuasion.*
William Beveridge: *Why I Am a Liberal.*
Jo Grimond: *The Liberal Future.*
Jo Grimond: *The Liberal Challenge.*
Jo Grimond: *Memoirs.*
George Watson (ed.): *The Unservile State.*
George Watson (ed.): *Radical Alternative.*
David Steel: *A House Divided.*

Index